THE DISCIPLE'S JOURNEY

*A 12-Week Road
Map for Following
Jesus in Every
Sphere of Life*

JIM PUTMAN

A NavPress resource published in alliance
with Tyndale House Publishers

To my Real Life Ministries team—for all that I have learned in our time together and for the relationships, support, and accountability we have shared for over twenty-five years.

CONTENTS

WEEK 9: THE HOME AND FAMILY SPHERE (CONTINUED)

WEEK 10: THE WORLD SPHERE

WEEK 11: THE SPIRITUAL SPHERE

WEEK 12: BRINGING IT ALL TOGETHER

Introduction

THE DISCIPLE'S JOURNEY

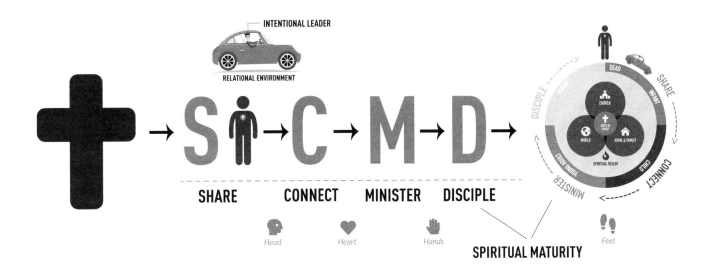

When we talk about discipleship, we are talking about a journey. Jesus has a goal for us and the people we will invest in and disciple. Yes, His ultimate end for us is heaven, but until then His goal for us is spiritual maturity.

What does that maturity look like? The invitation Jesus gave His disciples tells us. In the invitation is the definition, a simple explanation of what Jesus required of all His disciples. He said it this way in Matthew:

"Come and follow me, and I will make you fishers of men."
MATTHEW 4:19, WNT

If we break that passage down into three parts, we discover the definition of a disciple.

- *Come and follow me*: A disciple is one who is following Jesus.
- *And I will make (change) you*: A disciple is being changed by Jesus.
- *Fishers of men*: A disciple is on mission with Jesus.

Discipleship, then, is a journey in which you follow Jesus, are changed by Jesus, and learn to be on mission with Jesus. In this workbook, you will go through a set of lessons designed to help a believer in Jesus along this journey in four areas:

1

1. We want to help you understand that you are a disciple of Jesus and what that reality means.

2. We want you to learn to have an abiding relationship with Jesus daily. This workbook is designed to guide you through a three-month habit that you will be able to continue with when you are finished.

3. We want you to participate in a safe and encouraging small group where you learn to be in relationship with other believers. (If you are leading a group or individual through this book, please visit thedisciplesjourney.org for the Leader's Guide.)

4. We want you to learn to make disciples in every area of your life.

Jesus invited the first disciples to join Him on the journey of discipleship, and the disciples had to decide: Would they go on the journey or not? Those who agreed were invited to follow Him. Jesus told them—and continues to tell each of us—"I am going to take you as you are, and I am going to turn you into a different kind of person who cares about what I care about." After these disciples had a three-year journey with Jesus, in relationship with Him, being changed by Him, and growing into spiritually mature disciples, He told them,

> "Go and make disciples of all nations, baptizing them in the name of the Father and of the Son and of the Holy Spirit, and teaching them to obey everything I have commanded you. And surely I am with you always, to the very end of the age."
> MATTHEW 28:19-20

Jesus brought the disciples to the point where they were finally ready to go and make other disciples of Jesus. These men were still not completely mature. They would not be perfect until they went to be with the Lord after their time on Earth. However, they were ready to make disciples of Jesus because they were indwelled by the Holy Spirit and they understood who Jesus was and what He came to do. They understood His teachings, they had been changed by Jesus, and they were now ready to go on mission with Jesus.

The same is true of us! The Holy Spirit has been given to us as well, and we also have God's teaching within Scripture as a guide. God has given us everything we need to know as we grow as disciples and disciple others into maturity in every area of life.

This workbook will guide you through the disciple's journey, using God's Word as the map. As we look at what God's plan and commands are for a disciple, we will be utilizing the framework of the book of Ephesians, which begins with what God has done for us and our identity in Christ and then walks through five different areas of the disciple's life. In this workbook, we call these areas the Five Spheres:

1. the Abiding Sphere;
2. the Church Sphere;
3. the Home and Family Sphere;
4. the World Sphere; and
5. the Spiritual Sphere.

Each week's study includes five days of Scripture study and questions to help us understand the spheres and our journey of discipleship in more depth. At the end of each day, you will find an answer key for some of the questions from that day.

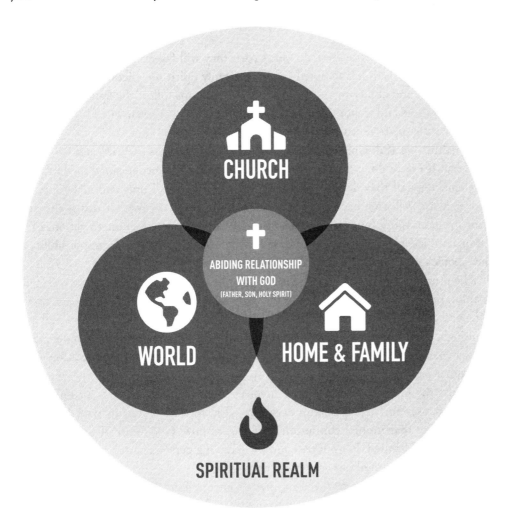

MAKING A COVENANT

As we look at Jesus' great commission command in Matthew 28, we discover that discipleship is not a solo venture:

> "Go and make disciples of all nations, baptizing them in the name of the Father and of the Son and of the Holy Spirit."
>
> MATTHEW 28:19

In fact, this verse shows us that discipleship has three parts:

1. God's part (*in the name of the Father and of the Son and of the Holy Spirit*);
2. the receiving person's part (*disciples of all nations*); and
3. my part (*go and make . . . baptizing them*).

When disciples of Jesus try to do God's part, they will fail every time. Only God can do His part. If a person has accepted Christ, the Holy Spirit now lives in them, and they have the power and ability to choose to make their actions follow the Spirit. I must trust that the Lord sees and is working in the life of a new believer, even when it doesn't seem that He is using me to do so.

Sometimes we as disciplemakers try to do the receiving person's part, and we can't do that either. If I have done my part to teach and encourage someone along the journey of disciplemaking and they decide to quit or get out of the car, I pray and make sure they know they are welcome back in the car—but ultimately I know that this is the other person's responsibility (not mine). Jesus Himself had people who chose to get out of the relational vehicle He was driving, and though He was sad, He didn't take responsibility for other people's decisions (John 6:66). I am only responsible for my part.

When (not *if*) a person we are seeking to disciple fails in their part, we often feel guilt. We think that we failed somehow, and the devil loves to pile on the guilt and shame by telling us we shouldn't continue trying. Learning boundaries is itself a journey we all must go through. Most importantly, we must all seek out wise counsel from other, more mature disciplemakers to help us know when we are moving away from our part into either God's or the other person's part.

Because the journey of discipleship involves more than just us, it is a commitment we must take seriously. Throughout Scripture, God formed covenants with His people to demonstrate that mutual commitment. Then, as now, God's part of the covenant is unbreakable and assured. For our part and the receiving person's part, a covenant can be a powerful representation of our commitment as well.

Here is a covenant to use when you invite someone into the journey of discipleship. May it help you as you go on this journey and learn to help others do so as well.

THE DISCIPLE'S JOURNEY COVENANT

- **I commit to listening to God's voice** through abiding in relationship with Him and fellow believers, accepting the truth that I have been given the Holy Spirit as God's indwelling gift.

- **I commit to being part of a local church**, knowing that abiding includes being a part of a local church body where I experience weekly spiritual feeding from spiritual fathers as they preach from Scripture.

- **I commit to using this workbook** to abide personally. I will abide through reading God's Word daily and praying with a journal I write my prayers in. Through this I learn to feed myself as well.

- **I commit to allowing myself to be discipled by another believer** throughout this study. I will abide through my relationship with a more mature believer to guide me. This is an act of humility that directly affects my spiritual growth to maturity. I acknowledge that without humility I am not and cannot become spiritually mature.

- **I commit to being part of a small group going through this workbook together** as we discuss and pray through what we are learning. I will be in a discipleship relationship with an Intentional Leader as well as with a small group pursuing discipleship in community. I will develop the habit of spending time in God's Word, journaling my prayer life, and meeting weekly with a group of believers as we work through this content together.

- **I commit to working through boredom and days of dryness** as I go through this workbook. I will finish this workbook even if I get bored or feel as though I am not getting out of it what I wanted. I acknowledge that perseverance is part of maturing. I understand that pushing through trials and distractions is as much a part of maturing as what we are learning.

- **I commit to fighting for relationship and dealing with inevitable issues** with those in my group when they occur. Should my Intentional Leader or someone else in the group irritate or hurt me, I will continue and not quit. I will learn to look past faults and confront in love to resolve issues when—not *if*—they occur. I acknowledge that learning to become one who loves broken people is as important as learning content.

- **I commit to being honest** when I don't know something or when I fail in something. I recognize that depth and maturity require the risk of honesty. I acknowledge that my willingness to be present and honest in community is as important as learning new content or skills.

- **I commit to being humble** and to allowing others to know my real situations and speak into them for my good. I will be vulnerable with my questions, rather than seeking to appear smart.

- **I commit to being open about my struggles and failures**, acknowledging that openness creates opportunities for growth in relationships. I will ask people to pray for me.

- **I commit to cultivating a sacred and safe place** for others in the group to be honest about their own struggles. If someone is struggling, I will pray for them and text or call them between group meetings to see how they are. I will help keep the group safe by not sharing with others things that are discussed within the group.

- **I commit to seeking wise counsel** throughout my journey, allowing people to speak into my life. I am signing my name to this commitment as a step toward accountability for myself and the group I am in.[1]

_____

Signature

---

1. If you are in the role of leader in your group, you cannot lead well unless you make this covenant alongside the rest of the group. One further commitment for leaders is that if someone misses the group, you need to commit to reaching out and checking on them. You will also need to pray for those you lead and be available if they need to talk outside the normal group time.

Part I

STARTING THE JOURNEY

When you decide to take a journey, there are several decisions you must make before you go.

1. What is the destination?
2. What vehicle am I taking?
3. Who is driving?
4. Where can I find a map?

For our journey of discipleship, we find the decisions listed above in the life and work of Jesus Christ and in His commands to the first disciples:

1. What is the destination? *Becoming spiritually mature disciples of Jesus.*
2. What vehicle am I taking? *A personal relationship with Jesus, as well as a relational environment with another follower of Jesus.*
3. Who is driving? *Jesus is ultimately driving, but on Earth another disciple drives to show us how to do the same.*
4. Where can I find a map? *Jesus holds the map, and the map exists in Scripture.*

THE MAP KEY

Because we are using a map (Scripture), we must also understand the map key: the labels we need to know for the journey ahead. Throughout this workbook, we will be using everyday terms to help us better understand and picture what God has laid out in His Word about the life of a disciple. To get us started, here are a few of the terms we will be using for this journey:

- **The Invitation:** While Jesus ultimately gives the invitation, a disciple who is following Jesus' directions (His words through Scripture) and His method of discipleship (through relationship) is the one who carries it. You must accept the invitation to hear the message and then become a disciple. As you do, you step into the relational vehicle that Jesus ultimately drives, but which on Earth is steered by a driver who is more experienced (spiritually mature) than you. That driver's role is not only to get you to the destination but to teach you how to help others get there as well.

- **The Journey:** This is the process that begins when we accept Jesus' invitation to follow Him and takes us on our path of spiritual growth throughout every area of our lives. The journey is completed when we reach our destination, which is heaven.

- **The Map:** God's Word as directed and empowered by God's Holy Spirit is the map for our journey.

- **Gas or Power Source:** The Holy Spirit gives us both the desire and the power to do what pleases God. Without abiding in Him, we would not get very far along on our journey—even if we had the map (Philippians 2:13).

- **The Relational Vehicles:** We will be using the language of different vehicles—motorcycle, car, van, bus, train—to represent the vehicles you are in as you go through this journey. Jesus discipled His followers while He was in relationship with them, so we refer to our vehicles as "relational environments": the contexts in which relational discipleship takes place.

- **The Intentional Leader:** Just as Jesus was the Intentional Leader in His relationships with His disciples, all discipleship relationships have an Intentional Leader. This is usually someone who is further along the journey than you are and who knows how to use the map and drive the vehicle (relational environment) toward the destination.

- **The Destination:** Our final destination is heaven, but while we live on Earth, our destination is to become more like Jesus. We do this as we live out a God-centered and God-powered missional life in the Five Spheres.

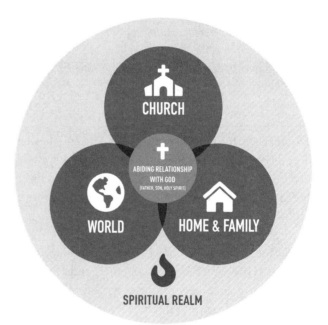

As we go on our discipleship journey, we become the driver people see physically while the Holy Spirit directs us. We drive His relational vehicle and invite people on the journey, taking the role of Intentional Leader with the people we disciple.

Week 1

THE BIG PICTURE

Day One

DO YOU KNOW YOU ARE A DISCIPLE OF JESUS?

GETTING STARTED

You have been introduced to the disciple's journey and some of the terms you need to know before setting out. And with this knowledge, you have made a commitment to start the journey. Now it is time to go deeper into what that will entail.

> *Lord Jesus: Help me see what You want me to see today. Expose any lies I may believe and lead me to Your truth. Help me trust and obey You and walk out what I'm learning in every sphere of my life.*

Do not merely listen to the word, and so deceive yourselves. Do what it says.

JAMES 1:22

Whether you grew up in the Christian church or became a Christian in your older years, did you know that you are supposed to be a disciple of Jesus? So many people have never had this truth shared with them.

A good friend once confessed to me that he had been a Christian for eighteen years and had never once been told that he was a disciple. He thought disciples were just the guys who followed Jesus in New Testament times. I told him that those men in Scripture *were* disciples but that Jesus had sent them out to make more disciples who would make more disciples, and so on. When he finally understood this truth, it changed his life—and because of that change, many other lives were changed.

1. What was your experience of accepting Christ like?

   ☐ I came forward at church or a church function to accept Christ during an invitation time.
   ☐ I was baptized as a child and went through a confirmation process.
   ☐ I was baptized as an adult to become part of a church.
   ☐ I prayed the salvation prayer with my parents or another Christian.
   ☐ Other: _____

 Scan QR code to access video podcasts and other content that accompanies this week's session.

MATTHEW 4:19, WNT

[Jesus said,] "Come and follow me, and I will make you fishers of men."

MATTHEW 28:18-20

Then Jesus came to them and said, "All authority in heaven and on earth has been given to me. Therefore go and make disciples of all nations, baptizing them in the name of the Father and of the Son and of the Holy Spirit, and teaching them to obey everything I have commanded you. And surely I am with you always, to the very end of the age."

ACTS 6:1-7

In those days when the number of disciples was increasing, the Hellenistic Jews among them complained against the Hebraic Jews because their widows were being overlooked in the daily distribution of food. So the Twelve gathered all the disciples together and said, "It would not be right for us to neglect the ministry of the word of God in order to wait on tables. Brothers and sisters, choose seven men from among you who are known to be full of the Spirit and wisdom. We will turn this responsibility over to them and will give our attention to prayer and the ministry of the word."

This proposal pleased the whole group. They chose Stephen, a man full of faith and of the Holy Spirit; also Philip, Procorus, Nicanor, Timon, Parmenas, and Nicolas from Antioch, a convert to Judaism. They presented these men to the apostles, who prayed and laid their hands on them.

So the word of God spread. The number of disciples in Jerusalem increased rapidly, and a large number of priests became obedient to the faith.

2. What happened after you accepted Christ?

☐ I was given a Bible and told to come back to church.
☐ I was told that I needed to follow a set of rules, but I wasn't sure which ones.
☐ I had someone ask me to start meeting with them, and they spent time helping me understand Scripture one-on-one.
☐ I was invited to an ongoing class.
☐ Other: _____

3. In your mind, is there a difference between being a Christian and being a disciple? Why?

_____

_____

4. Do any of the following statements resonate with you?

☐ *I thought a disciple was just a pastor who did that as a full-time job.*
☐ *I thought I was unqualified to be a disciple.*
☐ *No one has ever told me I was a disciple who was supposed to make disciples.*
☐ *I thought the disciples were some kind of special "saints." I am just a normal person who doesn't have much knowledge or skills worth using.*
☐ Other: _____

Jesus made it clear that He had a mission He wanted His disciples to join Him in. He focused on these disciples to help them truly grow so that they would then be able to do the same with others. His goal was to reach the whole world—but it started with intentionally giving time to the Twelve. Jesus knew that discipleship cannot happen in a mass training alone. Rather than for a lot of people to be discipled only a little or not at all, He wanted His disciples to really understand His teaching at a heart level.

Read Matthew 4:19 (see sidebar).

5. Jesus invited people into His personal mission. What was that mission?

_____

_____

Read Matthew 28:18-20 (see sidebar).

6. Jesus told His disciples to go into the world and make what? How were they to do that?

_____

_____

Read Acts 6:1-7 (see sidebar).

7. What did people call those who had accepted Christ? Underline the word *disciple* as often as you see it in this passage. What did the writer of Acts call the early believers?

_____

_____

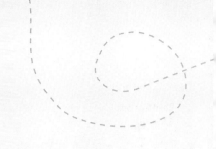

8. In many cases, instead of making disciples who can in turn make more disciples, spiritual leaders have made converts. Take a minute to look up the definitions of *disciple* and *convert*. What is the difference between the two?

_____

YOU ARE CALLED TO BE A DISCIPLE

The goal of this workbook is to help you understand who and what you are according to Scripture. First, let me make it clear: If you have truly accepted Jesus as Savior and Lord, you are a disciple. (I will define the term *disciple* more thoroughly later.) Jesus draws a disciple to Himself, but a disciple must also accept the invitation. If God drew you, then He has a purpose for you. That purpose includes the blessing of a relationship with you as well as a plan to bring glory to Himself through you. We can and should be confident in who God can help us become.

As you come to understand the people Jesus chose to be His disciples, you will develop the confidence that it's not about how great you and I are, but about how great our God is. Jesus did not choose people that the educated religious people of the day would have chosen. In fact, this is one of the reasons the religious elite rejected Jesus as the Messiah. Jesus chose as His disciples those who were considered uneducated (like Peter, James, and John—mere fishermen); those who were seen as betrayers of the Jewish people and too sinful to even touch (Matthew, a tax collector); those who were distrusted by authorities as radicals (Simon the Zealot). You get the point. None of us has an excuse for not being a disciple as Jesus defined the idea. God has proven He can do great things through broken people.

As you read the story of Jesus in the Gospels (Matthew, Mark, Luke, and John), you will see the constant failings of those who were already His disciples—and through this you will also see Jesus' grace.

9. Which of the statements below describe why you might not consider yourself an acceptable disciple?

☐ *I don't have a Bible college degree or enough biblical knowledge.* (Read Acts 4:13; see sidebar.)
☐ *I struggle with sin.* (Read Romans 7:14–8:39.)
☐ *I have a terrible past.* (Read Luke 5:27-29; see sidebar.)
☐ *I am not a good speaker or musician.* (Read Acts 4:13; see sidebar.)
☐ *I haven't had anyone tell me I was a disciple.* (You have now!)
☐ *I haven't had anyone disciple me.* (We are working on that now!)
☐ Other: _____

It is my hope that as you read Scripture from a discipleship mindset you will begin to see these excuses fall away from your thinking.

As disciples, we must learn that we are chosen because we are special to God even though we are broken. When we look at who we used to be, we can be encouraged as believers, but when we look at Jesus (the perfect one) we are humbled and continue to seek

ACTS 4:13
When they saw the courage of Peter and John and realized that they were unschooled, ordinary men, they were astonished and they took note that these men had been with Jesus.

ROMANS 7:14-21, NLT
So the trouble is not with the law, for it is spiritual and good. The trouble is with me, for I am all too human, a slave to sin. I don't really understand myself, for I want to do what is right, but I don't do it. Instead, I do what I hate. But if I know that what I am doing is wrong, this shows that I agree that the law is good. So I am not the one doing wrong; it is sin living in me that does it.

And I know that nothing good lives in me, that is, in my sinful nature. I want to do what is right, but I can't. I want to do what is good, but I don't. I don't want to do what is wrong, but I do it anyway. But if I do what I don't want to do, I am not really the one doing wrong; it is sin living in me that does it.

I have discovered this principle of life—that when I want to do what is right, I inevitably do what is wrong.

LUKE 5:27-29
After this, Jesus went out and saw a tax collector by the name of Levi sitting at his tax booth. "Follow me," Jesus said to him, and Levi got up, left everything and followed him.

Then Levi held a great banquet for Jesus at his house, and a large crowd of tax collectors and others were eating with them.

Read Romans 8 in your personal Bible.

PHILIPPIANS 3:12-14

Not that I have already obtained all this, or have already arrived at my goal, but I press on to take hold of that for which Christ Jesus took hold of me. Brothers and sisters, I do not consider myself yet to have taken hold of it. But one thing I do: Forgetting what is behind and straining toward what is ahead, I press on toward the goal to win the prize for which God has called me heavenward in Christ Jesus.

Notes and Thoughts

to grow spiritually into His image (Romans 8:29). When we are humble, He can use us. None of us will ever be done growing in our understanding, attitudes, or abilities as long as we live. You and I can become mature in Christ, but we will never be fully mature until Christ fully transforms us in our final destination: the new heaven and earth.

Read Paul's statement in Philippians 3:12-14 (see sidebar).

Notice that Paul, the greatest teacher in the New Testament (other than Jesus, of course), makes it clear that he is not finished in the process of spiritual growth. Each of us is on a lifelong journey with Jesus (still as His disciples) that will continue to shape and direct us (Hebrews 12:1-2).

One of my goals with this workbook is to teach you some basic principles that will continue to shape your growth in the future. There are key values we must pick up and carry as believers who have the Holy Spirit now living inside us. One of those values is humility. Pride says, *I am already perfect* or *I have grown enough.* Pride says, *I don't have to follow a disciplemaker and be taught or held accountable or learn.* Humility says, *I must be a lifelong learner as I continue to learn from Jesus through His Holy Spirit, who guides me by His Word, the Bible, and through those who were told to make disciples.* Every mature disciplemaker knows that he or she still needs accountability and friends to seek wise counsel from. Remember: It takes humility to become mature, and humility is a sign that you are mature.

DAY ONE REVIEW

1. What stood out to you or convicted you from today?

2. What were your expectations when you became a follower of Jesus?

3. Name some ways your expectations have changed since becoming a follower of Jesus.

4. Do you consider yourself a disciple? Why or why not?

5. Describe what you think someone who is spiritually mature looks like.

6. Does knowing you are a disciple change the way you look at your weekly calendar and activities? What should you take out? Is there anything you should add in?

Day Two

UNDERSTANDING THE BIG PICTURE

GETTING STARTED

If you didn't know this beforehand, hopefully by now you know that you are a disciple of Jesus. You also may have discovered some misconceptions you had about that term and what it means. Today we are going to talk about the bigger picture: God's overarching plan for mankind and salvation.

> *Lord Jesus: Help me see what You want me to see today. Expose any lies I may believe and lead me to Your truth. Help me trust and obey You and walk out what I'm learning in every sphere of my life.*

Christians often share the gospel with unbelievers in a way that is confusing. They talk about being saved and they ask people if they want to get saved. When unbelievers hear us say that Jesus died to save us, they often ask, "Saved from what? Why do I need to be saved?" They will say, "I am as good as anyone else, right?"

To help unbelievers comprehend their need for Jesus, we must help them understand the story of God and humankind from the beginning. The whole story also answers the fundamental questions that many nonbelievers have, such as the issue of pain and suffering on planet Earth. Non-Christians have a real struggle with understanding how there could be a good God in a world with so much pain and injustice: *If there is a good God, then why would He allow all this . . . ?* Because so many Christians have not been discipled, these same questions can cause them to doubt what they once believed themselves.

Why is there pain and sorrow if there is a good God? is a great question! There is also a good answer, and we find it in the overarching story of God. If we are going to stay secure as believers and be able to share with unbelievers, we need to understand that story. You cannot open a good book in the middle and quickly understand all the backstory. Jesus said that the New Testament is built upon the Old Testament, which means that to understand the gospel, we must go back to the beginning.

1. At some point in your life you will face doubts and struggles to reconcile what the world says with what you have believed. Have you ever been asked (or asked yourself) one of these questions?

    ☐ *Why do bad things happen to good people?*
    ☐ *Why doesn't God stop evil?*
    ☐ *Why do good things happen to bad people?*
    ☐ *If I am saved, then why does God allow me to hurt so much?*

We live in a spiritually dangerous world that seeks to challenge everything the Bible tells us. One of the most unfortunate things I deal with is people who were at one time raised in

GENESIS 2:15-25, NLT

The Lᴏʀᴅ God placed the man in the Garden of Eden to tend and watch over it. But the Lᴏʀᴅ God warned him, "You may freely eat the fruit of every tree in the garden—except the tree of the knowledge of good and evil. If you eat its fruit, you are sure to die."

Then the Lᴏʀᴅ God said, "It is not good for the man to be alone. I will make a helper who is just right for him." So the Lᴏʀᴅ God formed from the ground all the wild animals and all the birds of the sky. He brought them to the man to see what he would call them, and the man chose a name for each one. He gave names to all the livestock, all the birds of the sky, and all the wild animals. But still there was no helper just right for him.

So the Lᴏʀᴅ God caused the man to fall into a deep sleep. While the man slept, the Lᴏʀᴅ God took out one of the man's ribs and closed up the opening. Then the Lᴏʀᴅ God made a woman from the rib, and he brought her to the man.

"At last!" the man exclaimed.

"This one is bone from my bone,
and flesh from my flesh!
She will be called 'woman,'
because she was taken
from 'man.'"

This explains why a man leaves his father and mother and is joined to his wife, and the two are united into one.

Now the man and his wife were both naked, but they felt no shame.

Read Genesis 3 in your personal Bible.

the faith but were challenged with a question that they didn't know how to answer. Sadly, there were answers—but they couldn't find them. Those they knew who were Christians couldn't answer them, either, and would simply say something like "Well, you just have to have faith." Biblical relational discipleship, however, enables you to have relationships with more mature believers who can help you find real-life answers to your questions.

The first disciples often had questions they couldn't answer, and Jesus took the time in relationship to help them work through the challenges they were having, as well as questions unbelievers were bringing. As you go along on this journey, you will begin to be able to answer many different questions for yourself and others.

Understanding the big picture revealed in Genesis is vital if we are to understand salvation correctly. That's because context is important: Genesis sets the stage for the entire story of Jesus. The warnings and the Curse in Genesis reveal truths every disciple must learn.

Read Genesis 2:15 through Genesis 3 (see sidebar).

2. Circle any of the following statements that seem accurate.

    a. In the beginning God created a perfect world, and humans and God walked together. However, God gave people a choice. In a sense God said, "Live with me and let me decide the terms for what I have created or choose yourself as leader and ruler."
    b. The world was imperfect and painful to start with, so Adam and Eve were suffering from all kinds of struggles before they chose to disobey God. They didn't have enough, so the tree they were forbidden to eat from was important for their survival.
    c. God shared what the consequences would be if they disobeyed, and the devil deceived them by convincing them that God was not acting in their best interest.
    d. God is relational, and relationship requires choice. The result of self-rule is death in every part of creation. This is the Curse.
    e. God's response was to immediately kill Adam and Eve for what they had done.
    f. The serpent (the devil) forced Adam and Eve to trust themselves and his word rather than trusting God.
    g. God kicked Adam and Eve out of the Garden defenseless and without His help. They were truly on their own from then on.
    h. God is not only the Creator but also the Sustainer of life. To sin (rebel against God) is to separate from God, who is life itself. The result of being separated from life is death.[i]

As you read the whole story of God and His interactions with humans, you will see that God did allow humanity to choose relationship with Him. God made humans in His image, which means that we were created with the ability to choose relationship with God as well. God did not make us robots—He made us so much more than that. He made us with the ability to relate to Him and other humans. He made us with a soul that would last from conception through eternity. The body, too, would last unless humans chose sin—but with sin came the breakdown of the body and death.

God clearly told Adam and Eve the results of disobedience. He allowed them to choose whether to obey. Because He is a righteous and just God, there was a prescribed penalty for their disobedience, rebellion, and unbelief.

Look at it this way—you probably have a cell phone, right? If you keep it plugged into the charger, it will last indefinitely. If you pull it away from the charger, however, it starts to run on its battery, which doesn't last that long. In the same way, none of us last when we are separated from God because we have rebelled against Him. Eventual death is always the result. The entire world has been unplugged from the source (God), which means death is in every part of life. The big story of God, as it unfolds in the rest of Scripture, tells us that sin did come with a curse that spread to all humanity.

Paul sums it up in the New Testament (read Romans 5:12; see sidebar). Sin is like a virus that affects every person. Others have sinned against us, and that sin has affected us, but we have also sinned against others and affected them. God knew sin would affect the world when He told Adam and Eve to trust and obey Him. However, the whole story of God reveals that He also is a loving God, filled with grace for those who accept Him for who He is. He is righteous and right, loving and gracious.

God pursued Adam and Eve after the Fall. He found them and provided a sacrifice that resulted in coverings for their nakedness. He also continued relationship with Adam and Eve's family as they began to inhabit the earth. In fact, the whole Bible is a story about a God who pursues people and continually seeks to bring them back to Himself.

ROMANS 5:12, NLT
When Adam sinned, sin entered the world. Adam's sin brought death, so death spread to everyone, for everyone sinned.

3. Why do you think God allowed life to continue outside of the perfect Garden relationship that He created? Circle your response(s).

   a. God made us relational beings with the freedom to choose Him or not, and He allowed life to continue after the Fall so that we could experience life without His full presence and perhaps decide to trust Him.

   b. God allowed us to sin so that we could learn that He is trustworthy; that what He says is true; and that sin, rebellion, and lack of trust lead to death.

   c. God allowed sin because in choosing it, we would also learn He is a grace-filled God who forgives those who choose to receive forgiveness.

   d. God had a plan to eventually destroy and then remake a new heaven and a new earth with those who decided God was good and right.[ii]

God desires to close out the story of Earth's creation with a glorious ending. In the end, those who choose Him say that they now believe God knows all things, that He is right, He is good, He knows what we don't, and He is worthy of trust. God's people know that He will receive and restore them to the new heaven and new earth with all who have come to that same conclusion. We will dive into this more later, but the big-picture story of God and humans has a glorious ending for all who decide they want a relationship with God—just as He wants one with us.

Read Revelation 21.

4. Circle the words that describe what you read in Revelation 21.
   - new
   - relationship with God
   - a long life
   - a never-ending life with God and others who also now understand and love God

God did not make us robots—He made us so much more than that. He made us with the ability to relate to Him and to other humans.

- a place without dying or pain
- a new body
- a place without the devil, who made his own choice as one of God's created angels
- a place where the contamination of a sinful nature will be gone [iii]

Those who have ended their rebellion against God in their life on this broken planet will now enter a new heaven and new earth without sin, sin nature, or the devil. Things will again be as they were created to be.

A disciple is someone growing in their understanding of God's bigger story—the truth about where we come from and what happened to the world. A disciple knows who the enemy is, what the enemy's goals are, and how the enemy works. A disciple knows God's plan to save the world by the Cross as announced by His people, the church. A disciple is one who is . . . well, let's wait until tomorrow to look into that.

DAY TWO REVIEW

Jesus came to Earth to live among His creation and to explain where we came from, what happened, and how we got here. Now He is asking us to go on a journey called discipleship with Him. Jesus presented Himself as the one the Old Testament Scriptures prophesied about. He did miracles to prove it. He lived a life unlike any other. He was pure and wise and loving. He rose from the dead to prove He is who He said He was, and now He says, "Let's go on a road trip together." Are you willing to climb into the relational vehicle He is driving?

1. What stood out to you or convicted you from today?

2. Have you ever found yourself asking a question like *Why does God allow bad things to happen to good people?* Has this lesson changed your answer in any way?

3. If you were asked, "What do I need to be saved from?" what would your answer be after this lesson?

4. Do you tend to walk through your week with more of a focus on worldly issues or more of an eternal focus?

Notes and Thoughts

---

i. Answer: Statements a, c, d, and h are accurate.
ii. Answer: All the statements are correct.
iii. Answer: All the statements are correct.

Day Three

THE DEFINITION IS IN THE INVITATION: PART 1

GETTING STARTED

Now that we have a clearer view of God's plan for salvation, let's take a look at how He plans to utilize His disciples in that plan as we begin to join Him in His mission.

> *Lord Jesus: Help me see what You want me to see today. Expose any lies I may believe and lead me to Your truth. Help me trust and obey You and walk out what I'm learning in every sphere of my life.*

Yesterday we looked at the story of creation and how the world came to be the way it is. We're going to look at this from a different angle today and then begin to answer the question, *What is a disciple of Jesus?* On Day One we came to realize that we are all disciples who are called to make disciples. Now let's define the word *disciple* clearly from Jesus' perspective.

Read Luke 15:11-32.

Remember yesterday we asked the question *Why did God allow people to sin in the Garden of Eden?* The story of the Prodigal Son in Luke 15 answers this question. It also answers the question of why God allowed the world to continue in brokenness after sin. Do you see it?

1. Which of the following statements correlate with the story of the Prodigal Son? Circle your answers.

    a. God is the father in the story Jesus told.
    b. The son was allowed to leave the father rather than be put to death. (In that time period, if a Jewish son asked for his inheritance early, the father would have had the right to put the son to death.)
    c. The father let the son go because he didn't care about the son.
    d. The father allowed the son to go in hopes that the broken world would reveal that the father was right and that home with him was a far better choice.
    e. The older brother in the story had no sin.
    f. The older brother was just as guilty as the younger brother because, though he looked like he was at home and in agreement with the father, he did not have the heart of the father. He did not love his brother.
    g. This is a story about the prodigal sons (plural)—neither one understood the heart of the father.[i]

Our heavenly Father also pursued His prodigals (Israel) with love, sending them a message through God's only Son. Jesus came to tell the prodigal sons that they were loved and

He would lead them home if they would follow Him. Jesus later sent out the disciples, who would write the New Testament Scriptures, to tell the entire prodigal world that we can come home too. Now we as disciples live in the world to tell others the Father wants each person to come home if they are willing. He provided a pathway through Jesus if we will accept Him (John 14:6).

Read Hebrews 1:1-2 (see sidebar).

THE JOURNEY OF A DISCIPLE

When Jesus came to the world two thousand years ago, He spent time with some of the people He came into contact with and invited them to become His disciples. In inviting the disciples to come with Him, Jesus was inviting them into relationship. This invitation was an opportunity to enter a relational environment or vehicle.

Jesus offers us the same invitation. If we choose to get in, we start toward a final destination: the new heaven and new earth. But we still have a purpose while we live in this fallen world. Jesus' invitation to come and follow Him is a journey toward a changed life—a life of purpose—for as long as we live on Earth. We call this purpose *being a spiritually mature disciple.*

HEBREWS 1:1-2

In the past God spoke to our ancestors through the prophets at many times and in various ways, but in these last days he has spoken to us by his Son, whom he appointed heir of all things, and through whom also he made the universe.

Jesus' invitation to come and follow Him is a journey toward a changed life—a life of purpose—for as long as we live on Earth. We call this purpose being a spiritually mature disciple.

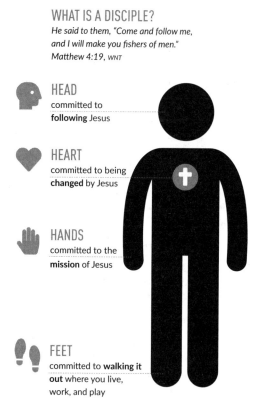

WHAT IS A DISCIPLE?
He said to them, "Come and follow me, and I will make you fishers of men."
Matthew 4:19, WNT

HEAD
committed to
following Jesus

HEART
committed to being
changed by Jesus

HANDS
committed to the
mission of Jesus

FEET
committed to **walking it out** where you live, work, and play

At Real Life Ministries (the church where I pastor), our key verse for defining a disciple is Matthew 4:19. We often say of that verse, as we read in the introduction to this workbook, "In the invitation [to be a disciple] is the definition [of a disciple]."

INVITED INTO RELATIONSHIP

Let's read this verse again together. Jesus invited the disciples to . . .

"Come and follow me, and I will make you fishers of men."
MATTHEW 4:19, WNT

The first part of the invitation tells us that in this relationship with Jesus, Jesus is the leader and we are the followers. In Eden humans were given a perfect world where we could walk with God in the Garden. It was beautiful and perfect. We had everything we needed.

What did we have to do to stay there? We had to trust and obey God. But we chose not to do that. We broke our relationship with Him. So God sent His only Son, Jesus, to bring us back. On the cross, Jesus died for our sins, paying the price for our entrance back into relationship with God. That sacrifice is what allows our entrance into the new heaven and new earth when this earthly life is over. Jesus is also the one who leads us back toward His design for living—and toward our purpose.

2. Based on what you have learned so far, which of the following answers describes a disciple of Jesus?

    a. A disciple understands who Jesus is and has decided to follow Him.
    b. A disciple recognizes that they have sinned. Disciples are prodigal children in need of being saved.
    c. A disciple has prayed a prayer of salvation and been baptized.
    d. A disciple is in a storm (life) but has built their life on the Rock (God).
    e. A disciple has lived in a faraway land of sin and rebellion but has heard the message from the Son of God that they can come home to the Father and is now following Him.
    f. A disciple not only hears the words of Jesus but also puts them into practice (meaning the disciple follows and obeys Jesus).[ii]

SAVED BY FAITH

Jesus is both our Savior and our Lord, offering us salvation as we submit to His authority to guide us into our purpose. We follow and He leads (Matthew 7:24-28).

Many people like the idea of Jesus as Savior but not as Lord. A form of Christianity has developed around the concept that faith saves (trusting Jesus has paid your price for sin)—which is true—but also that this does not need to lead to a changed life. The reality is that faith includes repentance, which is a change of heart that leads to a change of direction. Repentance renounces a self-ruled life and accepts the rule of the King of kings, who sits on the throne of our hearts. True faith acknowledges that we cannot pay for our own sin and live because we know that our sin equals death. True faith also accepts the rule that sin at its core is rebellion against God.

That's why, when we see that the heart of God toward us is good, our heart toward Him changes. We are so grateful that He has saved us and so saddened by our own sin, which we know has hurt Him and others, that what we want—what drives us—has changed. We no longer want to follow our own whims and ways: We want to follow God. Before we were Christians,

MATTHEW 7:24-28

[Jesus said,] "Everyone who hears these words of mine and puts them into practice is like a wise man who built his house on the rock. The rain came down, the streams rose, and the winds blew and beat against that house; yet it did not fall, because it had its foundation on the rock. But everyone who hears these words of mine and does not put them into practice is like a foolish man who built his house on sand. The rain came down, the streams rose, and the winds blew and beat against that house, and it fell with a great crash."

When Jesus had finished saying these things, the crowds were amazed at his teaching.

we wanted what we wanted—and our wants led to pain, struggle, and emptiness even in success. Now we understand things differently. True faith leads to obedience, which is following Jesus.

3. You may claim, "But I thought I was saved by faith apart from works!" Read the following Scriptures and draw a line to the truth each reveals:

Romans 4:13	Real faith leads to good works.
Romans 1:5	Abraham believed God versus just believing in God.
James 2:18-26	Obedience comes from faith.

Faith is not merely intellectual assent that Jesus is God's Son. Faith is not merely acknowledgment that we have sinned and need a Savior. Yes, Jesus came to save all who believe in Him, but faith in Him leads us to trust Him as our Savior and our Lord.

The key to a relationship with God is humility. Humility says, "I understand I need to be saved and cannot save myself. I cannot earn salvation or deserve it. Yes, Lord, I will let you save me!" Humility also says, "I will follow Jesus rather than go my own way. My way of seeing things can be—and often is—wrong, and Jesus is right." To be a disciple of Jesus means that we now learn truth as God sees it, and we learn to obey Him.

Growing in this humility also requires that we follow a human disciplemaker. Remember Matthew 28:19-20, where Jesus tells His disciples to make disciples, teaching them to obey all that Jesus commanded? Humility is a lifelong journey for all of us, requiring us to follow God and His delegated authority. When we become disciplemakers, we are also characterized by humility.

DAY THREE REVIEW

1. What stood out to you or convicted you from today?

2. Is there an area in your life where you need to humble yourself and submit to God's authority? What is it? What would humility and submission look like?

3. How much of your daily walk of faith involves a "me and Jesus" mentality, meaning you have not allowed God's people to play a part in your life of learning and support? Why might that be happening? What would change that?

4. What is one area of self-rule in your life that you can turn over to God this week?

---

i. Answer: The correct answers are a, b, d, f, and g.
ii. Answer: All the statements are correct.

THE DEFINITION IS IN THE INVITATION: PART 2

GETTING STARTED

As we have been talking about following Jesus, much of what we have discussed to this point has been the knowledge of who Jesus is, what He has done for us, and what response that should bring in our lives. Now that we are following Jesus and we have this knowledge about who He is, it's time to start looking at the ways He wants to change us from the inside out.

Lord Jesus: Help me see what You want me to see today. Expose any lies I may believe and lead me to Your truth. Help me trust and obey You and walk out what I'm learning in every sphere of my life.

Yesterday we looked at being changed at the head level. Today we are focusing on the heart.

When I was young, I felt that my parents' rules were meant to control me—to keep me under my parents' control. As I grew up and decided to go my own way, living how I wanted, I came to understand that what they had taught me was right and true. Doing things my own way was painful for me and others. I had hurt them so much over the years, seeking the approval of people who in the end didn't care about me. These other people were willing to hurt me to get what they wanted from me. And even if they wanted to help me, their "wisdom" just led to more or different pain. Some of these friends were willing to ignore the pain our actions were causing me because they just wanted what they wanted.

Yet my parents continued to love me even though I had hurt them the most. I came to realize that the reason they were worth listening to was because their heart for me was love. Not only were they right, but their heart for me extended to forgiveness even though I had hurt them. As I stopped running away from them and came toward them, we began to spend time together, and their presence in my life began to change me at the heart level. Though I still occasionally hurt them, I was brokenhearted when I did. Though I still failed, I no longer did it out of anger or on purpose. My parents were clear: The reason they were like this with me was because it was exactly how God in Christ Jesus had been with them.

INVITED TO CHANGE

The road trip of discipleship is the journey toward change. We talked earlier about how, in His time on Earth, Jesus was inviting His guys into the front seat—ultimately toward heaven, but in the meantime toward their purpose as disciples on planet Earth. On the

> As I stopped running away from them and came toward them, we began spending time together, and their presence in my life began to change me at the heart level.

MATTHEW 22:37-40

Jesus replied: "'Love the Lord your God with all your heart and with all your soul and with all your mind.' This is the first and greatest commandment. And the second is like it: 'Love your neighbor as yourself.' All the Law and the Prophets hang on these two commandments."

EXODUS 20:3-17

[God said,] "You shall have no other gods before me.

"You shall not make for yourself an image in the form of anything in heaven above or on the earth beneath or in the waters below. You shall not bow down to them or worship them; for I, the LORD your God, am a jealous God, punishing the children for the sin of the parents to the third and fourth generation of those who hate me, but showing love to a thousand generations of those who love me and keep my commandments.

"You shall not misuse the name of the LORD your God, for the LORD will not hold anyone guiltless who misuses his name.

"Remember the Sabbath day by keeping it holy. Six days you shall labor and do all your work, but the seventh day is a sabbath to the LORD your God. On it you shall not do any work, neither you, nor your son or daughter, nor your male or female servant, nor your animals, nor any foreigner residing in your towns. For in six days the LORD made the heavens and the earth, the sea, and all that is in them, but he rested on the seventh day. Therefore the LORD blessed the Sabbath day and made it holy.

"Honor your father and your mother, so that you may live long in the land the LORD your God is giving you.

"You shall not murder.

"You shall not commit adultery.

"You shall not steal.

"You shall not give false testimony against your neighbor.

"You shall not covet your neighbor's house. You shall not covet your neighbor's wife, or his male or female servant, his ox or donkey, or anything that belongs to your neighbor."

journey they were seated where they could watch how He would pay for the sin debt of all humankind. They would see—firsthand—Jesus become the Lamb of God who would take away the sins of the world. He was also showing them how to make disciples. These men were both the messengers and the messenger makers.

What use is good news if no one is around to tell it accurately and effectively? What good are messengers if the way they live their lives does not bring credibility to the message? Remember, Jesus invited His disciples to come and follow Him just as they were—but He would make them into something else. Within the invitation was the promise of relationship. To come and follow Him would mean that they could come and be with Him. This would include friendship, coaching, reshaping, and transformation. Jesus was going to reshape them. He was offering to be their Head (authority), but He was also going to change their hearts.

FAITH THROUGH LOVE

Yesterday we pointed out that real faith involves trusting Jesus not only as Savior but also as Lord. While faith leads to a growing obedience (Romans 1:5), faith also expresses itself through love.

> In Christ Jesus neither circumcision nor uncircumcision has any value. The only thing that counts is faith expressing itself through love.
> GALATIANS 5:6

Every command in Scripture is about love.

Read Matthew 22:37-40 and Exodus 20:3-17 (see sidebar).

Jesus said that everything written in the Law and the Prophets (all the Old Testament Scriptures) had to do with love in some way. Every command either protects or builds relationship with God and others.

1. Reread the list of the Ten Commandments from Exodus 20:3-17. How do you notice each of these commands creating or protecting relationships? What else stands out to you?

It is possible to follow Jesus without truly understanding the heart of Jesus. The story of the Prodigal Son reveals that while the older brother was with the father (living in the same house), he did not have the heart of the father toward his own brother. The apostle Paul affirms this reality that you can follow Jesus for reasons other than love.

Read 1 Corinthians 13:1-4 (see sidebar).

I CORINTHIANS 13:1-4

If I speak in the tongues of men or of angels, but do not have love, I am only a resounding gong or a clanging cymbal. If I have the gift of prophecy and can fathom all mysteries and all knowledge, and if I have a faith that can move mountains, but do not have love, I am nothing. If I give all I possess to the poor and give over my body to hardship that I may boast, but do not have love, I gain nothing.

Love is patient, love is kind. It does not envy, it does not boast, it is not proud.

In these verses, Paul tells us it is possible to do many things that might seem right but that do not mean much to God. Some might give all they have to the poor so that others will applaud them. Some might do good deeds in pursuit of fame or position. Others might become martyrs because they think doing so will earn them salvation. Many believe that spiritual maturity is knowing the Word and all of God's mysteries or that if you are gifted (speaking in the tongues of angels and men), you have achieved some special spiritual status.

Paul's point? None of it means a thing. No good deed or seeming spiritual maturity matters without love. God's Word is clear: As you follow Him, you will be changed at the heart level.

I can hear some of you saying, "But wait—I don't always love people well. In fact, I don't feel a thing a lot of the time." Well, God knew we needed to know what love really is from His perspective if we were to grow into the likeness of Christ. That is exactly what He gave us in 1 Corinthians 13:4-7.

THE RIGHT DEFINITION OF *LOVE*

The Greek word for "love" in this passage is *agapē*, which means an act of the will to give the other what they need rather than what they deserve. Grace flows out of this kind of love. In 1 Corinthians, Paul tells us what love *does* rather than how it *feels*: valuing God and others, giving of self for the other.

This kind of love is impossible without God's help. Remember, Scripture tells us that the Holy Spirit indwelled us when we were saved, and now He works in our hearts (Galatians 5:22-23; Philippians 2:13). The power to do so comes from God's Spirit working within us. Love looks like certain behaviors—and love looks like a person: Jesus Christ.

Our world defines *love* as an emotion. Love looks like strong romantic feelings, even lust. We believe that a good relationship is one that isn't hard work, one that just comes easily. If it's not, we say we must not have met our true soulmate. That is not how the Bible defines *love*.

From God's perspective we have several barriers keeping us from truly loving. Remember, we inherited a sinful nature—a spiritual virus or disease that causes us to be self-centered and rebellious. Sin destroys relationships. It makes us untrustworthy and blind. Left to itself, sin will cause us to destroy relationships. We also have a spiritual enemy who desires to destroy what God made perfect.

This is why Jesus had to come. He died for our sin, giving us the truth about what love is and does. Jesus is our model, and His Word is our guide. He also gave us other mature believers to help us understand and live out the truth. We are on a journey toward maturity, and maturity is what gives us the ability to be in a loving relationship with God and others.

DAY FOUR REVIEW

1. What stood out to you or convicted you from today?

2. Which of the concepts taught in 1 Corinthians 13:4-7 do you have the most trouble with? Why?

3. Is there a struggling relationship in your life right now where God is calling you to give love rather than what the other person might deserve? What can you do this week to extend God's grace in that relationship?

Day Five

THE DEFINITION IS IN THE INVITATION: PART 3

GETTING STARTED

- We are being changed at the head level (what we know and who we follow).
- We are being changed at the heart level (what love is and where it comes from).

Lord Jesus: Help me see what You want me to see today. Expose any lies I may believe and lead me to Your truth. Help me trust and obey You and walk out what I'm learning in every sphere of my life.

Jesus invited His disciples to go on a journey, to get into a vehicle of relationship with Him. Jesus Himself was the driver, and as He demonstrated where they were going and how to operate the relational vehicle, He was teaching those in the vehicle how to drive a relational vehicle themselves.

This journey would change the disciples at the heart level. They would learn to see people the way Jesus saw them. They would come to understand the real problems with the world: sin, the brokenness sin causes, and the devil, who keeps trying to sabotage the journey.

In the same way, a mature disciple of Jesus has responded to the gospel and gotten into the car, allowing Jesus to drive where He wants to take them. On the journey, we are changed at the heart level. We learn to be relational people who love God and others. And from that, we become people who live out the full definition of being a disciple of Jesus.

INVITED TO JOIN THE MISSION

Jesus said, "Come and follow me, and I will make you fishers of men" (Matthew 4:19, WNT). Once we accept the invitation into relationship and heart change, we step into the final part of Jesus' invitation. Our mission in life changes. We become committed to the mission of Christ—disciplemaking.

God the Father thought we were worth His Son's life, and Jesus (God the Son) agreed. If God, the Creator and Sustainer of the universe, is on a mission for the souls of men and He thought it was worth His own life—how can it not be worth ours as well?

When we realize who Jesus is and that He has a mission for regular people like us, we feel honored to be invited to join Him. And no matter how hard this mission seems, we can find confidence in this truth: Our mission leader rose from the dead and made it clear to us that He will also raise us to eternal life and victory with Him.

Becoming a fisher of men is built upon the fact that we are following Jesus and being changed by Jesus. We cannot just go straight to the mission without allowing our leader to change our hearts. If we try to move forward without heart change, then we are cut off

> When we realize who Jesus is and that He has a mission for regular, everyday people like us, we feel honored to be invited to join Jesus.

from the mind of Christ and the heart of Christ. If Jesus is not guiding us, we won't know what the right fight is, and even if we did, we would fight the right fight in the wrong way.

THE RIGHT HEART

A disciple's desire to reach the lost is born out of a love for God. God loves those who are lost so much that He was willing to give up His place in heaven to save them and us. If we truly love Him, then we will love those He loves.

As the heart of God grows in us, we begin to love people too. As a disciple follows Jesus, Jesus changes the disciple so that they desire to do what He desires them to do. Remember again the verse that defines all this: "Come and follow me, and I will make you . . ." (Matthew 4:19, WNT). Jesus changes us as we follow Him.

We cannot change ourselves because

- we don't know what we are supposed to look like in the first place, and
- we don't have the power to change ourselves.

Only through following Jesus and being changed by Him are we led to become fishers of men. As we understand His love for us and the lengths to which He will go to save us, we are grateful—and we want to express our gratitude in action.

THE PRODIGAL SON STORY REVISITED

Years ago my son, who is now a youth pastor, was a drug addict and was living in a homeless shelter. My wife and I had done all we could, and we could no longer protect him from himself. It was the most painful experience of our lives. While he was there, a pastor who had been serving in the homeless shelter recognized my son's last name. The pastor had gone through a training our church had done and read a couple of my books, and the material and training had helped him and his church. Without telling me, he began to visit my son and take him to lunch. He constantly pointed my son toward Jesus and back home to us, even when my son didn't want to hear it.

Eventually my son did come home, but he did not tell me about this pastor until many months later. When I found out, I looked up the pastor's number and called him to thank him. He told me that he just wanted to bless me for all he had learned. I told him there was no greater way to minister to my heart than to do what he did. There was no better way to love me than to love my prodigal son.

Now consider the heart of God the Father. There is no better way to thank Him for what He has done for us than to take part in His mission to save the lost and rebellious. John 3:16 tells us that Jesus came to the world because He loved His human creations. If we truly love Jesus, then we will recognize, understand, and join in His love for all those who are lost.

Understanding the spiritual reality that there are only two categories of people—saved and lost, each destined for a different experience of eternity—changes how we see every area of our lives. Just as in our life on Earth we learn skills that will help us make a living, understanding the spiritual reality moves us to learn tools and develop abilities to disciple others in every sphere of our lives.

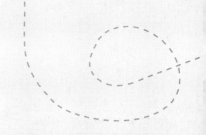

Read Matthew 6:22-33 (see sidebar).

1. This passage helps us understand Jesus' view of our time on planet Earth. What stands out to you as you read this passage?

_____

_____

Read Ephesians 2:1-10.

2. After reading this passage, which of these statements seem correct?

    a. Paul was a perfect man, and he had the right to be a disciple because of his obedience.
    b. Every person has sinned, and God has given us grace through faith.
    c. God saved us for a purpose He had in mind for us before the world was created.
    d. We are created anew even though we were once destroyed.
    e. You were saved *from* something *for* something.[i]

Read 2 Corinthians 5:14-21.

3. After reading this passage, which of these statements seem correct?

    a. What we do is compelled by fear that we won't earn salvation.
    b. What we do is compelled by our love for God and others.
    c. Disciples have been reconciled to God and given the ministry of reconciling others.
    d. We are ambassadors of our King, who is Jesus.
    e. Our message from the King is that people are going to hell but that God can—and wants to—save them.[ii]

As we think back to the definition of a disciple, we should be able to see that Jesus expected His disciples to follow Him. As they followed Him, their hearts would change. They then would see themselves as fishers of men: disciples who would make disciples. Making disciples was not just the job of the first disciples of Jesus—it is the role of every disciple. This does not mean that every person is called to quit their job and become a pastor, but it does mean that we are all disciples in every sphere of our lives.

4. Which of the following statements describes a disciple of Jesus?

    a. A disciple of Jesus serves God and others with resources (time, abilities, gifts, finances) regardless of earthly rewards.
    b. A disciple of Jesus already knows how to treat other people.
    c. A disciple of Jesus doesn't think or act differently after deciding to follow Jesus.
    d. A disciple of Jesus loves God and others (Romans 12:1-2; 1 Corinthians 13:1-7).
    e. A disciple of Jesus is committed to His mission and His team.
    f. A disciple of Jesus seeks to intentionally grow in their relationship with Jesus.[iii]

MATTHEW 6:22-33

[Jesus said,] "The eye is the lamp of the body. If your eyes are healthy, your whole body will be full of light. But if your eyes are unhealthy, your whole body will be full of darkness. If then the light within you is darkness, how great is that darkness!

"No one can serve two masters. Either you will hate the one and love the other, or you will be devoted to the one and despise the other. You cannot serve both God and money.

"Therefore I tell you, do not worry about your life, what you will eat or drink; or about your body, what you will wear. Is not life more than food, and the body more than clothes? Look at the birds of the air; they do not sow or reap or store away in barns, and yet your heavenly Father feeds them. Are you not much more valuable than they? Can any one of you by worrying add a single hour to your life?

"And why do you worry about clothes? See how the flowers of the field grow. They do not labor or spin. Yet I tell you that not even Solomon in all his splendor was dressed like one of these. If that is how God clothes the grass of the field, which is here today and tomorrow is thrown into the fire, will he not much more clothe you—you of little faith? So do not worry, saying, 'What shall we eat?' or 'What shall we drink?' or 'What shall we wear?' For the pagans run after all these things, and your heavenly Father knows that you need them. But seek first his kingdom and his righteousness, and all these things will be given to you as well."

ROMANS 12:1-2, NLT

And so, dear brothers and sisters, I plead with you to give your bodies to God because of all he has done for you. Let them be a living and holy sacrifice—the kind he will find acceptable. This is truly the way to worship him. Don't copy the behavior and customs of this world, but let God transform you into a new person by changing the way you think. Then you will learn to know God's will for you, which is good and pleasing and perfect.

1 CORINTHIANS 13:1-7

If I speak in the tongues of men or of angels, but do not have love, I am only a resounding gong or a clanging cymbal. If I have the gift of prophecy and can fathom all mysteries and all knowledge, and if I have a faith that can move mountains, but do not have love, I am nothing. If I give all I possess to the poor and give over my body to hardship that I may boast, but do not have love, I gain nothing.

Love is patient, love is kind. It does not envy, it does not boast, it is not proud. It does not dishonor others, it is not self-seeking, it is not easily angered, it keeps no record of wrongs. Love does not delight in evil but rejoices with the truth. It always protects, always trusts, always hopes, always perseveres.

Notes and Thoughts

Each of us is on a journey of discipleship, which means we may be immature and incomplete—but if we are not on the journey at all because we refuse to be, are we a disciple of Jesus? Let me say it another way: If being a disciple and a Christian are the same thing in Scripture and in the early church, can you say you are a Christian if you are not a committed growing disciple?

Just because you have decided to follow Jesus does not mean you do it very well at the beginning or will ever be perfect at it. But discipleship does involve commitment to the journey, no matter how far we have to go. We read in the Gospels that Jesus often asked the disciples why they had so little faith. We all have growth ahead of us. Even when we see ourselves as failures, we can be thankful that Jesus is a grace giver. Over time, each of us will be able to look back and be encouraged that we are not what we used to be. And we must continue to look at Jesus and His perfection to keep us humble and growing.

DAY FIVE REVIEW

1. What stood out to you or convicted you from today?

2. Describe some of the ways you are currently serving God and others with your resources (time, abilities, gifts, finances).

3. What are some ways you have seen Jesus change your heart or reshape the way you think since you began following Him?

4. Choose a person from one area of your life who does not know Jesus. What is one thing you can do this week to illustrate Jesus to them, either by word or action?

---

i.   Answer: The correct statements are b, c, d, and e.
ii. Answer: The correct statements are b, c, d, and e.
iii. Answer: The correct answers are a, d, e, and f.

JESUS' METHOD OF DISCIPLESHIP

Day One

JESUS: OUR MESSAGE AND MODEL

GETTING STARTED

- The good news of the gospel is most importantly about Jesus dying for our sins and rising from the dead.
- However, it is also important that Jesus made disciples. He knew He needed faithful messengers to deliver the Good News to the world (Romans 10:13-15).
- Jesus didn't just task His disciples with sharing the Good News; He showed His disciples how to be the kind of people who would bring credibility to the message. Through His life and message, He showed them what God's version of spiritual maturity looked like.
- Jesus also gave the disciples a model to follow in disciplemaking. When Jesus sent the disciples into the world to make disciples, He did not mean for them to just go and do it any way they wanted; He intended that they should do with others what He had done with them.

Lord Jesus: Help me see what You want me to see today. Expose any lies I may believe and lead me to Your truth. Help me trust and obey You and walk out what I'm learning in every sphere of my life.

ROMANS 10:13-15, NLT

For "Everyone who calls on the name of the Lord will be saved."
  But how can they call on him to save them unless they believe in him? And how can they believe in him if they have never heard about him? And how can they hear about him unless someone tells them? And how will anyone go and tell them without being sent? That is why the Scriptures say, "How beautiful are the feet of messengers who bring good news!"

JESUS' REPRODUCIBLE METHOD

Let's look back at our key verse on discipleship:

[Jesus said,] "Come and follow me, and I will make you fishers of men."
MATTHEW 4:19, WNT

We've talked about how the verse includes an invitation with a definition. But this verse also implies relationship. Jesus was saying, "Come be *with me*."

This verse also fits within a larger story that reveals how Jesus used relationship to disciple His people. We often read the Gospels to study Jesus and His teachings, but we miss that within the story of the Gospels is a method and model to follow. We should be

Scan QR code to access video podcasts and other content that accompanies this week's session.

JOHN 1:36-39

When he saw Jesus passing by, he said, "Look, the Lamb of God!"

When the two disciples heard him say this, they followed Jesus. Turning around, Jesus saw them following and asked, "What do you want?"

They said, "Rabbi" (which means "Teacher"), "where are you staying?"

"Come," he replied, "and you will see."

So they went and saw where he was staying, and they spent that day with him. It was about four in the afternoon.

looking at **how** Jesus shared, **when** Jesus shared, and **who** He shared **with**. We should look at **where** He was when He was teaching (on a mountainside, in a synagogue, at the Temple, looking over a city). While Jesus certainly spoke to crowds at times, most often He gave His disciples the time and explanation that others would have missed. Jesus was journeying with and teaching with His disciples in mind even when a crowd was present. He was modeling a lifestyle (how to deal with people, how to pray, etc.) in front of His disciples. He knew His desired outcome from the beginning, and He was working backward. He had a timeline and a process in mind. Jesus wanted the disciples to know the truth, to love God and others well, and to know how to fulfill the mission. He was teaching them lessons that had an application in every sphere of their lives.

JESUS' REPRODUCIBLE PROCESS

Jesus was a master coach and an intentional leader. He knew that real disciplemaking starts with a simple beginning and then moves on to more complex ideas as the disciples grow in maturity. Jesus didn't want His disciples to simply have knowledge about something; He wanted them to be able to do something well. Again, He had the end in mind. He was able to assess where each of His disciples was and how far they were from where they needed to be. He also knew what kinds of environments and lessons they needed to be able to move toward growth and the final destination. Jesus utilized a reproducible process that the disciples themselves could later repeat:

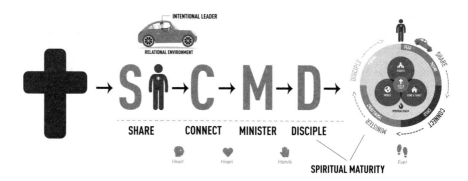

Share

Jesus SHARED who He was through performing miracles, fulfilling prophecies, teaching powerful lessons, and living a sinless life.

- God revealed who Jesus was through the proclamation of John the Baptist and the manifestation of the Holy Spirit descending on Jesus at His baptism. God spoke directly to those present at Jesus' baptism, declaring that Jesus was His Son, in whom He was well pleased.
- Jesus spent a lot of time with those who would become His disciples before He invited them to become disciples, sharing a glimpse of His power, authority, and mission before inviting them to follow. (See John 2:1-11 for an example.)
- As Jesus shared His life with His disciples, He shared more and more of Himself and His teachings.

Connect

Jesus then invited those who believed to CONNECT with Him in relationship.

- In connecting with His disciples, Jesus revealed—in increasing measure—who He was and what the truth was from His perspective (*head-level instruction*).
- Jesus modeled for the disciples what love looks like (*heart-level instruction*).
- Jesus showed the disciples how to live out being fishers of men by showing them what to do and when (*hand-level instruction*).

[Jesus said,] "Come and follow me, and I will make you fishers of men."

MATTHEW 4:19, WNT

"Anyone who loves their life will lose it, while anyone who hates their life in this world will keep it for eternal life. Whoever serves me must follow me; and where I am, my servant also will be. My Father will honor the one who serves me.

"Now my soul is troubled, and what shall I say? 'Father, save me from this hour'? No, it was for this very reason I came to this hour."

JOHN 12:25-27

Minister

Jesus then began to train His disciples for MINISTRY.

- At first Jesus had them do simple things like pass out the food when He fed the five thousand.
- As time went on, their tasks changed—He sent them out in pairs to preach all over Israel.
- During this portion of ministry, the disciples were casting out demons and healing the sick.
- When they returned, Jesus debriefed with them.

After this the Lord appointed seventy-two others and sent them two by two ahead of him to every town and place where he was about to go.

LUKE 10:1

Calling the Twelve to him, he began to send them out two by two and gave them authority over impure spirits.

MARK 6:7

Disciple

Finally Jesus went to be with the Father. He sent the disciples the Holy Spirit and then sent them to make DISCIPLES. Jesus' disciples repeated the process they had learned.

Then Jesus came to them and said, "All authority in heaven and on earth has been given to me. Therefore go and make disciples of all nations, baptizing them in the name of the Father and of the Son and of the Holy Spirit, and teaching them to obey everything I have commanded you. And surely I am with you always, to the very end of the age."

MATTHEW 28:18-20

Read Acts 2.

1. In Acts 2, which verses best describe the disciples SHARING who Jesus is?

2. Look back at the Matthew 28:18-20 passage. What similarities do you notice between Peter's message in Acts 2 and what Jesus commanded the disciples to do?

3. In Acts 2, which verses show the disciples CONNECTING with those who decided to follow Jesus?

    a. What verse in Acts 2 reveals who CONNECTED?

    b. Which verses show them CONNECTING with God?

    c. Which verses show them CONNECTING with one another?

4. Which verses in Acts 2 show that the early disciples were becoming MINISTERS?

    a. What verse shows who MINISTERED in the early church?

    b. Read Acts 6:1-7 (see sidebar). Which verses show that the disciples in the early church were beginning to make disciples who were moving into ministry?

    c. List the names of the ministers who began to take care of the Greek widows.

5. Read Acts 7:8-10 and Acts 8:4-6 (see sidebar). What verses show that those who MINISTERED in Acts 6 were becoming DISCIPLEmakers later?

> You have heard me teach things that have been confirmed by many reliable witnesses. Now teach these truths to other trustworthy people who will be able to pass them on to others.
>
> 2 TIMOTHY 2:2, NLT

6. **Go Deeper:** Do a little extra research online or read the letter of 1 Timothy to answer the following questions.

ACTS 6:1-7

In those days when the number of disciples was increasing, the Hellenistic Jews among them complained against the Hebraic Jews because their widows were being overlooked in the daily distribution of food. So the Twelve gathered all the disciples together and said, "It would not be right for us to neglect the ministry of the word of God in order to wait on tables. Brothers and sisters, choose seven men from among you who are known to be full of the Spirit and wisdom. We will turn this responsibility over to them and will give our attention to prayer and the ministry of the word."

This proposal pleased the whole group. They chose Stephen, a man full of faith and of the Holy Spirit; also Philip, Procorus, Nicanor, Timon, Parmenas, and Nicolas from Antioch, a convert to Judaism. They presented these men to the apostles, who prayed and laid their hands on them.

So the word of God spread. The number of disciples in Jerusalem increased rapidly, and a large number of priests became obedient to the faith.

a. Who was Paul, the writer of this passage?

b. Who was Timothy, the one being written to?

c. Who were Timothy's mother and grandmother?

d. What had Paul done in Timothy's life?

e. What did Paul want Timothy to do?

f. Did Timothy have some kind of higher education?

Based on what we see in Scripture, we can know unequivocally that we are all called to be and make disciples. Jesus gave us a model to follow and a process that anyone can reproduce. This journey takes time and intentionality, as well as commitment on the part of the disciple and the disciplemaker.

DAY ONE REVIEW

1. What stood out to you or convicted you from today?

2. Write down Jesus' purpose(s) for making disciples.

3. Why do you think Jesus chose that time in history to come to Earth?

4. Do you think Jesus could have reached more people if He had come at a time when He could have used technology? Why or why not?

5. How and when were you introduced to Jesus? As you look at your own discipleship journey, what parts align with the different elements of Jesus' process?

ACTS 7:8-10

[The disciple Stephen said,] "Then [God] gave Abraham the covenant of circumcision. And Abraham became the father of Isaac and circumcised him eight days after his birth. Later Isaac became the father of Jacob, and Jacob became the father of the twelve patriarchs.

"Because the patriarchs were jealous of Joseph, they sold him as a slave into Egypt. But God was with him and rescued him from all his troubles. He gave Joseph wisdom and enabled him to gain the goodwill of Pharaoh king of Egypt. So Pharaoh made him ruler over Egypt and all his palace."

ACTS 8:4-6

Those who had been scattered preached the word wherever they went. Philip went down to a city in Samaria and proclaimed the Messiah there. When the crowds heard Philip and saw the signs he performed, they all paid close attention to what he said.

Notes and Thoughts

Day Two

SHARING YOUR LIFE

> *Lord Jesus: Help me see what You want me to see today. Expose any lies I may believe and lead me to Your truth. Help me trust and obey You and walk out what I'm learning in every sphere of my life.*

Yesterday we went through Jesus' reproducible process: SCMD. Now let's start to break it down into parts. Remember that Jesus had an end in mind from the beginning. He was training His disciples to be fishers of men someday. Jesus began by SHARING Himself (via time, some shared experiences, and teaching), which led the disciples to believe Jesus was the promised Messiah. Because of what He shared, some were willing to take the next step when the time came for Jesus to invite them into CONNECTION. The disciples could not do all that Jesus could do, and they certainly were not Jesus, but Jesus wanted them to pick up parts of how He shared His life and truth to use later. He was modeling for them how to make disciples, and that would begin with sharing their lives and God's truth with others.

WHY SHARE?

Sharing is different from telling. The word *tell* does not connote kindness or giving more than just words. The word SHARE is a loving, relational word. It implies, *I have something and will offer it to you too so we both can have it.* Jesus came to Earth to share His very life, and He wants us to do the same. He modeled how to reach people by meeting them right where they were. Being in pain or discomfort was an opportunity for Jesus to share Himself, and He did not avoid giving of Himself sacrificially to those He wanted to save. In disciplemaking, we use the word in two senses: SHARE your life and SHARE the truth—the Good News! Today we will look at what it means to share your life, which involves not only coming alongside others in their openness or need but also sharing your struggles and your testimony of what God has done.

Sharing Your Life

We have already seen that as disciples we are learning to love others at the heart level while we walk with Christ. Now we are learning that Jesus changed His disciples as He shared His life with them—and He does the same for us.

Jesus came to Earth to SHARE His very life, and He wants us to do the same. He modeled how to reach people by meeting them right where they were.

1. Read the following examples of Jesus SHARING His life and His desire for us to SHARE ours. With these passages in mind, how has the word SHARE in the SCMD process changed meaning for you?

    - Luke 5:27-32
    - Luke 10:25-37
    - Luke 19:1-10
    - John 4:7-42

    _____

    _____

    _____

Read Luke 10:25-37.

2. Why do you think those who were supposed to SHARE with the robbed man walked around him? Circle the answers that you think may have been true.

    a. They thought it must be his own fault and that God was punishing him.
    b. They were on their way to do religious work and didn't have the time.
    c. They were too tired from doing religious work, and in their mind, their work was done.
    d. No one was around to see them do it and praise them for it.
    e. They had already given money in tithe, so the rest of their money was theirs.
    f. Other: _____

3. Read the following passages and notice the ways in which you see Jesus creating opportunities to SHARE the truth about Himself by sharing His life with others in their time of need or openness.

    - *Matthew 9:10-12*: Why do you think that Jesus spent time with Matthew (the tax collector) and his friends, even though they were disreputable?

    _____

    _____

    - *Luke 10:25-37*: What do you think Jesus wanted His followers to do with man who was left broken by robbers? Who do you consider the hero of the story? What does this teach you about who Jesus wants us to share our lives with?

    _____

    _____

    - *Luke 19:1-10*: Can you think of a reason Jesus chose to go to Zacchaeus's house to meet with him before sharing the truth with him?

    _____

    _____

    - *John 4:7-42*: What happened as a result of Jesus meeting the woman at the well?

    _____

    _____

MATTHEW 26:36-42

Then Jesus went with his disciples to a place called Gethsemane, and he said to them, "Sit here while I go over there and pray." He took Peter and the two sons of Zebedee along with him, and he began to be sorrowful and troubled. Then he said to them, "My soul is overwhelmed with sorrow to the point of death. Stay here and keep watch with me."

Going a little farther, he fell with his face to the ground and prayed, "My Father, if it is possible, may this cup be taken from me. Yet not as I will, but as you will."

Then he returned to his disciples and found them sleeping. "Couldn't you men keep watch with me for one hour?" he asked Peter. "Watch and pray so that you will not fall into temptation. The spirit is willing, but the flesh is weak."

He went away a second time and prayed, "My Father, if it is not possible for this cup to be taken away unless I drink it, may your will be done."

1 PETER 4:10

Each of you should use whatever gift you have received to serve others, as faithful stewards of God's grace in its various forms.

MATTHEW 5:27-32

[Jesus said,] "You have heard that it was said, 'You shall not commit adultery.' But I tell you that anyone who looks at a woman lustfully has already committed adultery with her in his heart. If your right eye causes you to stumble, gouge it out and throw it away. It is better for you to lose one part of your body than for your whole body to be thrown into hell. And if your right hand causes you to stumble, cut it off and throw it away. It is better for you to lose one part of your body than for your whole body to go into hell.

"It has been said, 'Anyone who divorces his wife must give her a certificate of divorce.' But I tell you that anyone who divorces his wife, except for sexual immorality, makes her the victim of adultery, and anyone who marries a divorced woman commits adultery."

Testimony Bullet Points

Sharing Your Struggles

When we look at Matthew 26:36-42, we discover something astounding. Some people believe they are mature because they are loving toward others, and that is partly true. But if we won't let anyone love us, we are not moving toward spiritual maturity. Maturity involves sharing all of life: learning to share our hurts and struggles with others and letting them love us too. In Matthew 26, Jesus, the Son of God, asks His friends to pray for Him because His soul is grieved. We are called on to confess our sins and share our burdens, and even Jesus shows us that love, by His definition, includes allowing others to see our struggles even as we see theirs.

4. Circle the things you think might be benefits of sharing your struggles.

   a. When you realize that everyone has struggles, you no longer believe the devil's schemes that something must be wrong with you.
   b. When you share your struggles, others get to use their gifts to help you through it, which leads to their growth.
   c. God's grace flows through others to us and through us to others (1 Peter 4:10).
   d. People who are broken and have no one to help them will see what they could have if they choose to follow Christ.

Sharing Your Testimony

When I use the word SHARE, it also implies that I am going to share something sacred to me with you. My story is sacred to me, and yours is sacred to you. Part of sharing is giving your testimony: the good news about what God has done. Jesus gave His testimony about where He came from when He told the disciples that He was sharing with them what He had seen and heard when He was with the Father (John 8:38).

The men who wrote Scripture give their testimony within the stories they tell. Notice that their stories demonstrate humility: They simply give the details of their interactions with Jesus in the New Testament, much of which is not flattering to them. The disciples don't try to make themselves the heroes—they are pointing to the hero: Jesus. We see the same posture when Paul gives his testimony while being tried by King Agrippa (Acts 26:4-18).

Guidelines for Sharing Your Testimony

- A good testimony can be told in five minutes or it can be much longer, depending on whom you are talking to and in what context.
- Start with where you were when Jesus found you.
- Talk about how you met Jesus.
- Be honest about where the Lord has brought you. Remember, the hero of this story is Jesus! You don't need to pretend you are perfect or without issues.
- Choose to share whatever parts are relevant and appropriate depending on the context. For example, don't tell a child the details of sin; don't share about past sexual issues with someone of the opposite gender other than your spouse.

Outlining Your Testimony

Take a few minutes to write your testimony out in bullet points in the space provided, and be ready to share it with your group. As you do, here are some things to remember:

- You may not be able to answer every question people ask about God, but you can tell your testimony about what God has done for you personally. Your story is indisputable.
- Telling your testimony reminds you of the good things God has done for you.
- Your testimony reveals who you were, shows you have the humility to talk about it, and will help others feel more comfortable and safe to open up themselves.
- Remember, your testimony is not declaring that you no longer have problems or failings. You are changing, but you are still reliant on God's continual grace.
- We do not glorify our past or exaggerate it for effect. We are sad about who we were and thankful for what God is doing in us now.

All of us can share what Jesus has done for us with someone else. Pray this week for God to show you someone you can begin to disciple by sharing your life.

DAY TWO REVIEW

1. What stood out to you or convicted you from today?

2. What did God reveal to you when it comes to sharing your testimony?

3. Talk or write about a time you shared something personal about yourself with someone else. What was the response?

Notes and Thoughts

Day Three

SHARING THE GOSPEL

GETTING STARTED

We have been talking about sharing our testimony with others, telling them what Christ has done in our life. Now we are ready to move on to sharing the gospel with others, telling them what Christ has done for all humankind and how they can respond to Him.

Lord Jesus: Help me see what You want me to see today. Expose any lies I may believe and lead me to Your truth. Help me trust and obey You and walk out what I'm learning in every sphere of my life.

When Jesus told the twelve to go and make disciples, He did not mean they should do it any way they wanted. Jesus knew the way He had taught them was the best way. And because the disciples had just been through the journey with Him personally, they would know what He meant when He gave them the mission.

Jesus' intention was to make and release disciples who would build His church (Matthew 16:18). When you look at Acts 2 (and, in fact, the rest of the book of Acts), you can see that the disciples did exactly what they had been trained to do:

- They shared the truth about Jesus (Acts 2:1-41).
- They connected in relationship with those who believed and were baptized (Acts 2:42-47).
- They began to train people within these connection groups to minister to one another and to those who were lost (Acts 4:34).
- Finally, they sent out disciples to make disciples (Acts 8:5).

The apostle Paul raised up Timothy and Titus, then sent them with others to various places, and the message spread. Jesus' process of "Share, Connect, train for Ministry, and then release to make Disciples" was reproduced again and again.

You have heard me teach things that have been confirmed by many reliable witnesses. Now teach these truths to other trustworthy people who will be able to pass them on to others.

2 TIMOTHY 2:2, NLT

Read 2 Corinthians 5:14 and 1 Peter 2:9-10 (see sidebar).

I have found that very few people share their faith with unsaved friends or those within their spheres of influence. That includes families! Most Christian parents say that, in part, they take their kids to youth group so their kids will know Jesus. A staggering number of

MATTHEW 16:18

"I tell you that you are Peter, and on this rock I will build my church, and the gates of Hades will not overcome it."

2 CORINTHIANS 5:14

Christ's love compels us, because we are convinced that one died for all, and therefore all died.

1 PETER 2:9-10

You are a chosen people, a royal priesthood, a holy nation, God's special possession, that you may declare the praises of him who called you out of darkness into his wonderful light. Once you were not a people, but now you are the people of God; once you had not received mercy, but now you have received mercy.

parents don't know how to share the gospel with their own kids. They don't know how, or don't believe it's their job, to make disciples of Jesus at home.

In contrast, most people hear a message from a pastor and receive Christ at an event, rather than having it SHARED with them by their parents or friends personally. Most of those who accept Christ are never personally CONNECTED with a more mature intentional believer for the purpose of a defined discipleship journey. Some results of this kind of Christianity include . . .

- Most Christians don't regularly share the gospel with others.[1]
- Only 32 percent of Christians between the ages of 23 and 75 attend church weekly.[2]
- Although many people may be connected to a group or club, most groups are not for the sole purpose of connection and Bible study.
- Around 20 percent of churchgoers serve in any way in the church.[3]
- Only 21 percent follow the biblical practice of tithing.[4]
- Only 4 percent of Christians have a biblical worldview.[5]

Do you remember our discussion about the difference between conversion and discipleship? It is my conviction that many Christians today don't demonstrate visible spiritual maturity because most have not been discipled—they have been merely converted. My hope is that through this journey of discipleship, your life will begin to demonstrate the fruit of spiritual maturity (Galatians 5:22-23).

SHARING THE GOSPEL

Jesus came to bring the Good News (the gospel) to announce that through Himself, a means to a restored relationship with God was now possible.

1. If you were given the opportunity right now to SHARE the truth about how to be saved, how would you explain it?

_____

_____

_____

Read Colossians 1:13-23 (see sidebar) to learn how Paul phrased the truth about how to be saved.

2. Which of the following concepts from our earlier lessons do you see in Colossians 1:13-23?

   a. Where did this world come from? What was it like in the beginning? (Genesis 2)
   b. What happened that changed it to what we have now? (Genesis 2–3)
      The choice and the Curse.
      The Curse spreads.
      We all have the Curse because we have all sinned (Romans 3:9-23).
   c. *God's Part*: What did God do about our choice and the Curse?
      He sent His Son to die in our stead if we will accept Him (Isaiah 53; Romans 5:6-11).

COLOSSIANS 1:13-23, NLT

For he has rescued us from the kingdom of darkness and transferred us into the Kingdom of his dear Son, who purchased our freedom and forgave our sins.

Christ is the visible image of the invisible God. He existed before anything was created and is supreme over all creation, for through him God created everything in the heavenly realms and on earth. He made the things we can see and the things we can't see— such as thrones, kingdoms, rulers, and authorities in the unseen world. Everything was created through him and for him. He existed before anything else, and he holds all creation together. Christ is also the head of the church, which is his body. He is the beginning, supreme over all who rise from the dead. So he is first in everything. For God in all his fullness was pleased to live in Christ, and through him God reconciled everything to himself. He made peace with everything in heaven and on earth by means of Christ's blood on the cross.

This includes you who were once far away from God. You were his enemies, separated from him by your evil thoughts and actions. Yet now he has reconciled you to himself through the death of Christ in his physical body. As a result, he has brought you into his own presence, and you are holy and blameless as you stand before him without a single fault.

But you must continue to believe this truth and stand firmly in it. Don't drift away from the assurance you received when you heard the Good News. The Good News has been preached all over the world, and I, Paul, have been appointed as God's servant to proclaim it.

ROMANS 5:6-11, NLT

When we were utterly helpless, Christ came at just the right time and died for us sinners. Now, most people would not be willing to die for an upright person, though someone might perhaps be willing to die for a person who is especially good. But God showed his great love for us by sending Christ to die for us while we were still sinners. And since we have been made right in God's sight by the blood of Christ, he will certainly save us from God's condemnation. For since our friendship with God was restored by the death of his Son while we were still his enemies, we will certainly be saved through the life of his Son. So now we can rejoice in our wonderful new relationship with God because our Lord Jesus Christ has made us friends of God.

d. *Our Part*: What must we do to accept Jesus' sacrifice and experience restored relationship?

> We must trust in Jesus as our Savior and Lord (John 3:16).

According to Scripture, believing is not mere intellectual assent (Acts 2:36-42). True belief leads to a changed heart, which leads to changed direction (repentance). When we believe, we confess that Jesus is Lord (we are not ashamed of Him), and we choose to be baptized to symbolize dying to the old life and being raised to live a new life. Baptism is a picture of cleansing from our sin and a new birth. This picture burns the spiritual truth in our mind.

As our time together goes on, we will keep coming back to your ability and willingness to share your faith. To become fishers of men, we must become comfortable with this concept of SHARING our lives, our testimony, and how to become a disciple.

3. As you reflect on the two parts of SHARING in the SCMD process (sharing your life and sharing the gospel), what was new to you or perhaps impacted you in a different way?

_____

_____

4. Of the different aspects of SHARING, which is the hardest for you? In the space below, write your reasons why.
   - sharing your life (presence, struggles, and testimony)
   - sharing the gospel

_____

_____

5. Take another look at the Scripture passages we read today and the order in which they are given. What are some ways to remember these passages so that you can have them ready when the opportunity arises?

_____

_____

Here are some ideas:

- Memorize the verses in sequence.
- Place the verses on the inside of the front cover of your Bible.
- Write them on a card you put in your wallet.

6. Practice going through the verses with your spouse or a friend in the group. Practicing with someone always helps you work through different kinds of responses before you are in a real situation.

5. Start praying for doors to open to share the gospel with the people you love and work with. Write their names here.

_____

Remember, we are not sent to make converts—we are sent to make disciples. Once we share our lives and the gospel with another person, we need to then CONNECT with them so they can be taught to obey all that Jesus commanded.[6]

DAY THREE REVIEW

Notes and Thoughts

1. What stood out to you or convicted you from today?

2. Share a recent choice or decision you made that emerged from the changes God has made to your heart and mindset.

3. What habit or tool do you already have, or are planning on implementing in your life, to help you remember Bible verses that talk about the gospel?

1. Aaron Earls, "Evangelism More Prayed for Than Practiced by Churchgoers," Lifeway Research, April 23, 2019, https://research.lifeway.com/2019/04/23/evangelism-more-prayed-for-than-practiced-by-churchgoers.
2. "A New Chapter in Millennial Church Attendance," Barna, August 4, 2022, https://www.barna.com/research/church-attendance-2022. This percentage is the average of the weekly church attendance of Millennials (39 percent), Gen Xers (31 percent), and Boomers (25 percent) according to a 2022 study.
3. Shari Finnell, "Declining Volunteerism Is Changing the Church Experience," Faith & Leadership, March 7, 2023, https://faithandleadership.com/declining-volunteerism-changing-the-church-experience. This statistic is as of March 2022, according to a study on the effect of the global COVID-19 pandemic on church involvement.
4. "What Is a Tithe?: New Data on Perceptions of the 10 Percent," Barna, September 7, 2022, https://www.barna.com/research/what-is-a-tithe.
5. Tracy F. Munsil, "Biblical Worldview Among U.S. Adults Drops 33% Since Start of COVID-19 Pandemic," February 28, 2023, https://www.arizonachristian.edu/2023/02/28/biblical-worldview-among-u-s-adults-drops-33-since-start-of-covid-19-pandemic. This statistic is from *American Worldview Inventory 2023*, which was created by Arizona Christian University's Cultural Research Center.
6. See addendum at the back of this workbook to find out how to use the concepts shared in *The Disciple's Journey* as a simple way to walk someone through the gospel of Christ.

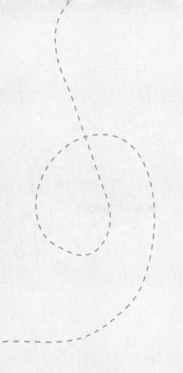

Day Four

CONNECT

GETTING STARTED

Hopefully you have found a tool or practice to help you remember the verses that talk about the gospel so you are ready to share them wherever you are. Today we are going to begin addressing the need we all have to be connected to both God and others.

Lord Jesus: Help me see what You want me to see today. Expose any lies I may believe and lead me to Your truth. Help me trust and obey You and walk out what I'm learning in every sphere of my life.

One day, Jesus made an astounding statement: "I am the way and the truth and the life. No one comes to the Father except through me" (John 14:6). Those who accepted this truth were invited to come and follow Him (Matthew 4:19). When Jesus said to come and follow Him, He was inviting people to be with Him in relationship—a CONNECTION. Before Jesus started sending the disciples out to do anything, He had to change their minds and hearts.

WHY WE DON'T KNOW HOW TO CONNECT

In our first week in this workbook, we discovered that we can look good and appear to be committed—and even be generous—but if we don't love, we are nothing. All those things can happen without love and for a reason other than love—but without love, none of it can lead to true CONNECTION.

In Jesus' time, the scribes and Pharisees (the religious leaders of the day) represented spiritual maturity to the Jewish people. Jesus made it clear that these men were not the models Jesus wanted His disciples to follow. He called the religious leaders whitewashed tombs (Matthew 23:24-27); they looked good on the outside but on the inside, they were filled with death. Even though some of these men were trying to honor God's law and serve His people, many of them missed that God created the law to reinstate love in a world that had lost sight of what love is. In another vivid metaphor, Jesus said that the religious leaders had strained out a gnat and swallowed a camel—they had completely missed the point.

Jesus came to Earth to tie the Old Testament teachings about God to a real, live, visible person who would show human beings what love was supposed to look like (Hebrews 1:2). Through His relationship with the disciples, Jesus showed them what relationship God's way looks like. He often said things that turned their understanding of love and following God upside down. For example:

"You have heard that it was said to the people long ago, 'You shall not murder, and anyone who murders will be subject to judgment.' But I tell you that anyone who is angry with a brother or sister will be subject to judgment. Again, anyone who says to a brother or sister, 'Raca,' is answerable to the court. And anyone who says, 'You fool!' will be in danger of the fire of hell.

"Therefore, if you are offering your gift at the altar and there remember that your brother or sister has something against you, leave your gift there in front of the altar. First go and be reconciled to them; then come and offer your gift."

MATTHEW 5:21-24

Jesus desired His disciples to love one another, rejecting pretense and choosing authentic relationship. When we are in safe relationships, we are not afraid of being judged or mocked. This safety allows us to be real, and we see each other for who we really are.

Of course, true vulnerability in authentic relationship eventually leads to conflict. People are broken, and the truth about that brokenness comes out as we spend time together. Love then must compel us to seek to resolve conflict well. This pursuit of loving one another is essential if you want to honor God and be close to Him.

1. Jesus is our model for love in action. Draw a connecting line from the New Testament verse to the corresponding teaching about what love looks like:

i. Matthew 18:21-35	a. Love those who don't love you back.
ii. Mark 9:35	b. He who wants to be first must be last.
iii. Matthew 5:46-48	c. Forgive others.
iv. Philippians 2:1-8	d. Love is revealed by how much it gives up.
v. John 15:13	e. The attitude and humility of Jesus demonstrate sacrificial love.*

Remember, Jesus taught His disciples about connection from within a connected relationship.

Read John 13:3-15 (see sidebar).

2. Based on John 13:3-15, how do you think Jesus knew His disciples needed this lesson?[i]

3. Why did Jesus choose to teach this lesson at that time?[ii]

4. How did Jesus teach this lesson?[iii]

---

* Answers: i=c, ii=b, iii=a, iv=e, v=d.

JOHN 13:3-15

Jesus knew that the Father had put all things under his power, and that he had come from God and was returning to God; so he got up from the meal, took off his outer clothing, and wrapped a towel around his waist. After that, he poured water into a basin and began to wash his disciples' feet, drying them with the towel that was wrapped around him.

He came to Simon Peter, who said to him, "Lord, are you going to wash my feet?"

Jesus replied, "You do not realize now what I am doing, but later you will understand."

"No," said Peter, "you shall never wash my feet."

Jesus answered, "Unless I wash you, you have no part with me."

"Then, Lord," Simon Peter replied, "not just my feet but my hands and my head as well!"

Jesus answered, "Those who have had a bath need only to wash their feet; their whole body is clean. And you are clean, though not every one of you." For he knew who was going to betray him, and that was why he said not every one was clean.

When he had finished washing their feet, he put on his clothes and returned to his place. "Do you understand what I have done for you?" he asked them. "You call me 'Teacher' and 'Lord,' and rightly so, for that is what I am. Now that I, your Lord and Teacher, have washed your feet, you also should wash one another's feet. I have set you an example that you should do as I have done for you."

5. At what time in the discipleship process did Jesus teach this lesson? Does this decision say anything about the disciples themselves?[iv]

6. What did Jesus want the disciples to do with what they learned?[v]

DAY FOUR REVIEW

1. What stood out to you or convicted you from today?

2. Write down and share a rule that God has given us. How do you see this command protecting and promoting relationship? (For example, you could look at Exodus 20:14, "You shall not commit adultery," from the Ten Commandments.)

3. Describe how you think Jesus might have felt when He found His disciples fighting among themselves. What might He have been thinking?

4. Consider the relationships you are currently in. Do they help you move forward in your discipleship journey, or do they hinder you? How?

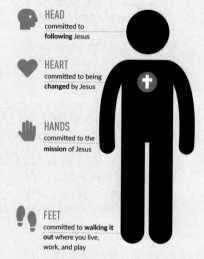

WHAT IS A DISCIPLE?
He said to them, "Come and follow me, and I will make you fishers of men."
Matthew 4:19, WNT

HEAD
committed to **following** Jesus

HEART
committed to being **changed** by Jesus

HANDS
committed to the **mission** of Jesus

FEET
committed to **walking it out** where you live, work, and play

---

i. Answer: The disciples had been fighting with one another about who was the greatest. Jesus knew they needed this lesson because He was with them and knew what they needed.

ii. Answer: Jesus knew His crucifixion was drawing near, and with it the end of His discipleship journey with the disciples. He knew that they would remember His last lesson.

iii. Answer: Jesus modeled service, rather than just teaching a lesson about service.

iv. Answer: Jesus had taught the disciples this lesson several times. Humans are hardheaded. He taught and loved them anyway.

v. Answer: Jesus wanted His disciples to model this servant-hearted love for the people they would disciple.

Day Five

THE HEART TO MINISTER

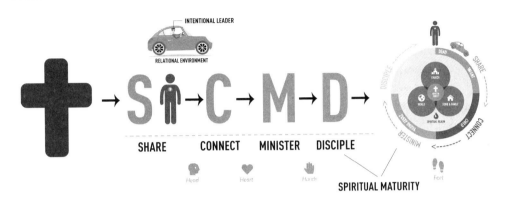

INTENTIONAL LEADER

RELATIONAL ENVIRONMENT

+ → S ⫯ → C → M → D →

SHARE   CONNECT   MINISTER   DISCIPLE

Head   *Heart*   *Hands*   *Feet*

SPIRITUAL MATURITY

GETTING STARTED

- As we go back to the journey visual above, we can see Jesus SHARED who He was and invited the disciples to follow Him, and they agreed to do so.
- In CONNECTION the disciples are learning what truth and love look like in action.
- The disciples are also learning about every rule God has given and the relational reason behind it.

Lord Jesus: Help me see what You want me to see today. Expose any lies I may believe and lead me to Your truth. Help me trust and obey You and walk out what I'm learning in every sphere of my life.

As the disciples experience SHARING and CONNECTION, they are beginning to see the spiritual and physical needs around them as an opportunity to MINISTER. Jesus is a God of reconciliation. He sees the brokenness of the world, and He knows that brokenness exists because people choose to rebel against Him. To one degree or another, it is our (humankind's) fault that we are in this state. God could have just destroyed us. He could have let us go our own way to our eventual demise. Instead, He chose to make the first move toward reconciliation.

Read Ephesians 2:3-5 (see sidebar).

God moved first, and He sends us into the world to the lost to announce His first move. Our first move, then, is to become ministers of reconciliation between God and man (Romans 5:8-13; John 3:16; 1 John 4:19).

EPHESIANS 2:3-5

All of us also lived among them at one time, gratifying the cravings of our flesh and following its desires and thoughts. Like the rest, we were by nature deserving of wrath. But because of his great love for us, God, who is rich in mercy, made us alive with Christ even when we were dead in transgressions—it is by grace you have been saved.

ACTS 17:26

"From one man he made all the nations, that they should inhabit the whole earth; and he marked out their appointed times in history and the boundaries of their lands."

JOHN 6:44

"No one can come to me unless the Father who sent me draws them, and I will raise them up at the last day."

EPHESIANS 2:8-10

It is by grace you have been saved, through faith—and this is not from yourselves, it is the gift of God—not by works, so that no one can boast. For we are God's handiwork, created in Christ Jesus to do good works, which God prepared in advance for us to do.

1 PETER 4:10

Each of you should use whatever gift you have received to serve others, as faithful stewards of God's grace in its various forms.

THE ROAD TRIP

On the journey of discipleship, we see that not only was Jesus driving the car (relational environment) toward His personal destination but He was also preparing His disciples to be able to teach others how to take the journey toward spiritual maturity too. Jesus was like a driving instructor. His goal was that, by the end of the process, the disciples would both be able to get to the destination themselves and teach others to make the road trip.

Like every young adult, I had to take driver's training to get my license. However, I had already learned to drive when my grandfather, and later my father, taught me to drive in the hayfield where my grandparents lived. Even earlier than that, my dad would let me sit in his lap as he drove on the back roads. I learned to steer with my dad's hands inches away from mine in case he needed to take the wheel. In a sense, this is what Jesus intended the journey of discipleship to look like.

I am so grateful that my disciplemaker (my father) not only shared the gospel with me but also knew I had experiences, skills, and giftings that God wanted me to use in the body of Christ. My father didn't think his job with me was over when I received Christ. He knew that my journey was just starting: I needed someone to help me know what God had commanded and to support me as I made mistakes.

My past experiences had left me broken and ashamed, and I did not understand how God could redeem me or my past. My disciplemaker helped me see that God could use even my past sin issues to help others because I was able to understand where people were coming from.

Even for those parts of my past that I wasn't ashamed of, I did not see how what I had learned could be connected to the Lord's work after salvation. I was an athlete—how could I use my experiences to help the church? Would the church allow me to use those gifts even if they could be helpful? My disciplemaker helped me find my place.

1. Read the following list of verses and draw a line from each one to its corresponding statement.

i. Psalm 139:13-16	a. Choosing to obey makes you a utensil for special work.
ii. Acts 17:26	b. Every saved person is to serve in the church.
iii. John 6:44	c. God knit you together the way He wanted you.
iv. Matthew 10:29-31	d. God delivers His grace to others through you.
v. Ephesians 2:8-10	e. Those who have been saved have a purpose.
vi. Ephesians 4:11-13	f. God gave leaders the role of equipping (coaching).
vii. 1 Corinthians 12:4-27	g. God knows what is happening around you.
viii. 2 Timothy 2:20-21	h. God placed us in our slice of history.
ix. 1 Peter 4:10	i. God drew you to Himself, which means He knows you.*

* Answers: i=c, ii=h, iii=i, iv=g, v=e, vi=f, vii=b, viii=a, ix=d.

Jesus revealed to the disciples that their identity did not lie in how other people viewed them (as mere uneducated fishermen or tax collectors). He taught them how to use their experiences, skills, spiritual abilities, and authority to serve, protect, and equip others. God has created each of us with abilities and a purpose, but because of sin, we became broken. Once we were saved, the Holy Spirit moved inside us and now makes us into new creatures for God's purpose. The purpose of a disciplemaker is to work with God (via His Holy Spirit and His Word) to make disciples who now are part of God's plan and team.

GROWING IN MATURITY IN EVERY AREA

Jesus was an intentional disciplemaker leading the disciples through a process to help them be able to know and follow His commands. He was making these men into lovers of God and others. And He was teaching these men the skills they would need to be fishers of men. When Jesus went to sit at the right hand of the Father, He sent God the Holy Spirit to indwell His disciples.

Jesus does the same for us. On the journey of discipleship, He is like the navigational system in your car as well as the gas in the engine that powers the transformation within those traveling.

Looking back at Jesus' relationship with His disciples, we see Jesus having His disciples begin to MINISTER in small ways over time. They would do chores when Jesus would do a miracle, like picking up the extra loaves and fish. They would go ahead of Him and arrange for food and lodging. They acted as bodyguards when the crowds surrounded and pressed in on Jesus. They would bring to Jesus people who had questions and wanted to talk to Him. But as time went on, Jesus began to increase the level of their MINISTRY.

Read Luke 9:1-10; 10:1-12; and Mark 9:19-29.

2. Circle the reasons why you think Jesus sent the disciples out in twos.

   - support and encouragement
   - accountability
   - different individual insights that might make them a good team
   - protection
   - just a random number
   - for practice
   - to humble them when they started getting proud
   - to help them fight discouragement and temptation when they faced their internal battle with the enemy

3. What did Jesus do with the disciples after they came back from assignments?

_____

_____

Jesus knew that His men had to practice their MINISTRY to grow in their abilities and faith. You can only get so good while sitting on the bench. Jesus also knew that His disciples would make mistakes and require coaching. He debriefed with them about the

LUKE 9:1-10

When Jesus had called the Twelve together, he gave them power and authority to drive out all demons and to cure diseases, and he sent them out to proclaim the kingdom of God and to heal the sick. He told them: "Take nothing for the journey—no staff, no bag, no bread, no money, no extra shirt. Whatever house you enter, stay there until you leave that town. If people do not welcome you, leave their town and shake the dust off your feet as a testimony against them." So they set out and went from village to village, proclaiming the good news and healing people everywhere.

Now Herod the tetrarch heard about all that was going on. And he was perplexed because some were saying that John had been raised from the dead, others that Elijah had appeared, and still others that one of the prophets of long ago had come back to life. But Herod said, "I beheaded John. Who, then, is this I hear such things about?" And he tried to see him.

When the apostles returned, they reported to Jesus what they had done. Then he took them with him and they withdrew by themselves to a town called Bethsaida.

LUKE 5:16
Jesus often withdrew to lonely places and prayed.

situations they had encountered. He was getting them ready for the upcoming mission, and He increased the training as the time for His departure came closer. He also sought to give His disciples rest and time with Him, knowing this rhythm was crucial if they were to finish the race. Jesus modeled rest and time with God often (Luke 5:16).

4.   Every disciple is different. Circle which of the actions below is the hardest for you.
   • going out in faith when you are given an assignment
   • receiving coaching
   • failing
   • resting
   • going with others because you prefer to be alone

5.   Why is that action hard for you? Share with your group.

Notes and Thoughts

DAY FIVE REVIEW

1.   What stood out to you or convicted you from today?

2.   Share about a time in your life when your past or what others thought of you influenced your decisions or actions.

3.   Is there a gift or an ability God has given you that you are not currently using to minister to others? What is holding you back? What is one step you can take this week toward using that gift in ministering (serving) in your church or group?

UNDERSTANDING SPIRITUAL GROWTH

Day One

THE PROCESS OF MATURITY

GETTING STARTED

- Discipleship is like a road trip.
- As believers we SHARE our lives with other believers.
- We SHARE our lives with the lost in the hope that they will want to know what makes us different.
- We invite those who respond favorably into a relational vehicle to CONNECT, where we show them how to follow Jesus. We tell them, "We will learn to do this together."
- In that relational vehicle we CONNECT with them and help them make the most important connections of their lives—to God through Jesus, our Savior and Lord (John 14:6).
- In this CONNECTION we start to help them discover the truths we find in Scripture and how to apply them.
- We know that every believer has been saved for a purpose. Each person has gifts, abilities, and resources they can use to serve God. We help them discover this truth as well.

JOHN 14:6

Jesus answered, "I am the way and the truth and the life. No one comes to the Father except through me."

Lord Jesus: Help me see what You want me to see today. Expose any lies I may believe and lead me to Your truth. Help me trust and obey You and walk out what I'm learning in every sphere of my life.

Spiritual growth doesn't happen all at once, but rather over time. This week we are going to learn about the spiritual stages of development that we all go through on our journey toward spiritual maturity. Remember, Jesus invited His disciples into a journey where He would take them as they were and then make them into something completely different—in the same way an infant grows into a child and a child grows into an adult.

 Scan QR code to access video podcasts and other content that accompanies this week's session.

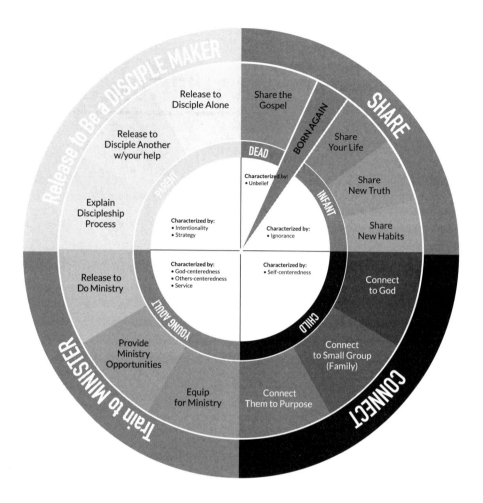

1. Assess where you are in your spiritual growth process. Circle the description you think best fits:

   - spiritually dead
   - a spiritual infant
   - a spiritual child
   - a spiritual young adult
   - a spiritual parent

2. Why did you choose that answer? At the end of the day, we will see if your response has changed.

Let's look at how Scripture describes spiritual growth. Jesus describes the process of becoming part of the family of God as a new birth. He used this language so that everyone could understand the spiritual growth cycle.

Read John 3:3-5 (see sidebar).

JOHN 3:3-5

Jesus replied, "Very truly I tell you, no one can see the kingdom of God unless they are born again."

"How can someone be born when they are old?" Nicodemus asked. "Surely they cannot enter a second time into their mother's womb to be born!"

Jesus answered, "Very truly I tell you, no one can enter the kingdom of God unless they are born of water and the Spirit."

3. Using the following Scripture, fill in the blank for the following statements:

The true light that gives light to everyone was coming into the world. He was in the world, and though the world was made through him, the world did not recognize him. He came to that which was his own, but his own did not receive him. Yet to all who did receive him, to those who believed in his name, he gave the right to become children of God—children born not of natural descent, nor of human decision or a husband's will, but born of God.

JOHN 1:9-13

    a. Jesus tells Nicodemus that if he wants to enter the family of God and the promised Kingdom of God, he must be _____.

    b. All humans are God's creation, but we only become children of God when we _____.

4. Using the following Scripture, fill in the blank to indicate what stage we were in before we were born again.

As for you, you were dead in your transgressions and sins, in which you used to live when you followed the ways of this world and of the ruler of the kingdom of the air, the spirit who is now at work in those who are disobedient. All of us also lived among them at one time, gratifying the cravings of our flesh and following its desires and thoughts. Like the rest, we were by nature deserving of wrath. But because of his great love for us, God, who is rich in mercy, made us alive with Christ even when we were dead in transgressions—it is by grace you have been saved.

EPHESIANS 2:1-5

I was dead because I have _____, and to be separated from God who is life, is to start the process of dying.

5. Referencing the corresponding Scripture reading, fill in the blanks in the following statements:

Read 1 Corinthians 3:1-4 (see sidebar).

    a. Paul describes a new or an immature believer as an _____.

Read 2 Corinthians 5:17 (see sidebar).

    b. As a believer, I am a _____ _____.

6. John uses the same kind of language. Underline the words in the following verse that describe stages of human and spiritual development:

I am writing to you, fathers,
    because you know him who is from the beginning.
I am writing to you, young men,
    because you have overcome the evil one.

1 CORINTHIANS 3:1-4

Brothers and sisters, I could not address you as people who live by the Spirit but as people who are still worldly—mere infants in Christ. I gave you milk, not solid food, for you were not yet ready for it. Indeed, you are still not ready. You are still worldly. For since there is jealousy and quarreling among you, are you not worldly? Are you not acting like mere humans? For when one says, "I follow Paul," and another, "I follow Apollos," are you not mere human beings?

2 CORINTHIANS 5:17

If anyone is in Christ, the new creation has come: The old has gone, the new is here!

MATTHEW 4:19, WNT

[Jesus said,] "Come and follow me, and I will make you fishers of men."

I write to you, dear children,
> because you know the Father.

I write to you, fathers,
> because you know him who is from the beginning.

I write to you, young men,
> because you are strong,
> and the word of God lives in you,
> and you have overcome the evil one.[i]

I JOHN 2:13-14

The final stage of spiritual growth is that of a parent (a disciple who makes disciples).

7. Read the following Scripture passages and circle *True* or *False* next to each of the corresponding statements.

I am writing this not to shame you but to warn you as my dear children. Even if you had ten thousand guardians in Christ, you do not have many fathers, for in Christ Jesus I became your father through the gospel. Therefore I urge you to imitate me. For this reason I have sent to you Timothy, my son whom I love, who is faithful in the Lord. He will remind you of my way of life in Christ Jesus, which agrees with what I teach everywhere in every church.

> Some of you have become arrogant, as if I were not coming to you.

I CORINTHIANS 4:14-18

I am writing to Timothy, my true son in the faith.

> May God the Father and Christ Jesus our Lord give you grace, mercy, and peace.

I TIMOTHY 1:2, NLT

In fact, though by this time you ought to be teachers, you need someone to teach you the elementary truths of God's word all over again. You need milk, not solid food! Anyone who lives on milk, being still an infant, is not acquainted with the teaching about righteousness. But solid food is for the mature, who by constant use have trained themselves to distinguish good from evil.

HEBREWS 5:12-14

Whatever you have learned or received or heard from me, or seen in me—put it into practice. And the God of peace will be with you.

PHILIPPIANS 4:9

a. True/False: Every believer can become mature enough to make disciples.
b. True/False: Spiritual parenting is not that important in the discipleship process.
c. True/False: Modeling maturity is very important.
d. True/False: Personal commitment to learning is just as important for the learner as it is for the disciplemaker.
e. True/False: The further along in the growth cycle you are, the more valuable you are to God.[ii]

Remember that every child of God in every stage of development is equally important to God. A spiritual young adult may be more useful to the mission than an infant, but age and stage are not a measure of value.

8. According to the definition of a disciple in Matthew 4:19, what is a mature believer capable of teaching?

9. Read the following Scriptures and underline an essential key to growth:

Like newborn babies, crave pure spiritual milk, so that by it you may grow up in your salvation.

I PETER 2:2

You must remain faithful to the things you have been taught. You know they are true, for you know you can trust those who taught you. You have been taught the holy Scriptures from childhood, and they have given you the wisdom to receive the salvation that comes by trusting in Christ Jesus. All Scripture is inspired by God and is useful to teach us what is true and to make us realize what is wrong in our lives. It corrects us when we are wrong and teaches us to do what is right.

2 TIMOTHY 3:14-16, NLT

THE DISCIPLESHIP WHEEL

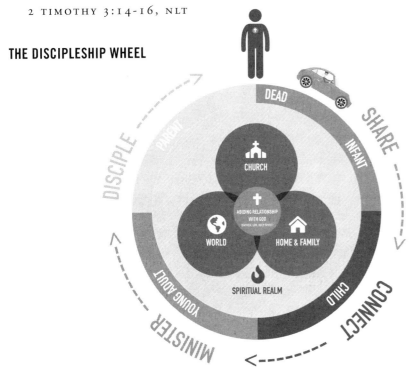

The Discipleship Wheel helps us understand the stages of development that exist on the disciple's journey and discover where we and those we are discipling are at in the process. The outside wheel reveals the process that we identified in the last week: SHARE, CONNECT, MINISTER, and DISCIPLE. The inside wheel reveals the five stages of spiritual development that disciples go through in their journey: dead, infant, child, young adult, parent.

As you look at the spiritual wheel, you see how the SHARE, CONNECT, train to MINISTER, and release to DISCIPLE portions correspond to the five stages of spiritual development:

1. Dead

- We SHARE our lives with the dead in the hope that we will get to SHARE the gospel with them at some point.

2. Infant

- Once someone is born again, they become an infant, and we continue to SHARE our lives with them as a parent does a newborn infant.

3. Child

- We CONNECT the disciple to truth and relationship with others in the relational vehicle, moving toward spiritual growth and maturity.

- As time goes on, we CONNECT the disciple to the truth as Jesus did with His disciples.

- We then begin to help CONNECT the disciple to their purpose: to serve. At first, this involves simple things they learn: love those around them, see the needs and meet them.

4. Young Adult

- As time goes on, we intentionally start to help the disciple understand that they were saved for a purpose. We are intentionally training them for MINISTRY.

5. Parent

- Just as a parent raises their children to someday be parents as well, so we are making disciples who become DISCIPLEmakers.

FINAL THOUGHTS

God's plan is to give a born-again infant a spiritual parent—as well as spiritual aunts and uncles, even older brothers and sisters—to help them grow up. Think about it this way: When a person is born again, they are like a spiritual infant in the things of God. It doesn't matter how old or skilled they are in the things of the world—spiritual rules and values are very different from worldly rules and values.

If a physical baby was born and the parents did not care for the child and protect the child, what would happen? This kind of profound neglect would be called abuse in the

> When a person is born again, they are like a spiritual infant in the things of God. It doesn't matter how old or skilled they are in the things of the world—spiritual rules and values are very different from worldly rules and values.

physical world. In the same way, when someone is a spiritual infant, a spiritual parent must help protect them from and walk them through many things. All of us, as believers, have an enemy who wants to destroy us. New believers have been thrown into a battle they don't know how to fight.

This is what making disciples is all about: feeding and caring for a spiritual infant as they grow into childhood. The spiritual child needs different kinds of food and protection along the growth cycle. The child must eventually learn how to feed themselves—and how to feed others. The goal of every parent is to help their child grow into maturity and be able to have a family of their own. This is what discipleship is all about.

DAY ONE REVIEW

1. What stood out to you or convicted you from today?

2. After going through today's study, do you still see yourself at the same stage of spiritual development that you identified at the beginning? Why or why not? Share with your group.

3. Every disciple of Jesus is able to disciple others to their same level of maturity. Read the story of Jesus with the woman at the well in John 4:1-30. How did the woman respond when Jesus shared who He was?

   • Where did the woman go? What did she do?

   • What stage of spiritual growth do you think she was in?

   • What does this story say to you about your own ability to share about Jesus and disciple someone?

---

i. Answer: You should have underlined the words *children*, *young men*, and *fathers*. John is not writing exclusively to men here, but rather indicating the various stages of spiritual growth.

ii. Answer: True: a, c, and d; False: b and e.

Day Two

THE STAGES OF GROWTH

GETTING STARTED

We have discovered that spiritual growth can be compared to physical growth in some ways and that we all go through a pathway of development in our journey to maturity. In this section we will take a closer look at what each stage of spiritual growth looks like. This will help us identify where we are in our own journey. Identifying the growth stage of the people we are discipling can help us determine what tools and teaching they need from us.

Lord Jesus: Help me see what You want me to see today. Expose any lies I may believe and lead me to Your truth. Help me trust and obey You and walk out what I'm learning in every sphere of my life.

In sports, a good coach knows what a good player looks like, sees strengths and encourages their development, and points out weaknesses that need to be corrected.

When my children were growing up, I worked hard to discern the right thing to teach at the appropriate age. When my kids were infants and later in the terrible twos, I wished so badly for the time when they would be able to express themselves in words, rather than just crying. I was exhausted by the miniature emotional cyclones hitting my house at every turn, but I had to teach them what they were able to learn at the stage they were in. When a baby acts like a baby, that is normal. But I had to always keep in mind the final outcomes that I hoped to see in them—because when a teenager acts like a baby, that is unhealthy.

This strategy presupposes that each stage of development has characteristics I can recognize, enabling me to match the appropriate lesson to the appropriate stage of development. The same is true of spiritual growth. If I am going to be a mature disciple of Jesus, I need to know what a mature disciple looks like. I have to be able to assess myself against what God would have me be, so I can confess my shortcomings and continue on. If I am going to disciple another person, I must evaluate where they are in comparison to the desired scriptural outcome so I can gently help them make course corrections.

In sports, a good coach knows what a good player looks like. He can see strengths and encourage them, and he can point out weaknesses that need to be corrected. He also creates environments and methods for improvement. Jesus is the epitome of a great coach. He did this with His disciples, and they did this with others later as well. As a church we desire to train our people to be able to recognize a mature disciple.

1. Let's review our definition from Matthew 4:19 again. Fill in the blanks.

A disciple is _____ Jesus, being _____ by Jesus, and committed to the _____ of Jesus.

In the physical world, we can easily determine when we are dealing with an infant or a child, but spiritually, it's not as easy. A seventy-year-old business tycoon can be powerful in personality and highly skilled in the human realm, but if he has just been born again or has not been discipled into maturity, he is still an infant spiritually. We risk harm to the person and to the church when we put a spiritual infant into a major spiritual role in God's family, the church.

Jesus gave us a way to determine where a person is in their spiritual growth. Discipleship is a relational process, and in relationship, we get to see how a person acts, not just what they know theoretically or educationally.

Read Matthew 7:15-19 and Luke 6:43-45 (see sidebar).

DETERMINING THE STAGE

In a discipleship relationship, we will see and hear things that indicate where the disciple is spiritually. If we listen to *ourselves* honestly, we can learn where we are too. When we do and say things that are contrary to what God has revealed in His Word and different from what the Holy Spirit would want, we are revealing what is in our heart.

Because of this reality, two things are true:

- Noticing traits and behaviors that fit into one of the stages equips us to assess where we or others are. When we know what stage someone is in, we can help them grow.

- No matter how long we have been a disciple, every one of us can act like a child at times. This may not mean we are a child spiritually, but realizing we are acting like one should bring conviction. Physically, I am a fifty-four-year-old parent and pastor, but I still catch myself saying some childish things sometimes. When—not if—that happens, I must confess it to the Lord and apologize.

The stage tells us how to know where people are at so we can help them grow, much like a coach assessing their team. The coach can tell where the team is at and take the appropriate actions to help them improve their skills.

Your value is not determined by your stage. An infant in a family is just as valuable as the teenager or the parent. The growth stages laid out here are not a tool to discover your value. Your value is high because you are one of God's children. Your stage of maturity just reveals where you need to grow so that you can experience more of what God intended for you.

SPIRITUALLY DEAD TO BORN AGAIN

You can assess where a person is in their spiritual growth by the kinds of things they say. We have all sinned, but a spiritually dead person has not believed.

2.   What kind of things do you think a spiritually dead person might say? (Example: "I am as good as anyone else; why do I need to be saved?")

MATTHEW 7:15-19

"Watch out for false prophets. They come to you in sheep's clothing, but inwardly they are ferocious wolves. By their fruit you will recognize them. Do people pick grapes from thornbushes, or figs from thistles? Likewise, every good tree bears good fruit, but a bad tree bears bad fruit. A good tree cannot bear bad fruit, and a bad tree cannot bear good fruit. Every tree that does not bear good fruit is cut down and thrown into the fire."

LUKE 6:43-45

"No good tree bears bad fruit, nor does a bad tree bear good fruit. Each tree is recognized by its own fruit. People do not pick figs from thornbushes, or grapes from briers. A good man brings good things out of the good stored up in his heart, and an evil man brings evil things out of the evil stored up in his heart. For the mouth speaks what the heart is full of."

The change that occurs when a person has saving faith is the result of being born again.

3. What happens when we are born again? For each of the following statements, circle *True* or *False*.

    a. True/False: The Holy Spirit moves inside us.
    b. True/False: We are invited into a spiritual relational environment and family.
    c. True/False: We suddenly understand for ourselves what the Bible says.
    d. True/False: We immediately know right from wrong.[i]

4. What is the next step for a born-again believer? For each of the following statements, circle *True* or *False*.

    a. True/False: They seek to understand what God wants for them because they do not know.
    b. True/False: They won't do anything next because they don't know what they are supposed to do.
    c. True/False: They make gathering with other believers as the body of Christ a priority.
    d. True/False: They read their Bible.
    e. True/False: They continue in a relationship with the one who shared the gospel with them so they can grow.
    f. True/False: They go to Sunday school.
    g. True/False: They check the salvation box and go on with life.
    h. True/False: If they haven't already had a discipleship relationship with a more mature believer, they begin one.[ii]

5. Which of the questions surprised or intrigued you? Write them here to discuss with your group.

THE SPIRITUAL INFANT

When we are born again, we become an infant in Christ. Some familiar words that describe a human infant also apply to a new believer.

6. What are some characteristics of a spiritual infant? Circle the answers below that you agree with.
    * excitement
    * innocence
    * ignorance
    * vulnerability
    * other: _____

The word *ignorance* does not mean "stupidity," but rather indicates that someone does not yet have knowledge. A new believer, like an infant, is at the very beginning of their knowledge of spiritual matters.

7. What kinds of questions would you expect from a spiritual infant? (Examples: "When we die, does the Bible say we will be reincarnated?" "How do I answer my friend's questions about Jesus?" "Is there a real heaven or hell?" "Does my dog go to heaven when she dies?")

_____

_____

An infant in Christ has been given a new identity "in Christ," but they don't know this yet. As a result, they still define themselves in ways they did before they were born again ("I am an athlete"; "I am good at my job"; "I am beautiful"; etc.).

When we are born again, we become an infant in Christ.

8. What does an infant need? Mark the answers that you agree with:

    a. a spiritual family and parent to help them grow
    b. the Word of God explained to light their path
    c. spiritual protection offered by more mature believers
    d. nothing because God will now protect them and guide them Himself
    e. friendship and/or family because they may not have Christian relationships
    f. to learn how the enemy will attack
    g. to learn their new identity in Christ [iii]

What happens when a person becomes an infant but does not receive parenting? The answer shows up in the statistics we read earlier regarding how much Christians are engaged in community and intentional growth:

- Most Christians don't regularly share the gospel with others. [1]
- Only 32 percent of Christians between the ages of 23 and 75 attend church weekly. [2]
- Although many people may be connected to a group or club, I have found that most groups are not for the sole purpose of connection and Bible study.
- Around 20 percent of churchgoers serve in any way in the church. [3]
- Only 21 percent follow the biblical practice of tithing. [4]
- Only 4 percent of Christians have a biblical worldview. [5]

9. What is your reaction to those statistics? What do you think the impact might be on the current state of the church?

_____

_____

Remember: The end goal for maturity on this spiritual journey is that you will learn to drive a relational vehicle yourself and help others learn to do the same. I suggest you start praying now about whom to invite on this journey with you.

10. List some names you can start praying for to join you on the journey.

_____

_____

DAY TWO REVIEW

1. What stood out to you or convicted you from today?

2. Think back to how you behaved and spoke before you began to follow Jesus. What would have indicated to others that you were spiritually dead?

3. Which characteristics of a spiritual infant did you exhibit after you began following Jesus?

4. Is there someone in your life right now who is either spiritually dead or a spiritual infant? What is one thing you could share with them or do for them this week that would point to Jesus?

1. Aaron Earls, "Evangelism More Prayed for Than Practiced by Churchgoers," Lifeway Research, April 23, 2019, https://research .lifeway.com/2019/04/23/evangelism-more-prayed-for-than-practiced-by-churchgoers.
2. "A New Chapter in Millennial Church Attendance," Barna, August 4, 2022, https://www.barna.com/research/church -attendance-2022. This percentage is the average of the weekly church attendance of Millennials (39 percent), Gen Xers (31 percent), and Boomers (25 percent) according to a 2022 study.
3. Shari Finnell, "Declining Volunteerism Is Changing the Church Experience," Faith & Leadership, March 7, 2023, https:// faithandleadership.com/declining-volunteerism-changing-the-church-experience. This statistic is as of March 2022, according to a study on the effect of the global COVID-19 pandemic on church involvement.
4. "What Is a Tithe?: New Data on Perceptions of the 10 Percent," Barna, September 7, 2022, https://www.barna.com/research /what-is-a-tithe.
5. Tracy F. Munsil, "Biblical Worldview Among U.S. Adults Drops 33% Since Start of COVID-19 Pandemic," February 28, 2023, https://www.arizonachristian.edu/2023/02/28/biblical-worldview-among-u-s-adults-drops-33-since-start-of-covid-19 -pandemic. This statistic is from *American Worldview Inventory 2023*, which was created by Arizona Christian University's Cultural Research Center.
i. Answer: True: a, b, d; False: c.
ii. Answer: True: a, c, d, e, f, h; False: b, g.
iii. Answer: All are correct except for d.

Day Three

THE CHILD AND YOUNG ADULT STAGES

GETTING STARTED

Yesterday we worked through the first few steps of the spiritual road trip and how it correlates to spiritual growth. Remember that when you trust Jesus as your Lord and Savior, you are born again.

> *Lord Jesus: Help me see what You want me to see today. Expose any lies I may believe and lead me to Your truth. Help me trust and obey You and walk out what I'm learning in every sphere of my life.*

Someone SHARED the truth of the gospel with you, and you made the decision to die to your old way of doing things. You have now been raised to a new kind of life. Public confession in baptism is commanded in Scripture and burns into your mind what you have just done.

Read Acts 2:36-38; Romans 6:1-5; and 10:9-10 (see sidebar).

Baptism reminds you that you are forgiven and is a physical picture of the cleansing the Holy Spirit has done in you. Baptism is a picture of being born again: You have moved from spiritual death to new life in Christ as an infant.[1]

The Holy Spirit enters you when you receive Jesus by faith, and now you have the energy—the gas—for the journey of discipleship. You are then invited to CONNECT in a relational vehicle (or environment) where you will receive real teaching and the support you need to be changed.

As time goes on in this relational vehicle, you begin to understand the Word of God (all Jesus commanded) and your relationship with God and others. You should have a spiritual family protecting you, connecting with you, and helping you learn spiritual truths that are different from the physical truths you know. You are not expected to take care of yourself without help any more than a physical infant or child would in a family. You are also not just thrown into the minivan with the other six kids to fend for yourself. In other words, spiritual parents ease the infant into interactions with others who may unintentionally confuse or hurt them.

As you grow, you will be challenged and able to take on more and more. You will learn to feed yourself as well as sit at the dinner table with the CONNECT group you are doing this study with, as well as with your larger church family. You will be able to see the bigger picture—beyond your own thoughts, emotions, and desires to the needs of others.

ACTS 2:36-38

[The apostle Peter said,] "Therefore let all Israel be assured of this: God has made this Jesus, whom you crucified, both Lord and Messiah."

When the people heard this, they were cut to the heart and said to Peter and the other apostles, "Brothers, what shall we do?"

Peter replied, "Repent and be baptized, every one of you, in the name of Jesus Christ for the forgiveness of your sins. And you will receive the gift of the Holy Spirit."

ROMANS 10:9-10, NLT

If you openly declare that Jesus is Lord and believe in your heart that God raised him from the dead, you will be saved. For it is by believing in your heart that you are made right with God, and it is by openly declaring your faith that you are saved.

ROMANS 6:1-5, NLT

Well then, should we keep on sinning so that God can show us more and more of his wonderful grace? Of course not! Since we have died to sin, how can we continue to live in it? Or have you forgotten that when we were joined with Christ Jesus in baptism, we joined him in his death? For we died and were buried with Christ by baptism. And just as Christ was raised from the dead by the glorious power of the Father, now we also may live new lives.

Since we have been united with him in his death, we will also be raised to life as he was.

THE SPIRITUAL CHILD

Today we will look at the child and young adult stages of the spiritual growth cycle. What can a spiritual child do?

Generally, children can communicate as well as learn to do some chores. Intentional parents start early to help their kids learn that being part of a family involves contributing to it. Kids will often do the right thing when others are looking (and especially to get an allowance). A child is expected to act like a child, and so good parents will teach appropriate lessons and discipline in love so that their child has the tools to become a healthy adult. Remember, a good parent has an endgame in mind—we are modeling parenting to future parents. Maturity means becoming responsible, hardworking, loving, and so on.

It's the same in the spiritual parenting process. Although it can be hard to tell that you are dealing with a spiritual child when they are in a physically mature body, the relationship helps you observe what stage they are in.

1. Consider the following characteristics of a child. After each phrase, write what this might look like in a spiritual child.

   • They understand basic communication.

   • They know they have a family and some of what that means. (For instance, I learned I was a Putman and was told that meant something.)

   • They can do simple tasks for the good of themselves and others.

   • They are innocent in some ways, but you can see their self-centeredness coming through at times.

   • Their priority (and first word) is often *me, mine, I.* Sharing isn't normal, and the selfish nature is certainly evident.

   • Children are concerned about what is fair in their own eyes.

   • They will do what they are told . . . as long as they get what they want out of it.

   • Because children are naïve, they are often easy to fool. They cannot discern who is dangerous and who isn't.

2. What kinds of things might you expect to hear from a spiritual child?[i]

3. What does a spiritual parent need to do to help a spiritual child grow toward spiritual maturity? For each of the following statements, circle the appropriate response (*True* or *False*):

   a. True/False: Give them what they want.
   b. True/False: Explain to them why you are doing what you are doing.
   c. True/False: Not expect them to do anything to contribute.
   d. True/False: Encourage them and celebrate when they do what is right, even when they are not rewarded immediately.
   e. True/False: Protect them from being uncomfortable.
   f. True/False: Confront them lovingly when they are being childish and selfish.
   g. True/False: Let them be spiritual children—they will grow out of it on their own.
   h. True/False: Model what maturity looks like.
   i. True/False: Ask for forgiveness when you do wrong and tell them why you are sorry.
   j. True/False: Give them a high-level spiritual job because they have great talent and giftings.
   k. True/False: Have them lead if they are leaders in the business world.[ii]

THE SPIRITUAL YOUNG ADULT

The next stage of spiritual growth is what we call the spiritual young adult. When we are in this stage, we may look like a parent in many ways, but we are not quite adults. A spiritual young adult needs to continue to be connected (we never graduate from connection to God and others!) but now moves into more specific training in ministry. With coaching, young adults are able to do many things. They can babysit occasionally for someone else, but they are not quite responsible or intentional enough to parent by themselves. They can disciple someone up to the level of growth they themselves have reached, but they are not yet responsible or intentional enough to model parenthood to others.

Jesus saw that His disciples had grown in many ways (certainly not in every way), and He also knew the time was coming for Him to depart. Remember, His whole goal was to make them into disciples who could *make* disciples. With that in mind, Jesus intentionally gave them opportunities to practice.

A spiritual young adult . . .

- knows who they are in Christ and how to point out who others are in Christ, but does not know how to help people grow in their new identity intentionally;
- is zealous, but often without wisdom;
- has learned the truths of Scripture but has not yet learned to apply them in the right way at the right times;
- can be idealistic and see things in black and white, without nuance;
- can be naive about other people's motives;
- can be irresponsible occasionally;
- can be passionate for Jesus;
- wants to do something on their own;

Notes and Thoughts

- brings energy but doesn't always see the bigger picture of spiritual adulthood. Their view is limited by their lack of knowledge and experience;
- can be idealistic about what people should do;
- can get discouraged when they fail; and
- is dealing with more and more complex issues and needs deeper answers.

4. What kinds of things might you expect to hear from a spiritual young adult?[iii]

HELPING SPIRITUAL YOUNG ADULTS GROW

While a spiritual infant needs nurturing and a spiritual child needs guidance, a spiritual young adult needs specific lessons about what it means to follow Jesus, to be changed by Jesus, and to be committed to the mission of Christ. Because of the shift the Holy Spirit has made in their heart—taking them from a self-focus to an others-focus—the spiritual young adult can now start applying what they learn about God without (necessarily) becoming legalistic or getting confused by things that may seem unfair or uncomfortable. This investment in a spiritual young adult's growth moves them from knowing truth to discerning how to apply it appropriately.

Key Lessons in Following Jesus

A spiritual young adult needs to be taught how to . . .

- be faithful to God even when we don't understand what He is doing;
- go against the flow of our culture even if we have to stand alone;
- remain in Christ and stay committed to Him even when He prunes us;
- do His will no matter what; and
- discern His calling to serve, including when and where to serve in everyday life.

Key Lessons in Being Changed by Jesus

A spiritual young adult needs to learn . . .

- to become God- and others-centered for the sake of Christ;
- to forgive others even when they wrong us over and over;
- to value others above self and to become a servant; and
- how to pursue unity, deciding wisely how and on what we can be unified even through differences.

Key Lessons on Being Committed to the Mission of Christ

A spiritual young adult needs to learn how to . . .

- prioritize time so they can serve the Lord and His mission in every area of life;

LUKE 9:1-6

When Jesus had called the Twelve together, he gave them power and authority to drive out all demons and to cure diseases, and he sent them out to proclaim the kingdom of God and to heal the sick. He told them: "Take nothing for the journey—no staff, no bag, no bread, no money, no extra shirt. Whatever house you enter, stay there until you leave that town. If people do not welcome you, leave their town and shake the dust off your feet as a testimony against them." So they set out and went from village to village, proclaiming the good news and healing people everywhere.

- identify giftings and use them for Christ's mission;
- allocate time and other resource wisely; and
- share the gospel and look for ways and places to do it.

Read Luke 9:1-6 (see sidebar).

5. Based on what we learned in Week 2 about this story, along with any new observations from reading the passage again, why did Jesus send the disciples out without Him? Mark the answer(s) you agree with:

    a. To give them a chance to practice what He would later send them out to do.
    b. So He could debrief with them what happened and put more detail and instruction into their training.
    c. To humble them and let them learn through experience that ministry is not quite so simple so that they would listen, watch, and learn from Him more carefully.
    d. Other: _____

6. Notice that Jesus did not send out individuals, but rather groups of two on extended missions. Why do you think this is? Circle *True* or *False* next to each of the following statements.

    a. True/False: Relationships give support in stressful situations.
    b. True/False: Relationships multiply the wisdom you have—you can talk things out and hear different perspectives.
    c. True/False: Relationships provide a mix of giftings that help you meet different situations better.
    d. True/False: The God of relationships wanted to show those who are lost without Him what His help in relationship would produce in their relationship with others.
    e. True/False: When you become a spiritual parent you won't need relationships anymore—until then you should work in at least twos.[iv]

As believers, we learn in relationship so that we can become relational people. The spiritually mature know they always need relationships to survive and thrive in this life.

Read Ecclesiastes 4:8-12 (see sidebar).

THE EXPERIENCE MINDSET

Every coach knows that players cannot get good at the game when they're just sitting on the bench. Your team has to play and fail if they are ever going to succeed. In the same way, every good driving teacher knows kids have to get out of the classroom and into the driver's seat to learn to drive. As you are on this journey of discipleship, remember it takes courage: to go out on your own and, eventually as a spiritual parent, to let your "kids" go out and fail.

ECCLESIASTES 4:8-12, NLT
This is the case of a man who is all alone, without a child or brother, yet who works hard to gain as much wealth as he can. But then he asks himself, "Who am I working for? Why am I giving up so much pleasure now?" It is all so meaningless and depressing.
Two people are better off than one, for they can help each other succeed. If one person falls, the other can reach out and help. But someone who falls alone is in real trouble. Likewise, two people lying close together can keep each other warm. But how can one be warm alone? A person standing alone can be attacked and defeated, but two can stand back-to-back and conquer. Three are even better, for a triple-braided cord is not easily broken.

7. Consider what you've learned about each of the stages of spiritual development, both the descriptions and the kinds of statements each stage might use. Which stage seems to represent your life most of the time?

DAY THREE REVIEW

1. What stood out to you or convicted you from today?

2. Name a characteristic that you think separates a spiritual child from a spiritual young adult.

3. How do you think a spiritual child and a spiritual young adult might each react to serving in a ministry that is not their first choice or passion? What phrases might you hear them say?

4. Who is one person in your life who is further along in their discipleship journey than you are? Make a commitment to connect with them this week and ask them what they think you need to do to go deeper in your spiritual growth.

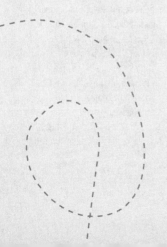

1. We'll explore more about what baptism means for us being "in Christ" in week 4, day 1.
   i. Examples: "I love my small group. I love that everyone knows my name and loves me. Don't you branch (split up) my group!"; "I told someone at work about Jesus, but I don't know what to do next with them. Can I bring them to our group so you can disciple them?"
   ii. Answer: True: b, d, f, h, i; False: a, c, e, g, j, k.
   iii. Examples: "Our group needs to branch (split into smaller groups) because we need room for a friend I have been witnessing to"; "Have you noticed that our church isn't reaching a particular group? How could we help make that happen?"
   iv. Answer: True: a, b, c, d; False: e.

Day Four

THE SPIRITUAL PARENT

GETTING STARTED

As we progress from spiritual infancy to spiritual parenthood, we must remember the SCMD process. Both Jesus, and then the early church that mimicked Him, SHARED who Jesus was and the gospel message He came to bring us. He then invited those who accepted the message into a CONNECT environment where people became part of a family. From there these disciples learned how to live out the truth in love and service to others (MINISTRY). Finally, they were sent out to make DISCIPLES themselves.

Let's review our road trip analogy:

Jesus invited His disciples on a journey to spiritual maturity. Remember that a disciple is one who is _____ Jesus, being _____ by Jesus, and is committed to the _____ of Jesus. We learn this in a relational _____ as we go through the SCMD process.

Lord Jesus: Help me see what You want me to see today. Expose any lies I may believe and lead me to Your truth. Help me trust and obey You and walk out what I'm learning in every sphere of my life.

Further along the path toward spiritual maturity, people often stall because they don't think they can or should be a spiritual parent. If we have made it too comfortable in a spiritual family, they will not want to start a family of their own. In addition, the enemy and other voices tend to convince them that this stage is only for the pastor. (Yet Jesus chose ordinary, unschooled men to be His disciples.)

Unfortunately, many pastors think this as well. Most pastors forget that their job is not just to transfer information but also to coach disciples into their own ability to make disciples. Winning on God's team is not about being a professional all-star player who attracts and gathers a crowd but rather about being a coach who raises up people to become players and coaches themselves.

When we get to the last stage of the spiritual journey, we never stop being a disciple of Jesus and we never stop learning from other believers. Humility is the trademark of a disciple of Jesus. As men who knew who Jesus was and understood the big picture (Jesus said, "You are my friends"), the disciples had learned what love looks like. After the Resurrection and the arrival of the promised Holy Spirit, they moved from seeking position and authority as a privilege to understanding humble-servant leadership. Jesus sent them out to preach the gospel in its entirety to the world—to build Christ's church via the process of discipleship.

> **Most pastors forget that their job is not just to transfer information but also to coach disciples into their own ability to make disciples.**

THE SPIRITUAL PARENT

A spiritual parent is a mature disciplemaker, capable of making disciples who make disciples. The key words that describe a spiritual parent are *intentional* and *purposeful*. While none of us are ever completely mature, spiritual parents . . .

- understand the big picture: the gospel, the mission, and God's plan to restore and reconcile the world after judgment;

- have seen in Jesus the picture of maturity: how to love, how to fight, how to see the world;

- understand how to complete God's mission via the relationship and process they have just been through;

- are intentional in how they disciple others, keeping the end in mind (disciples who make disciples) as they go;

- see people the way Jesus does through the power of the Holy Spirit, valuing every person and knowing that all who have been saved are saved for a purpose that utilizes their experiences and gifts; understand what every sphere of life should look like from God's view of each life; and seek forgiveness from God and from others when—not if—they fail.

What kinds of things might you expect to hear from a spiritual parent?[i]

DAY FOUR REVIEW

1. What stood out to you or convicted you from today?

2. Put yourself in the mindset of Jesus' disciples after He died and rose again. What are some concerns they might have had about their qualifications to preach the gospel to the world?

3. What are some concerns you have about being a disciple?

4. Consider your relationships in your church body and small group. What is a responsibility or need you see there that you have had the tendency to view as the "pastor's job"? What would it look like for you to fill that need?

_____

_____

_____

---

i. Examples: "I have a person ready to start another group"; "One of the people in my group is starting to look like a spiritual young adult—it's time to give them some responsibility"; "I have been spending time with a person at work, and they just received Jesus. I need to introduce them to my group."

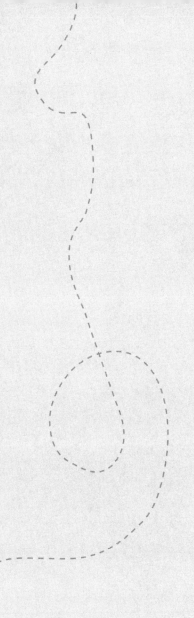

Day Five

IDENTIFYING A STAGE

GETTING STARTED

Yesterday you may have been surprised to find that you are not the only one who feels unqualified to disciple others. Hopefully you realize by this point that discipleship isn't just the job of the paid pastor or employee but the call given to all followers of Jesus. Just remember that everyone is in a different spot in their journey—but whatever stage of maturity you are at today, you can disciple someone else to that same level.

Lord Jesus: Help me see what You want me to see today. Expose any lies I may believe and lead me to Your truth. Help me trust and obey You and walk out what I'm learning in every sphere of my life.

I grew up as a disciple of wrestling and later became a disciplemaker in wrestling—a coach. I was able to coach because I was familiar with the rules, knew the nuances of wrestling, and could generally do the moves at the right time and in the right way. When I watched any wrestling practice anywhere, I could figure out who the beginners were, who the intermediate were, who the varsity were, and even who the possible state champions were.

As you grow into maturity in your journey of discipleship, you will understand more fully Jesus' mission and goals and what Kingdom wins look like. You can watch and listen to those who are growing disciples and be able to tell where they are in their journey toward maturity. And just like a coach, you as a spiritual parent can create a lesson in the right environment to help someone else grow.

Identifying the spiritual stage of a disciple, including yourself, involves a commitment to honesty, relationship, clarity, and grace. Being aware of the dynamics of spiritual maturity and the stages of growth will help you stay on the road during your discipleship journey. Here are some key principles to keep in mind:

- **Look for Consistency:** The stage you are really in is the one you are in consistently. A beginner in wrestling can occasionally pull off something that looks like a great move, but their performance over time demonstrates whether it was more of a fluke than a consistent pattern.

- **Assess Patterns, Not Moments:** A mature disciple, no matter how long they have been a disciple, can have a childish moment. That happens to all of us. Time spent with the disciple tells you where they are consistently.

> As you grow into maturity, you are able to watch and listen to those who are growing disciples and be able to tell their spiritual growth stage.

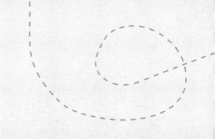

- **Your Value Is in Who You Are, Not Where You Are:** A person is not valuable because of where they are in their journey. You bear God's image. You are in Christ. That is the source of your value. In spiritual growth stages, value remains the same but usefulness to the mission differs (2 Timothy 2:20-21).

- **Don't Rush the Process:** If you see an act of immaturity in a new believer, and you are led to be part of their discipleship process, then help them mature if they are willing. Immature disciples may not be ready for your teaching at that exact moment. You may have to choose the right time for the right lesson.

- **Give Grace:** If a disciple you know to be consistently mature makes a childish mistake, give them grace. Any one of us can do the same thing (and have). Encourage them if you are in a position to do so, look past their faults, and pray for them.

- **Pay Attention to the Results:** You are not a spiritual parent unless you have spiritual children. Young adults could produce children, but they haven't yet. And if they did, those children probably would not be intentionally parented well. A spiritually mature parent has kids and is parenting them well.

- **Remember What Is True:** The devil will seek to either puff you up with pride or accuse you of unworthiness and drive you into the ground with discouragement. Keep your eyes focused on Christ, and don't allow your successes or failings to define you.

1. Based on what you now know about the process and stages of spiritual growth, circle either *True* or *False* next to the following statements:

   a. True/False: When you see an act of immaturity from a believer, you know they are an infant or a child.

   b. True/False: When you see immaturity in a believer, it's your invitation to correct them.

   c. True/False: When you act in an immature way in front of other believers, it's their invitation to correct you.

   d. True/False: God loves every child in His family the same, but their ability to do complex and important work differs.

   e. True/False: Proximity is one of the most important aspects of truly knowing where a person is in their discipleship journey.[i]

Really knowing someone takes time and regular relationship so you can see the unfiltered, honest behaviors and hear the words that come from their mouths. Anyone can look good in short stints, but over time true colors come out. When that happens, a disciple-maker can debrief the beliefs and emotions associated with the actions and words. Creating a safe place to be honest allows us to get to the heart of the matter. That's when we can lead those we are discipling into the right kind of environment and lessons that will help them take the next step.

2 TIMOTHY 2:20-21, NLT
In a wealthy home some utensils are made of gold and silver, and some are made of wood and clay. The expensive utensils are used for special occasions, and the cheap ones are for everyday use. If you keep yourself pure, you will be a special utensil for honorable use. Your life will be clean, and you will be ready for the Master to use you for every good work.

JOHN 6:1-11

Some time after this, Jesus crossed to the far shore of the Sea of Galilee (that is, the Sea of Tiberias), and a great crowd of people followed him because they saw the signs he had performed by healing the sick. Then Jesus went up on a mountainside and sat down with his disciples. The Jewish Passover Festival was near.

When Jesus looked up and saw a great crowd coming toward him, he said to Philip, "Where shall we buy bread for these people to eat?" He asked this only to test him, for he already had in mind what he was going to do.

Philip answered him, "It would take more than half a year's wages to buy enough bread for each one to have a bite!"

Another of his disciples, Andrew, Simon Peter's brother, spoke up, "Here is a boy with five small barley loaves and two small fish, but how far will they go among so many?"

Jesus said, "Have the people sit down." There was plenty of grass in that place, and they sat down (about five thousand men were there). Jesus then took the loaves, gave thanks, and distributed to those who were seated as much as they wanted. He did the same with the fish.

READ JOHN 6:12-71 IN YOUR PERSONAL BIBLE.

Read John 6:1-71.

2. What verse in John 6 tells you that Jesus was being intentional about what He was doing?

3. What stage of maturity do you think Jesus' disciples were at? What brought you to this conclusion?

4. In this passage, what stands out to you about the way Jesus taught? What kind of relational environments do you see in this passage? Did this have any bearing on the lesson's effectiveness?

5. As you go through John 6, you see Jesus and His disciples, Jesus and the crowd, Jesus and the Pharisees/religious leaders. Based on what you read, which of the following statements do you agree with?

   a. While Jesus was teaching crowds to some degree, as well as arguing with His critics, His main goal was to teach the disciples in those environments.
   b. Jesus was teaching the disciples how to deal with critics.
   c. Jesus was doing these miracles to reveal who He is: the Son of God.
   d. Jesus was showing the disciples that He cared about the hungry and hurting and that they should too.
   e. Jesus was putting the guys to work in simple ways that they could do at this point in their journey.
   f. Jesus was preparing the people for deeper teaching that the disciples would give after He rose from the dead and sent them into the world.
   g. Jesus was teaching the disciples that they should care about the God who gave bread more than about the bread itself.
   h. Jesus was preparing the disciples for His later teaching on Communion.[ii]

DAY FIVE REVIEW

1. What stood out to you or convicted you from today?

2. At the beginning of this week, you identified where you thought you were spiritually. Has that changed? Why or why not?

3. As you reflect on this week's Scripture readings, what are some of the relational environments where you noticed Jesus at work?

4. Which of those environments do you think were most effective when it came to teaching His disciples?

5. What are a few of the relational environments in your life right now where discipleship could happen? Do you see spiritual growth happening there, either in you or in others? Why or why not?

---

i.   Answer: True: d, e; False: a, b, c.
ii. Answer: All these statements are true.

Part II

THE FIVE SPHERES

So far we have worked through a simple understanding of the journey to spiritual maturity. Although growing to maturity is not simple, I hope you understand in general what maturity looks like. Our road trip analogy helps us go a step further. Remember our destination: spiritual maturity, which is becoming more like Jesus. We are following Jesus—who is changing us at the heart level—so we can be about His mission on Earth (Matthew 4:19). Jesus' road map for doing this was the SCMD process (Week 2), which we see in His relationship with the disciples.

Fill in the blanks to recall the key components of the journey:

In Matthew 4:_____, Jesus says, "Come and _____ me, and I will make you _____ of _____" (WNT).

Fill in the blanks below from the journey visual:

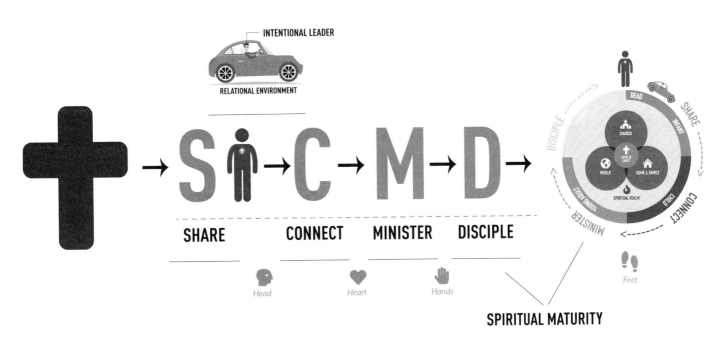

Spiritual maturity begins with accepting Jesus as our driver and getting into the relational vehicle He has invited us into. He is the one with the skills and directions to get us to His destination. He has given us His Holy Spirit as our guide, His Word as a map, and His people as our teachers.

JESUS AS OUR ARCHITECT

To use a different analogy, we could say that Jesus is the great Architect who has designed and built the world we are living in (read Psalm 19:1). He has a set of plans for our personal lives as well—plans for every part of our lives.

Imagine our life is like a house (read Matthew 7:24-27). God has given us a set of plans that will help us build a safe house on the rock (a firm foundation), and those plans are different from the world's plans. You may see a stark divide between what God gives you and what our cultural norms say. But the world's plans will eventually leave us with a huge problem. God can see all potential problems from His perspective, and He developed His plans from an understanding of those potential problems and His children's needs.

For instance, in the area of family, your understanding of the God-designed roles and responsibilities of a father and husband may clash with what your human father taught you. But only God has the right to define a father's role and way of doing things. Some men provide for their family and externally do the sorts of things the Bible says they should, but they do not have the heart of love that Jesus showed toward those in His life. Many fathers are not sacrificial, humble, or loving. God is our example of a Father, and He does the right things for the right reasons.

In the same way, God's plans for our lives include being on mission with Him, making disciples. Some of us may do the right things that Scripture says and may even love the way Scripture says we should (though no one is perfect); but we are missing the spiritual source of power that enables us to live out our God-given purpose with intentionality. We are not making disciples who make disciples.

When we don't teach the truth of the gospel, that we are saved for God's purposes and are hoping for eternal life together, we are living with an incomplete set of plans. Our plans from the Father include functions, heart, and purpose.

When we turned to God, we recognized that we had been living in a ramshackle spiritual house and needed to be saved. But do we find even now that parts of our lives are still wobbling on a faulty foundation? Even our foundation is faulty! Discipleship leads us to follow Jesus, who gives us new plans for every area of our lives. He changes our hearts from being centered on self to having love for God and others. He shows us that our mission is to make disciples and encourage disciples in every area of our lives.

The apostle Paul, one of Jesus' chosen apostles, shows us what it means to reflect Jesus' heart for disciplemaking. In the book of Colossians, he wrote that his goal was to present everyone mature and complete in Christ Jesus (Colossians 1:28). In other words, his mission was to make disciples, much like a parent's role is to raise a child to maturity. Paul's letter to the church in Ephesus goes further, giving us a framework that builds upon itself to create a picture of the life of discipleship. Paul deals with every major category of the Christian life and breaks it down into five different areas, which we call the Five Spheres:

1. the Abiding Sphere;
2. the Church Sphere;
3. the Home and Family Sphere;
4. the World Sphere; and
5. the Spiritual Sphere.

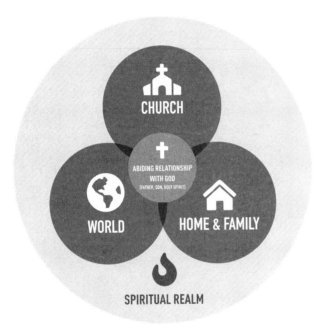

The rest of this workbook is dedicated to looking at the book of Ephesians as a guide and starting point for every area of our lives.

THE FOUNDATION OF THE FIVE SPHERES

Day One

EPHESIANS AND THE FIVE SPHERES

In the letter called Ephesians, Paul is writing to disciples of Jesus who are part of a church in Ephesus. Following Jesus' resurrection and ascension to heaven, the original disciples of Jesus made disciples, meaning that everyone in the early church called themselves a disciple.

In the first chapter of Ephesians, Paul makes two points that are foundational to the journey of discipleship:

- God has provided salvation and restoration for a fallen people. As we abide "in Christ," we remember who God is and who we are now in Christ. We remember how powerful God is and that He knows the future from the beginning.

- As we reflect on who He has made us when we first believed, we remember what He is capable of doing. Thinking about and reflecting on Him changes how we see the world.

Paul writes about what born-again disciples have "in Christ."

1. As you read the passage, underline every time you see "in Christ" or a variation of that phrase.

Paul, an apostle of Christ Jesus by the will of God,
> To God's holy people in Ephesus, the faithful in Christ Jesus:
> Grace and peace to you from God our Father and the Lord Jesus Christ.
> Praise be to the God and Father of our Lord Jesus Christ, who has blessed us in the heavenly realms with every spiritual blessing in Christ. For he chose us in him before the creation of the world to be holy and blameless in his sight. In love he predestined us for adoption to sonship through Jesus Christ, in accordance with his pleasure and will—to the praise of his glorious grace, which he has freely given us in the One he loves. In him we have redemption through his blood, the forgiveness of sins, in accordance with the riches of God's grace that he lavished on us. With all wisdom and understanding, he made known to us the mystery of his will according to his good pleasure, which he purposed in Christ, to be put into effect when the times reach their fulfillment—to bring unity to all things in heaven and on earth under Christ.

When we abide with Christ, we remember who He is and what He has done. We remember how powerful He is and that He knows the future from the beginning.

 Scan QR code to access video podcasts and other content that accompanies this week's session.

In him we were also chosen, having been predestined according to the plan of him who works out everything in conformity with the purpose of his will, in order that we, who were the first to put our hope in Christ, might be for the praise of his glory. And you also were included in Christ when you heard the message of truth, the gospel of your salvation. When you believed, you were marked in him with a seal, the promised Holy Spirit, who is a deposit guaranteeing our inheritance until the redemption of those who are God's possession—to the praise of his glory.

EPHESIANS 1:1-14

2. How many times was "in Christ" or a variation of the phrase used? _____ ⁱ

3. Which verse tells you how you get "in Christ"? _____ ⁱⁱ

4. Which verse tells us about the Holy Spirit moving inside us? _____ ⁱⁱⁱ

WHAT DOES "IN CHRIST" MEAN?

The overarching story of God detailed in Scripture shows us the choice He gives us: between identifying ourselves with Adam (our sin nature) or identifying ourselves with the perfect God-man, Jesus. God created a perfect world where God and humans walked together, and He gave humans the ability to choose for themselves whether they wanted a relationship with Him. When Adam and Eve sinned, they rejected their trust relationship with God. The Curse, which included physical death, was the result, and because all people eventually sinned, death came to all humanity (Romans 5:12). But God responded by showing grace to His creation: He sent Jesus to the cross to die in our place, offering life and restored relationship to all who would repent and receive Him as Lord and Savior.

Read Romans 5:15 (see sidebar).

Identifying with Adam represents rebellion and refusing to trust God, which results in separation from God. On the other hand, we can choose to identify with Jesus—the One who chose to obey and trust God. Jesus not only did what was right but also became our sacrifice for all human sins—from those of Adam and Eve to those who live today. Our part is to receive Jesus as our sacrifice for sin and as our Lord.

5. Read these Scripture passages, then circle *True* or *False* for each of the statements that follow.

Christ has indeed been raised from the dead, the firstfruits of those who have fallen asleep. For since death came through a man, the resurrection of the dead comes also through a man. For as in Adam all die, so in Christ all will be made alive. But each in turn: Christ, the firstfruits; then, when he comes, those who belong to him. Then the end will come, when he hands over the kingdom to God the Father after he has destroyed all dominion, authority and power.

1 CORINTHIANS 15:20-24

ROMANS 5:12, NLT

When Adam sinned, sin entered the world. Adam's sin brought death, so death spread to everyone, for everyone sinned.

ROMANS 5:15, NLT

There is a great difference between Adam's sin and God's gracious gift. For the sin of this one man, Adam, brought death to many. But even greater is God's wonderful grace and his gift of forgiveness to many through this other man, Jesus Christ.

Because one person disobeyed God, many became sinners. But because one other person obeyed God, many will be made righteous.

ROMANS 5:19, NLT

Well then, should we keep on sinning so that God can show us more and more of his wonderful grace? Of course not! Since we have died to sin, how can we continue to live in it? Or have you forgotten that when we were joined with Christ Jesus in baptism, we joined him in his death? For we died and were buried with Christ by baptism. And just as Christ was raised from the dead by the glorious power of the Father, now we also may live new lives.

Since we have been united with him in his death, we will also be raised to life as he was. We know that our old sinful selves were crucified with Christ so that sin might lose its power in our lives. We are no longer slaves to sin. For when we died with Christ we were set free from the power of sin. And since we died with Christ, we know we will also live with him. We are sure of this because Christ was raised from the dead, and he will never die again. Death no longer has any power over him. When he died, he died once to break the power of sin. But now that he lives, he lives for the glory of God.

ROMANS 6:1-10, NLT

a. True/False: If I am "in Christ," then I am a disciple of Jesus.
b. True/False: I am "in Christ" because I have accepted what Jesus did for me on the cross and have decided to surrender my life to His leadership.
c. True/False: If I am not "in Christ," I am "in Adam."
d. True/False: If I am "in Adam," it means my sin nature still controls and reigns in my life.
e. True/False: If I am "in Adam," it means I will be judged for my sin outside of Christ.
f. True/False: If I am "in Christ," the Holy Spirit lives in me and changes my heart.
g. True/False: Baptism is a picture of the decision I have made to be "in Christ."
h. True/False: If I am "in Christ," I can continue to sin because Jesus paid the price for my sin.
i. True/False: If I am "in Christ," I still struggle with sin, but I want to do what God would have me do.
j. True/False: If I am "in Christ," I can count on being raised from the dead just like Jesus was.
k. True/False: If I am "in Christ," then I am no longer a slave to sin but I still struggle with the presence of sin.[iv]

BAPTISM: A PICTURE OF CHOOSING TO BE "IN CHRIST"

When we looked at the spiritual child stage in Week 3, we learned that baptism is an act of obedience that reveals we have a new Lord. Baptism burns into our minds the decision we have made and its implications. The act of baptism was the normative way disciples accepted Jesus in the first church (Acts 2:38). The Holy Spirit was also promised to those who had made Jesus Savior and Lord: Now not only am I "in Christ," but also His Spirit

ACTS 2:38

Peter replied, "Repent and be baptized, every one of you, in the name of Jesus Christ for the forgiveness of your sins. And you will receive the gift of the Holy Spirit."

JOHN 3:3-5

Jesus replied, "Very truly I tell you, no one can see the kingdom of God unless they are born again."

"How can someone be born when they are old?" Nicodemus asked. "Surely they cannot enter a second time into their mother's womb to be born!"

Jesus answered, "Very truly I tell you, no one can enter the kingdom of God unless they are born of water and the Spirit."

Notes and Thoughts

(the Holy Spirit) is now in me. Baptism also represents the new birth we have in Christ. Jesus characterized being born again as being born of water and Spirit. We are born again and start our new journey.

In witnessing a baptism, other disciples are also reminded of the decision they made before. Baptism says,

- *I am making a public declaration that I am not ashamed of Jesus. I agree that I have sinned and confess it publicly. I also understand that I was destined to spiritual death as a result.*

- *In baptism, I identify with Jesus, who physically died because of my sin so I only have to die figuratively in my baptism. Just as Jesus was raised from the dead, I, too, will be raised to life upon my physical death or upon Jesus' second coming because I trust Him for salvation and lordship.*

Read John 3:3-5 (see sidebar).

DAY ONE REVIEW

1. What stood out to you or convicted you from today?

2. After today's lesson, how would you describe the implications of the statement *I am "in Christ"*? Has your previous understanding of "in Christ" changed in any way? If so, how?

3. Have you made a public declaration of your new birth in Christ by being baptized? If so, share your experience with the group. If not, write down or share with the group why you have not taken that step.

4. What are you currently doing to daily remind yourself of what it means to be "in Christ"?

5. Pick two or three of the true "in Christ" statements from question 5 (see page 81) and put them somewhere you will see every day (such as your bathroom mirror or your car dashboard). Make a point to review them daily.

---

i. Answer: Ten.
ii. Answer: Ephesians 1:7.
iii. Answer: Ephesians 1:13.
iv. Answer: All are true except for h.

Day Two

THE ABIDING SPHERE

GETTING STARTED

In your quiet time today, read Ephesians 1:1–2:10. Make sure you are praying that the Lord will help you understand His Word clearly. You might start a prayer journal to write down what you are learning as well as your prayers to the Lord. It's helpful to look back at what you have prayed for in the past and see how many things the Lord has done for you that you may have forgotten.

Lord Jesus: Help me see what You want me to see today. Expose any lies I may believe and lead me to Your truth. Help me trust and obey You and walk out what I'm learning in every sphere of my life.

Now that we are "in Christ," we have been given a new identity. When we think of our identity, we are considering who we are at our very core. Who are you—really?

When we think of our identity, we are considering who we are at our very core.

1. What are some words that describe you when you were "in Adam"—how you defined yourself before Jesus?

    _____

    _____

    _____

2. How did you come to believe this about yourself?

    _____

    _____

3. What influences most shaped your belief about who you are? Circle your answers.
    - my parents
    - school
    - sports
    - a hobby
    - a relationship
    - an experience
    - culture

4. Identify a story that reveals how you came to think you are who you are, and write it briefly here. Share this story in your group.

    _____

    _____

    _____

PSALM 139:13, NLT

You made all the delicate, inner parts of my body and knit me together in my mother's womb.

EPHESIANS 2:1-10, NLT

Once you were dead because of your disobedience and your many sins. You used to live in sin, just like the rest of the world, obeying the devil—the commander of the powers in the unseen world. He is the spirit at work in the hearts of those who refuse to obey God. All of us used to live that way, following the passionate desires and inclinations of our sinful nature. By our very nature we were subject to God's anger, just like everyone else.

But God is so rich in mercy, and he loved us so much, that even though we were dead because of our sins, he gave us life when he raised Christ from the dead. (It is only by God's grace that you have been saved!) For he raised us from the dead along with Christ and seated us with him in the heavenly realms because we are united with Christ Jesus. So God can point to us in all future ages as examples of the incredible wealth of his grace and kindness toward us, as shown in all he has done for us who are united with Christ Jesus.

God saved you by his grace when you believed. And you can't take credit for this; it is a gift from God. Salvation is not a reward for the good things we have done, so none of us can boast about it. For we are God's masterpiece. He has created us anew in Christ Jesus, so we can do the good things he planned for us long ago.

Read Psalm 139:13; Ephesians 2:1-10; and Colossians 1:15-19 (see sidebar).

As disciples of Jesus, we have come to understand that who we are at our core is who God has made us to be. God knit us together in our mother's womb (Psalm 139:13) and has saved us for a purpose. When we believe, we are created anew in Christ Jesus to be God's masterpiece (Ephesians 2:8-10).

Earlier in Ephesians 2, however, we see that while we were created for God's great purpose, sin marred the beautiful picture that God intended. Now, apart from God, we deserve God's wrath. But when we are "in Christ," the Master begins to rebuild His intended purpose for us and in us. We are new because He gives us a new identity. We are now who God says we are rather than who we thought we were or who the world told us we were.

You may be asking, *What new identity do I have in Christ?* Paul tells us the answer.

5. Underline the words or phrases in the following passages that tell you your new identity "in Christ."

Paul, an apostle of Christ Jesus by the will of God,

To God's holy people in Ephesus, the faithful in Christ Jesus:

Grace and peace to you from God our Father and the Lord Jesus Christ.

Praise be to the God and Father of our Lord Jesus Christ, who has blessed us in the heavenly realms with every spiritual blessing in Christ. For he chose us in him before the creation of the world to be holy and blameless in his sight. In love he predestined us for adoption to sonship through Jesus Christ, in accordance with his pleasure and will.

EPHESIANS 1:1-5

Consequently, you are no longer foreigners and strangers, but fellow citizens with God's people and also members of his household.

EPHESIANS 2:19

Speaking the truth in love, we will grow to become in every respect the mature body of him who is the head, that is, Christ.

EPHESIANS 4:15

I AM A DISCIPLE OF JESUS

The disciples were told to go and make disciples of Jesus, and they did. Each of us who is a disciple of Jesus is told to make disciples too. Embracing God's vision for us leads us to behave differently. Because God has foreknowledge of the future, He knew we would choose Him just as He chose us. We were part of God's plan for our slice of history, which He planned before He even made the world.

Read Acts 17:22-28 (see sidebar).

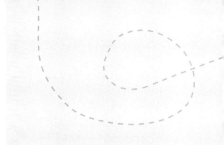

Through Paul's message to the Ephesians, we find that we are spotless and blameless in God's sight because of what Jesus did for us. We are adopted children of God.

Isn't that amazing? God wanted to be your Father. You are a chosen citizen of the Kingdom of heaven that never ends. You are part of a new nation that includes every race under heaven. You are a member of God's household and part of His body, the church. These realities suggest that you have a significant and useful purpose and a mission.

As humans who live down here on planet Earth, we fit into categories and use certain words to describe where we came from or what we do. We have résumés and a status based on characteristics and achievements. However, those things are merely where we live and what we do—they are not our most important identity.

Years ago on a visit to India, I came across another man from America. Trying to get to know him, I asked him what he did. His answer surprised me and has influenced the way I think ever since. He said, "I am a follower of Jesus who pay his bills by being a doctor." So often we think where we live, what we do, or what we have defines who we are. As disciples of Jesus, we care most about what our Savior and Lord says we are.

Right now, so many American Christians are upset about the direction our country is going. If I place my identity as an American before my identity as being "in Christ," then when America is shaken, so is my faith and everything else in my life. If America is in decline, affecting my job and my livelihood, and my job is one of my most important "identity" factors, then I am a mess. If my possessions matter most and I am in danger of losing them, I am truly shaken.

But if I am who Jesus says I am—if my identity is a child of the Most High God and my citizenship is in heaven—then I may be unsettled by what is happening in America, which affects the lesser things, but I am still solid. My true identity and purpose are not shaken.

THE ENEMY'S TACTICS

The enemy wants you to forget your new identity and fall back into your old understanding of things. The devil wants you to believe that any other identity is better than the one God offers. He did this in the Garden, and he still does it today. The devil told Adam and Eve that the identity of the one who knows and decides right from wrong was the identity of the one who trusts and walks with God. Who was right?

The devil loves to pull us back into our past identities. He wants you to believe that God "in Christ" does not see you as made new. When we fail in some way or we are in a time of confusion and don't know what to do and God isn't making it clear, the devil says, "The reason you are struggling is because God is angry at you or you disappointed Him in some way." If the devil can get us to forget our new identity, we will turn to old-identity behaviors. Our vision of ourselves determines our behaviors in all the spheres of our lives. I often hear Christians say things like "I am a sinner saved by grace." This is true, but I think that declaring you are still a sinner can make it feel more difficult to say no to sin. What if instead we claimed our new identity—that we are saints who are "in Christ" and who struggle with sin?

COLOSSIANS 1:15-19

The Son is the image of the invisible God, the firstborn over all creation. For in him all things were created: things in heaven and on earth, visible and invisible, whether thrones or powers or rulers or authorities; all things have been created through him and for him. He is before all things, and in him all things hold together. And he is the head of the body, the church; he is the beginning and the firstborn from among the dead, so that in everything he might have the supremacy. For God was pleased to have all his fullness dwell in him.

ACTS 17:22-28

Paul then stood up in the meeting of the Areopagus and said: "People of Athens! I see that in every way you are very religious. For as I walked around and looked carefully at your objects of worship, I even found an altar with this inscription: TO AN UNKNOWN GOD. So you are ignorant of the very thing you worship—and this is what I am going to proclaim to you.

"The God who made the world and everything in it is the Lord of heaven and earth and does not live in temples built by human hands. And he is not served by human hands, as if he needed anything. Rather, he himself gives everyone life and breath and everything else. From one man he made all the nations, that they should inhabit the whole earth; and he marked out their appointed times in history and the boundaries of their lands. God did this so that they would seek him and perhaps reach out for him and find him, though he is not far from any one of us. 'For in him we live and move and have our being.' As some of your own poets have said, 'We are his offspring.'"

1 CORINTHIANS 1:2

To the church of God in Corinth, to those sanctified in Christ Jesus and called to be his holy people, together with all those everywhere who call on the name of our Lord Jesus Christ—their Lord and ours . . .

Read 1 Corinthians 1:2 (see sidebar).

6. Do the words used in this passage to identify God's people reflect how you see yourself in Christ? Why or why not?

Remember, we reveal where we are at in the stages of spiritual growth by what worries us or gives us a sense of pride. The overflow of our mouths and the worries in our hearts that we keep hidden reveal what we are abiding in.

7. Abiding in who God is (His identity) gives us peace when things happen that threaten our view of life. Have you experienced this reality? If so, how?

Notes and Thoughts

DAY TWO REVIEW

1. What stood out to you or convicted you from today?

2. How do you think that abiding in our identity in Christ can help us when something happens that threatens who we think we are?

3. Consider how you see yourself in the different areas of your life. Does your identity change according to where you are or who you are around? What would it look like to be a disciple of Jesus consistently in every area of your life?

Day Three

THE PURPOSE OF ABIDING

GETTING STARTED

Yesterday we walked through what it means to have a new identity "in Christ." God offers us this identity. Paul was writing in a new way what Jesus had already taught His disciples.

> *Lord Jesus: Help me see what You want me to see today. Expose any lies I may believe and lead me to Your truth. Help me trust and obey You and walk out what I'm learning in every sphere of my life.*

Read John 15:1-17.

Jesus wants us to be "in Him" in an ongoing way—to remain or abide in Him. This means that we stay in Him no matter what happens on our discipleship journey. Being "in Christ" is like being grafted into the root of a vine, which provides the power to survive and thrive. According to Jesus, the Father is the gardener who tends the plant.

Abiding or remaining in Christ is remembering who He is. Because of who He is, I can have peace no matter what the world throws at me. So often we abide in something that is unreliable and we become shaken. If most of our abiding is in a news program, we'll be left angry or afraid. If we abide in social media content, we won't know where to turn when life gets hard. When we abide in the wrong thing, we get the wrong kind of spiritual fruit. Abiding in Christ gives us stability and hope.

1. Read the following statements and circle either *True* or *False*.

   a. True/False: The devil wants to get me to abide in something that is unreliable so that I become unstable.

   b. True/False: When I forget that God knows the future already and is working out His plan perfectly, I become afraid, angry, or unstable.

   c. True/False: Sometimes it looks like God is not in control, and this leads to me taking matters into my own hands to protect myself.[i]

ABIDING LEADS TO SANCTIFICATION

The big Bible word that describes this process of spiritual growth at the hands of our Master Teacher is *sanctification*. Sanctification is the "process of being made holy resulting in a changed lifestyle for the believer."[1]

Read John 17:15-17 and 1 Corinthians 6:9-11 (see sidebar).

JOHN 17:15-17

[Jesus said,] "My prayer is not that you take them out of the world but that you protect them from the evil one. They are not of the world, even as I am not of it. Sanctify them by the truth; your word is truth."

1 CORINTHIANS 6:9-11

Do you not know that wrongdoers will not inherit the kingdom of God? Do not be deceived: Neither the sexually immoral nor idolaters nor adulterers nor men who have sex with men nor thieves nor the greedy nor drunkards nor slanderers nor swindlers will inherit the kingdom of God. And that is what some of you were. But you were washed, you were sanctified, you were justified in the name of the Lord Jesus Christ and by the Spirit of our God.

GALATIANS 5:22-24

The fruit of the Spirit is love, joy, peace, forbearance, kindness, goodness, faithfulness, gentleness and self-control. Against such things there is no law. Those who belong to Christ Jesus have crucified the flesh with its passions and desires.

When we become disciples of Jesus, we are justified (declared righteous because of what Jesus has done for us). That's when we start the process of becoming what we were declared to be. This is called the process of sanctification.

In John 15:3, Jesus told His disciples that they were "already clean because of the word [Jesus had] spoken to [them]." What does this mean? Jesus had already called them, and they had answered the call in faith. They were declared clean (justified) because of their faith. They were now allowing Jesus to change them, and they were committed to His mission. Jesus said that as they remained in Him, they would be sanctified (made holy or set apart). Each of us is sanctified as we abide in who Jesus is and who He says we are now.

2. What is the purpose of pruning a fruit tree? (An online search might help expand your answer to this question.)

_____

_____

3. What does Jesus want His disciples to understand through this analogy?

_____

Read Galatians 5:22-24 (see sidebar).

4. What reason would God have for pruning us? Circle *True* or *False*.

   a. True/False: If I obey God, He will not prune me.
   b. True/False: He is getting me ready for new things by eliminating wasted energy.
   c. True/False: He is aligning my expectations with the reality that I will go through things I don't understand or like.
   d. True/False: He is telling me I will need to persevere when things don't go the way I want.
   e. True/False: Sometimes we go through tough things so God can show others who we are in tough times, which can draw them to what makes us strong.
   f. True/False: The purpose of pruning is so that I will bear spiritual fruit and bring glory to God.[ii]

What other reasons might God have for pruning us?

_____

JOHN 15:7-14

[Jesus said,] "If you remain in me and my words remain in you, ask whatever you wish, and it will be done for you. This is to my Father's glory, that you bear much fruit, showing yourselves to be my disciples.

"As the Father has loved me, so have I loved you. Now remain in my love. If you keep my commands, you will remain in my love, just as I have kept my Father's commands and remain in his love. I have told you this so that my joy may be in you and that your joy may be complete. My command is this: Love each other as I have loved you. Greater love has no one than this: to lay down one's life for one's friends. You are my friends if you do what I command."

5. Read John 15:7-14 and fill in the blanks:

   a. I am declared _____ because I believe what Jesus has spoken to me.
   b. John 15:7: If you remain in Him and His Word _____ in you, you can ask for what you want and He will give it to you. (Read verse 7 and 1 John 5:14-15.)
   c. If God's Word remains in me, it will change me and thus change what I ask for. When you ask anything in accordance with _____ will, it will be done for you.
   d. John 15:8: If you show yourselves to be Jesus' disciples, it will bring much _____ to the glory of the Father.

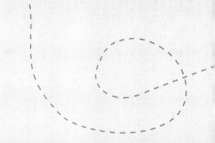

e. John 15:9-10: Jesus said that to remain in Him you must _____ Him.

f. John 15:12: His commands are all about _____.

g. John 15:13-14: Love looks like what? _____.[iii]

6. After Jesus warns us about abiding, He tells us that the Father will prune us. Why do you think He speaks that warning at that point in His teaching?

We are most tempted to separate from the Lord when we don't understand what He is doing. The enemy loves to do what he has always done—get us to doubt God and go our own way. Jesus gives us a warning just as He did in the Garden of Eden. If you don't stay connected to the Source of life, you will wither and die. Jesus warns us of the end: Those branches that die are cut off and thrown into the fire.

DAY THREE REVIEW

1. What stood out to you or convicted you from today?

2. What activity, person, or situation in your life are you prone to abide in rather than Jesus?

3. Share about a time when you believe God was pruning you.

4. As you look at your schedule this week, what are some things you might need to prune or cut away so that you can spend that time abiding in Jesus?

---

1. *Holman Concise Bible Dictionary*, s.v. "sanctification" (Nashville: Holman, 2010), 554.

i. Answer: All these statements are true.

ii. Answer: True: b, c, d, e, f; False: a.

iii. Answer: a. clean, b. remains, c. His, d. fruit, e. obey, f. love, g. obedience.

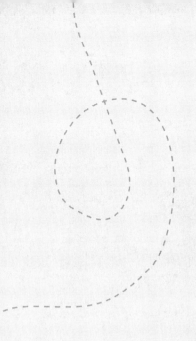

Day Four

GOOD WORKS

GETTING STARTED

On this journey with Jesus, we are starting to realize who He is (Mark 4:35-41), and we are "in Christ" when we choose to identify ourselves with Jesus rather than with Adam. As we abide in Him, it calms us in the storms of life.

> *Lord Jesus: Help me see what You want me to see today. Expose any lies I may believe and lead me to Your truth. Help me trust and obey You and walk out what I'm learning in every sphere of my life.*

When we abide in Jesus, we are also abiding in our newly given identities. God identifies us with Christ when we choose Jesus as He has chosen us. Jesus on the cross was clothed in our sin, and now we are clothed in Christ. He took what we deserved, and we got what Jesus deserved. We call this the great exchange. How amazing!

On the cross we see that God hates sin and will judge it. It's a warning to all who choose to continue to identify with Adam instead of identifying with Jesus. If Father God judged His own Son, then we can be sure He will judge those who reject His identity and the identity He made available to us in Christ.

At the same time, on the cross we see how much the Father (and the Son) love us. God was willing to allow Jesus to identify with Adam so we wouldn't have to. As a result, we are given a new identity "in Christ," and we are new creatures in Christ.

> In Christ Jesus you are all children of God through faith, for all of you who were baptized into Christ have clothed yourselves with Christ. There is neither Jew nor Gentile, neither slave nor free, nor is there male and female, for you are all one in Christ Jesus.
>
> GALATIANS 3:26-28

BACK TO EPHESIANS

Read Ephesians 2:1-10 (see sidebar).

When we were saved by grace through faith, we were saved from the wrath of God and given a new identity. That new identity leads to good works which God has planned for us to do. As we read through the rest of Ephesians, we will see the five different areas—the Five Spheres—where those good works are supposed to be lived out:

1. the Abiding Sphere;
2. the Church Sphere;

MARK 4:35-41

That day when evening came, [Jesus] said to his disciples, "Let us go over to the other side." Leaving the crowd behind, they took him along, just as he was, in the boat. There were also other boats with him. A furious squall came up, and the waves broke over the boat, so that it was nearly swamped. Jesus was in the stern, sleeping on a cushion. The disciples woke him and said to him, "Teacher, don't you care if we drown?"

He got up, rebuked the wind and said to the waves, "Quiet! Be still!" Then the wind died down and it was completely calm.

He said to his disciples, "Why are you so afraid? Do you still have no faith?"

They were terrified and asked each other, "Who is this? Even the wind and the waves obey him!"

3. the Home and Family Sphere;
4. the World Sphere; and
5. the Spiritual Sphere.

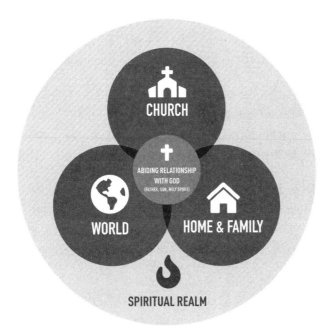

The good works God wants us to do concern the rebuilding of our lives that had been built on faulty architectural plans and on the quest for the wrong identity. We start with the Abiding Sphere because that rebuilding must come from God, not us.

1. Reread Ephesians 2:1-10, and circle *True* or *False* for the following statements.

   a. True/False: Only some humans were dead because of sin.
   b. True/False: We are saved from death and now are created anew in Jesus.
   c. True/False: Good works give us access to God's grace.
   d. True/False: We were saved by grace through faith for good works.
   e. True/False: We used to be dead, but now we have a new identity.
   f. True/False: The enemy directed our old way of living.[i]

2. As we come to understand that Jesus has given us architectural plans (commands to be taught and followed by disciples) for every sphere of our lives, we recognize some clear implications. Mark the following statements *True* or *False*.

   a. True/False: If you choose to ignore God's good works (His architectural plans) in one part of your life, then that area will be far weaker than it should be and dangerous for every person who shares that part of your spiritual house with you.
   b. True/False: Even if you choose to not let God rebuild an area according to His plans, the devil can't try to get into the rest of the house through that area.

EPHESIANS 2:1-10

As for you, you were dead in your transgressions and sins, in which you used to live when you followed the ways of this world and of the ruler of the kingdom of the air, the spirit who is now at work in those who are disobedient. All of us also lived among them at one time, gratifying the cravings of our flesh and following its desires and thoughts. Like the rest, we were by nature deserving of wrath. But because of his great love for us, God, who is rich in mercy, made us alive with Christ even when we were dead in transgressions—it is by grace you have been saved. And God raised us up with Christ and seated us with him in the heavenly realms in Christ Jesus, in order that in the coming ages he might show the incomparable riches of his grace, expressed in his kindness to us in Christ Jesus. For it is by grace you have been saved, through faith—and this is not from yourselves, it is the gift of God— not by works, so that no one can boast. For we are God's handiwork, created in Christ Jesus to do good works, which God prepared in advance for us to do.

c. True/False: A disciple of Jesus cannot keep the world's architectural plans separate from what Jesus wants to do in other areas.

d. True/False: God has plans for every part of our lives.

e. True/False: I can be saved and seem mature in one area of my life but still be immature in another.

f. True/False: As you walk through SCMD, you learn to share your life with others and connect at a deep relational level, but that doesn't impact other parts of your life.

g. True/False: Becoming like Jesus as you walk with Him helps you become better and more stable (as God sees it) in every sphere of life.

h. True/False: Once you've covered enough ground on your journey, you won't fall back into old patterns.[ii]

Abiding with Jesus daily gives us time to spiritually sit at Jesus' feet and learn His way of thinking and doing. Abiding doesn't just mean we learn His architectural plans for life (His commands so we can obey them)—it also means we are doing life with Jesus. As we do, He helps us build out the plans He gives us. Jesus helps us evaluate our work as we do it. His Holy Spirit speaks in a quiet voice, and we must stop to listen, rather than trying to discern it amid all the noise of life.

Spending time with Jesus allows the Lord to correct and encourage us as we build. The truth is, Jesus doesn't want to send us out to do anything apart from Him. He wants us to walk with Him, which means we need to spend time in conversation with Him. When we stay connected to Him, He will often reveal how we are falling back into old identities and where and how the enemy is trying to infiltrate our thinking and planning.

Read Micah 6:8 (see sidebar).

3. Abiding helps us deal with many issues in our lives. Which of the following do you deal with the most?

- I get discouraged and need Jesus to encourage me when things aren't going well.
- I forget the plans and need to spend time with the Architect again to be reminded.
- I tend to want to run ahead of Jesus and do things my own way. I need Him to pull me back alongside Him.
- I need to see the people around me the way Jesus does. If I get angry or discouraged with them, they become my enemies rather than my colaborers.
- Other: _____

The truth is, many have heard the gospel and accepted it as truth. However, in their discipleship they were not intentionally taught God's commands in every area, so they have lived in ignorance in one or more of the spheres. As we look at the other spheres in the weeks ahead, consider which of the spheres you feel the most ignorant or confused about and which you would say is the most important to you.

MICAH 6:8:8

He has shown you, O mortal,
what is good.
And what does the LORD
require of you?
To act justly and to love mercy
and to walk humbly with
your God.

DAY FOUR REVIEW

1. What stood out to you or convicted you from today?

2. What are some of the things or plans your life was built on before you became a disciple of Jesus?

3. Name some of the things God, as the Architect, would like to see you build your life on now.

4. Think about your life in the areas of Home and Family, World (including work), and Church. Which area stands out as needing more of God's presence? Pray that God will show you how He might want to do some remodeling in that area.

---

i. Answer: True: b, d, e, f; False: a, c.
ii. Answer: True: a, c, d, e, g; False: b, f, h.

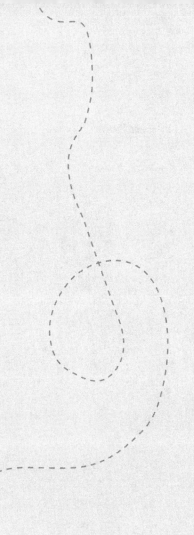

Day Five

THE BIG PICTURE

GETTING STARTED

You are now "in Christ," and God sees you in your new identity, as a new creature in Christ. Abiding is spending time with the Lord so we can be constantly reminded of God's perspective of us and the world we live in. When we spend time abiding, we are putting on spiritual glasses that help us see into the spiritual reality we are dealing with.

> *Lord Jesus: Help me see what You want me to see today. Expose any lies I may believe and lead me to Your truth. Help me trust and obey You and walk out what I'm learning in every sphere of my life.*

God is a God of relationship. As God gives us His architectural plans, His biggest concern is relational. He cares about the relationships you have in every sphere of your life. Physical things pass away, but human beings were built for eternity and relationships with God and others. When we abide, we spend time with our relational God, who wants to teach us how to live relationally in every sphere of our lives.

Jesus said that apart from Him we can do nothing. Oh, we can do plenty, but not much that is eternally and spiritually good without Him. That's why abiding is so important.

Read John 15:4 (see sidebar).

1. When Jesus tells us that we produce fruit when we remain in Him, what kind of fruit does He mean?

   _____

   _____

Read the following passages and answer the questions.

> The fruit of the Spirit is love, joy, peace, forbearance, kindness, goodness, faithfulness, gentleness and self-control. Against such things there is no law.
> GALATIANS 5:22-23

2. In John 15 Jesus said we must remain in Him to bear fruit. Paul says above that the Holy Spirit produces good fruit. Which one of the fruits listed above do you think you most lack? How might spending time with Jesus change that?

   _____

   _____

> This is the message we have heard from him and declare to you: God is light; in him there is no darkness at all. If we claim to have fellowship with him and yet

JOHN 15:4

[Jesus said,] "Remain in me, as I also remain in you. No branch can bear fruit by itself; it must remain in the vine. Neither can you bear fruit unless you remain in me."

walk in the darkness, we lie and do not live out the truth. But if we walk in the light, as he is in the light, we have fellowship with one another, and the blood of Jesus, his Son, purifies us from all sin.

1 JOHN 1:5-7

3. Based on this verse, where does fellowship with people start? Some people say that they are "good with God," but their interactions and relationships have constant friction. How can this be?

Not only does this time abiding with God give us a new identity, but it also gives us wisdom to live out that new identity.

The wisdom that comes from heaven is first of all pure; then peace-loving, considerate, submissive, full of mercy and good fruit, impartial and sincere. Peacemakers who sow in peace reap a harvest of righteousness.

JAMES 3:17-18

Not only does time abiding with God give us a new identity, but it also gives us wisdom to live out that new identity. Biblical wisdom is being able to discern what is true, what is ethically right, and what should be done in different situations.

4. Where does wisdom come from?

You were once darkness, but now you are light in the Lord. Live as children of light (for the fruit of the light consists in all goodness, righteousness and truth).

EPHESIANS 5:8-9

5. In Ephesians 5:8-9, what promise is given to those who abide in Jesus?

We have not stopped praying for you since we first heard about you. We ask God to give you complete knowledge of his will and to give you spiritual wisdom and understanding. Then the way you live will always honor and please the Lord, and your lives will produce every kind of good fruit. All the while, you will grow as you learn to know God better and better.

We also pray that you will be strengthened with all his glorious power so you will have all the endurance and patience you need. May you be filled with joy, always thanking the Father. He has enabled you to share in the inheritance that belongs to his people, who live in the light. For he has rescued us from the kingdom of darkness and transferred us into the Kingdom of his dear Son, who purchased our freedom and forgave our sins.

COLOSSIANS 1:9-14, NLT

Do you not know? Have you not heard? The Everlasting God, the LORD, the Creator of the ends of the earth does not become weary or tired. His understanding is inscrutable. He gives strength to the weary, and to him who lacks might He increases power. Though youths grow weary and tired, and vigorous young men stumble badly, yet those who wait for the LORD will gain new strength; they will mount up with wings like eagles, they will run and not get tired, they will walk and not become weary.

ISAIAH 40:28-31, NASB

This is what the LORD says: "Cursed are those who put their trust in mere humans, who rely on human strength and turn their hearts away from the LORD. They are like stunted shrubs in the desert, with no hope for the future. They will live in the barren wilderness, in an uninhabited salty land. But blessed are those who trust in the LORD and have made the LORD their hope and confidence. They are like trees planted along a riverbank, with roots that reach deep into the water. Such trees are not bothered by the heat or worried by long months of drought. Their leaves stay green, and they never stop producing fruit.

JEREMIAH 17:5-8, NLT

Scripture shows us that not only do we get the right plans from abiding in Jesus but as we walk with Him, we gain the strength to live out what God directs us to do. God never wants to send us anywhere alone, but He invites us to go with Him into the plans He has for us. If we try to pull off God's commands for building our lives on Him *without* God—without Him in us and without walking with Him daily—then our plans just become nice ideas.

DAY FIVE REVIEW

1. What stood out to you or convicted you from today?

2. Name some of the benefits that come from abiding in Christ.

3. Will you make any changes after this week's lesson to the time or the way in which you abide?

Week 5

THE ABIDING SPHERE

Day One

ACTIVELY ABIDING

GETTING STARTED

Using the journey analogy, we have been invited by Jesus and His representatives into relational environments (2 Corinthians 5:20). We move through the SCMD process on our journey toward spiritual maturity. On this journey, we are allowing God to change the way we see Him and ourselves. We are accepting a new identity that is not dictated by the world or the enemy. God also helps us learn how to rebuild our spiritual lives into what He would have us be in every sphere. We now have a personal relationship with Jesus, which means knowing Him—not just knowing about Him.

Lord Jesus: Help me see what You want me to see today. Expose any lies I may believe and lead me to Your truth. Help me trust and obey You and walk out what I'm learning in every sphere of my life.

Read Ephesians 1:17 (see sidebar).

When I was a wrestler, my coaches taught me the importance of drilling. A wrestler must practice the same move over and over with a partner. Drilling speeds up over time, with each person working on the same move as coaches help them fine-tune it. Every wrestler—from little kids to high school and college athletes to Olympic wrestlers—has to rehearse these fundamentals. The moves you learn over thousands of attempts are embedded in your muscle memory, becoming second nature. Then, in a live match, you're able to make snap decisions and react on the fly to what your opponent does. If you don't practice what you are learning, you will not be able to make instinctive decisions on a moving target.

Abiding with Christ works the same way. If you don't abide privately (through consistent devotional life), you won't wrestle well (make the right decisions) when the real game is taking place. The matches of life expose our private practice of abiding for what it is. If you don't make wise decisions based on God's Word when it counts, it's often because something is missing in your routine. If you don't have endurance in times of suffering or overwhelm, it's probably because you lacked the discipline to persevere in your spiritual life.

This week we will explore the Abiding Sphere in depth because abiding in Christ is central to every other sphere in life.

Ephesians 1:17

I keep asking that the God of our Lord Jesus Christ, the glorious Father, may give you the Spirit of wisdom and revelation, so that you may know him better.

 Scan QR code to access video podcasts and other content that accompanies this week's session.

1 JOHN 4:1-6

Dear friends, do not believe every spirit, but test the spirits to see whether they are from God, because many false prophets have gone out into the world. This is how you can recognize the Spirit of God: Every spirit that acknowledges that Jesus Christ has come in the flesh is from God, but every spirit that does not acknowledge Jesus is not from God. This is the spirit of the antichrist, which you have heard is coming and even now is already in the world.

You, dear children, are from God and have overcome them, because the one who is in you is greater than the one who is in the world. They are from the world and therefore speak from the viewpoint of the world, and the world listens to them. We are from God, and whoever knows God listens to us; but whoever is not from God does not listen to us. This is how we recognize the Spirit of truth and the spirit of falsehood.

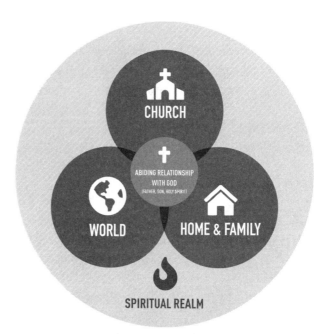

We abide through spending time with God in a daily, practical way: reading Scripture and connecting with Him in prayer. Let's look at how time in the Word of God helps us abide in who God is and remember who we are in Christ.

THE SOUND OF GOD'S VOICE

We all have a voice in our heads, and this voice makes us unique out of all creation. Our experiences, our personality, and the teaching of others help shape that inner voice. However, we have to pay attention to the role the spiritual realm plays in what we listen to. The enemy can tempt us to live out our old identity. He recognizes the specific sinful bent that we deal with and will try to tempt us to give in to it. His isn't the only or most important voice from the spiritual realm, though. The Holy Spirit also speaks to believers via thoughts, impressions, instincts, and more.

So, when our inner voice speaks, how do we discern whose voice it is—the voice of our sinful nature, the enemy, or the Holy Spirit?

When our family moved to Idaho, our three sons were still small, and being in a new place with a new church meant that we were surrounded by people we did not yet know. A child had recently been taken from a store in Oregon (where we used to live), and it had unsettled us. So we created a plan with our kids: If we sent anyone to pick them up from anywhere, we would tell our kids ahead of time. If we hadn't told them this and someone said, "Your dad and mom sent me to pick you up," our sons would know that person was not being truthful.

We also shared with our kids that we would not even send someone they knew to pick them up without giving them a code word. We made it clear that they could know we would never contradict ourselves by telling them to do something through someone else.

In the same way, this is why we must abide in Scripture—we must be taught by more mature believers to read Scripture and understand the Word of God so that we cannot be fooled by false teachers. **The Holy Spirit of God never contradicts the Word of God.**

BECOMING FAMILIAR WITH GOD'S VOICE

The Lord draws us to Himself through the Holy Spirit's work in our lives. First, the Holy Spirit works through other disciples to point us to Jesus. Once we have received Him, the Holy Spirit then moves inside us and works in our lives. And just as God's Spirit uses people and circumstances to draw us to Him, He also uses other people to help us learn how to grow in Him.

Through the work of the Holy Spirit, via the Word of God and the people of God, we begin to change. Part of this growth requires pruning, which also happens through God's Word, His people, and our circumstances. As we talked about last week, this is called sanctification: the process through which God is making us holy (set apart for His purposes).

1. Read the verses and match each verse to the correct statement.

i. Jude 3-5	a. If an angel teaches a different gospel, they are condemned.
ii. Galatians 1:6-8	b. The "faith" has already been delivered once and for all time.
iii. 2 Timothy 4:1-4	c. You test a false prophet by comparing them to Scripture.
iv. 1 John 4:1-6	d. People will want to change truth so that they like it.
v. John 10:1-5	e. God's sheep know His voice and will not follow another.*

Many people today claim that they will teach you the Word of God and how to properly understand it. You must be very careful not to be fooled by voices that are not God's. Here are some good things to consider when trying to discern the Lord's voice:

- **Be familiar enough with Scripture that you recognize when something is off.** Bank tellers are trained to identify counterfeit money through becoming so familiar with the real thing that they can feel when something is off. We need to be familiar with God's Word in the same way.

- **Read the whole context of a passage.** You must know what the Scripture as a whole says on a subject before you really know what a particular passage means. Also remember that the language of that day will help you understand the meaning far better than how our language today defines something because nuance can be lost in translation.[1]

- **Look at new understandings with discernment and caution** (Jude 3). Make sure you find out how something would have been understood by the people it was written to, rather than depend on an interpretation that developed later.

- **Ask a mature believer how to understand something before you make up your mind.** A wise person seeks wise counsel. We all need a disciplemaker as we grow into maturity.

---

* Answers: i=b, ii=a, iii=d, iv=c , v=e.

GALATIANS 1:6-8

I am astonished that you are so quickly deserting the one who called you to live in the grace of Christ and are turning to a different gospel—which is really no gospel at all. Evidently some people are throwing you into confusion and are trying to pervert the gospel of Christ. But even if we or an angel from heaven should preach a gospel other than the one we preached to you, let them be under God's curse!

2 TIMOTHY 4:1-4

In the presence of God and of Christ Jesus, who will judge the living and the dead, and in view of his appearing and his kingdom, I give you this charge: Preach the word; be prepared in season and out of season; correct, rebuke and encourage—with great patience and careful instruction. For the time will come when people will not put up with sound doctrine. Instead, to suit their own desires, they will gather around them a great number of teachers to say what their itching ears want to hear. They will turn their ears away from the truth and turn aside to myths.

2. Reflecting on what you have learned so far about abiding in God's Word, mark the following statements *True* or *False*. God's Word . . .

   a. True/False: reminds you of who you are "in Christ."
   b. True/False: reminds you of who God is and what He can do, no matter what happens in the world.
   c. True/False: convinces God to do what you want Him to do.
   d. True/False: helps you become familiar with who God is and how He views things.
   e. True/False: helps you understand God's architectural plans for every part of your life.[i]

DAY ONE REVIEW

1. What stood out to you or convicted you from today?

2. Why is it important that we be able to recognize God's voice?

3. What are some key things we can do to make sure we are understanding Scripture correctly?

4. Take a deeper look at three of today's passages (Galatians 1:6-8; 2 Timothy 4:1-4; 1 John 4:1-6) by filling out the chart below. How does knowing more about the origin of these letters help you better understand their respective messages?

Passage	Author	Approximate Year Written (AD)	Original Audience
Galatians 1:6-8			
2 Timothy 4:1-4			
1 John 4:1-6			

---

1. I often refer people to the Bible Hub app to dig deeper in Scripture. You can reference word meanings in the original biblical languages and compare Bible translations there.

i. Answer: True: a, b, d, e; False: c.

Day Two

THE ENEMY OF THE TRUTH

GETTING STARTED

We now know the importance of discerning between God's voice, our own inner voice, and the voice of Satan, our enemy. Today we will talk about how to recognize the lies of the enemy and stand on the Truth.

> *Lord Jesus: Help me see what You want me to see today. Expose any lies I may believe and lead me to Your truth. Help me trust and obey You and walk out what I'm learning in every sphere of my life.*

The enemy wants you to fall for all sorts of lies. He tells you that you cannot trust what God says about truth. He seeks to convince you that your identity is not who God says you are or who you should be. He assures you that you would be better off with an identity you create for yourself. This is the same tactic he used in the Garden with Adam and Eve. He was wrong, and they believed him. But now, because God has made a way for us to identify with Jesus, we can choose—by faith—the identity that God gives us. Abiding is how we stay rooted in that identity.

1. Read the passages below and match each passage with the correct statement.

i. 2 Timothy 3:16	a. God's Word will never disappear.
ii. Luke 21:33	b. The Holy Spirit taught and reminded the apostles.
iii. 1 Peter 1:22-24	c. God's Word is imperishable and saves us.
iv. John 14:26	d. God's Word keeps my way pure.
v. Psalm 119:9-11	e. The key to right living is rightly understanding truth.
vi. 2 Timothy 2:15	f. All Scripture is God-breathed.*

In Matthew 4:4-10, Jesus modeled for us how to defeat the enemy. As you read this passage you will see that the enemy attacked Jesus with questions, just as he did Adam and Eve in the Garden of Eden. In a sense he was saying, *Are you really the Son of God? If you are, why are you out here hungry and alone? And even if you are, is God really a good Father? If He is, why are you out here struggling? Take matters into your own hands!* As you read, notice how Jesus counters Satan's questions with truths from Scripture. We can use this same strategy when we are being tempted to doubt God's goodness.

---

* i=f, ii=a, iii=c, iv=b, v=d, vi=e.

MATTHEW 4:4-10

Jesus answered, "It is written: 'Man shall not live on bread alone, but on every word that comes from the mouth of God.'"

Then the devil took him to the holy city and had him stand on the highest point of the temple. "If you are the Son of God," he said, "throw yourself down. For it is written:

"'He will command his angels
concerning you,
and they will lift you up
in their hands,
so that you will not
strike your foot
against a stone.'"

Jesus answered him, "It is also written: 'Do not put the Lord your God to the test.'"

Again, the devil took him to a very high mountain and showed him all the kingdoms of the world and their splendor. "All this I will give you," he said, "if you will bow down and worship me."

Jesus said to him, "Away from me, Satan! For it is written: 'Worship the Lord your God, and serve him only.'"

Read Matthew 4:4-10 (see sidebar on previous page).

2.   Based on Matthew 4:4-10, mark the following statements *True* or *False*.

   a.   True/False: The devil often comes at us when we are alone and struggling.
   b.   True/False: The devil sought to get Jesus to question God's love and care because Jesus was hungry and alone.
   c.   True/False: The Holy Spirit led Jesus into the desert.
   d.   True/False: Jesus used Scripture to defeat the devil.
   e.   True/False: The devil used Scripture in context against Jesus.
   f.   True/False: Jesus showed that knowing all Scripture helps us defeat the enemy, who misuses Scripture.
   g.   True/False: Jesus knew Scripture well enough to know when the devil was asking Him to sin.
   h.   True/False: People do not live by physical bread for their physical body alone, but people truly live spiritually when they consume spiritual bread, which is the Word of God.
   i.   True/False: The devil tried to give Jesus what looked like a different and easier way to become King than the path that God was taking Him on.
   j.   True/False: Jesus was showing the disciples how to defeat the devil as well.[i]

Abiding in Christ through His Word helps you remember not only who God is but also who you are. Abiding helps us see how God works. When we have wrong expectations of God, we are easily disappointed, and the devil takes advantage of that disappointment.

Reading Scripture reminds us of how God worked in the past and what it looks like to remain in Him as He works. Consider people like Abraham, Joseph, Moses, and David. God called them and then shaped them through a set of difficult circumstances that got them ready for how God would use them. He put them into eternally significant struggles so they could participate in the work of God to restore the new heaven and new earth, where God will again be with us.

Here is what these stories teach us: When we are tempted to feel like God is letting us down, God is pruning us to reshape us into our God-given identity. He uses circumstances to shape us and move us to where He wants to use us.

Abiding helps keep our eyes on the big picture so we can get through all the seemingly little pictures of life without quitting. God's Word is truly a light unto our path (Psalm 119:105).

DAY TWO REVIEW

1.   What stood out to you or convicted you from today?

_____

_____

_____

2. Name some ways the enemy might use your identity to steer you away from truth.

_____

_____

3. What does the story of Jesus' temptation in the wilderness reveal about the timing of Satan's attacks?

_____

_____

4. Share about a time in your life when you were tempted to take matters into your own hands rather than trusting God. What is something you would do differently in that situation now?

_____

_____

---

i. Answer: Every answer is true except e.

Day Three

HOW TO PRAY

GETTING STARTED

Abiding in Christ involves regularly reading God's Word and praying in such a way that it changes you from who you were in Adam to who you are in Christ. Abiding also guides us on the pathway that God would have us walk as His disciples.

Lord Jesus: Help me see what You want me to see today. Expose any lies I may believe and lead me to Your truth. Help me trust and obey You and walk out what I'm learning in every sphere of my life.

MATTHEW 28:19

[Jesus said,] "Go and make disciples of all nations, baptizing them in the name of the Father and of the Son and of the Holy Spirit."

When we abide in Jesus, we obey the commands He has given us. Obeying His voice makes us one of His disciples as well (Matthew 28:19). We hear Him speak through Scripture, and we converse with His Spirit through prayer. As we grow in our understanding of who God is and how He works, our conversation with Him changes.

1. Read Matthew 6:5-15 and answer the following questions about God's desire for our prayer life.

   [Jesus said,] "When you pray, don't be like the hypocrites who love to pray publicly on street corners and in the synagogues where everyone can see them. I tell you the truth, that is all the reward they will ever get. But when you pray, go away by yourself, shut the door behind you, and pray to your Father in private. Then your Father, who sees everything, will reward you.

   "When you pray, don't babble on and on as the Gentiles do. They think their prayers are answered merely by repeating their words again and again. Don't be like them, for your Father knows exactly what you need even before you ask him! Pray like this: 'Our Father in heaven, may your name be kept holy. May your Kingdom come soon. May your will be done on earth, as it is in heaven. Give us today the food we need, and forgive us our sins, as we have forgiven those who sin against us. And don't let us yield to temptation, but rescue us from the evil one.'

   If you forgive those who sin against you, your heavenly Father will forgive you. But if you refuse to forgive others, your Father will not forgive your sins.
   MATTHEW 6:5-15, NLT

   a. What does the Father see? Underline the verse that tells us the answer.

   b. What does the Father want us to avoid? Circle the phrases that tell us the answer.

There is a progression in Jesus' prayer that will lead to a progression of change in our lives. As we spend time with God in prayer, we live increasingly engaged in the spiritual realm, where His values, our identity, and the identity of others come to the forefront.

Jesus says we can call God *our Father*. Let's spend some time looking at those two key words:

- **Father:** Through faith in Jesus, we can call God our Father. Our new identity is being children of God. (Read John 1:12.)

- **Our Father:** Because we are children of God, we also have brothers and sisters. We are recognizing it's not just me and Jesus, but rather me, Jesus, and brothers and sisters. Everyone else who is a child of God has a new identity too! Seeing ourselves as part of the family of faith changes our relationships within the family of faith.

2. Part of abiding is gleaning from Scripture what God would have us do and then applying these truths to our lives in wise ways. With that in mind, reread Matthew 6:5-15 and answer the following questions.

    a. *Our Father in heaven*: How does focusing on heaven change your thinking? (Read Colossians 3:1-2.)

    _____

    b. *May your name be kept holy*: Write below reasons you have to praise and worship God. How does focusing on who God is and what He has done change your prayer life?

    _____

    c. *May your Kingdom come soon. / May your will be done*: What do you need to submit to God's will and perspective?

    _____

    d. *Give us today the food we need*: Why did Jesus tell us to pray about this basic need? What is Jesus trying to teach us about prayer and what matters? (Read Matthew 6:25-33.)

    _____

    e. *Forgive us our sins, as we have forgiven those who sin against us*: Remember, Jesus sums up all the commands in love for God and others (see Matthew 22:37-40). Can you see Jesus leading His disciples toward love for one another in this prayer? What stands out to you about this progression?

    _____

    f. *Don't let us yield to temptation*: Jesus acknowledges that the disciples have an external enemy who fights against the changes God is implementing in them. If

JOHN 1:12, NLT

To all who believed him and accepted him, he gave the right to become children of God.

COLOSSIANS 3:1-2, NLT

Since you have been raised to new life with Christ, set your sights on the realities of heaven, where Christ sits in the place of honor at God's right hand. Think about the things of heaven, not the things of earth.

MATTHEW 6:25-33, NLT

[Jesus said,] "That is why I tell you not to worry about everyday life—whether you have enough food and drink, or enough clothes to wear. Isn't life more than food, and your body more than clothing? Look at the birds. They don't plant or harvest or store food in barns, for your heavenly Father feeds them. And aren't you far more valuable to him than they are? Can all your worries add a single moment to your life?

"And why worry about your clothing? Look at the lilies of the field and how they grow. They don't work or make their clothing, yet Solomon in all his glory was not dressed as beautifully as they are. And if God cares so wonderfully for wildflowers that are here today and thrown into the fire tomorrow, he will certainly care for you. Why do you have so little faith?

"So don't worry about these things, saying, 'What will we eat? What will we drink? What will we wear?' These things dominate the thoughts of unbelievers, but your heavenly Father already knows all your needs. Seek the Kingdom of God above all else, and live righteously, and he will give you everything you need."

God wants to change us in the direction of things above, what would the devil's goals be?

ROMANS 12:1-2, NLT

And so, dear brothers and sisters, I plead with you to give your bodies to God because of all he has done for you. Let them be a living and holy sacrifice—the kind he will find acceptable. This is truly the way to worship him. Don't copy the behavior and customs of this world, but let God transform you into a new person by changing the way you think. Then you will learn to know God's will for you, which is good and pleasing and perfect.

Read Romans 12:1-2 (see sidebar).

3. Reflecting on what you have learned about prayer, mark the following statements *True* or *False*:

   a. True/False: Prayer is about talking God into what you want Him to do.
   b. True/False: Prayer is about telling God what you have done for Him, or what you will do for Him, so that you can get Him to give you what you want.
   c. True/False: As you pray through the Lord's Prayer, you begin to recognize what He has done for you and who He is, which leads you to tell God that you want His will to be done.
   d. True/False: As you remember who you are "in Christ," you no longer value some things as much because they are no longer your most important identity.[i]

DAY THREE REVIEW

1. What stood out to you or convicted you from today?

2. After working through the Lord's Prayer, what about your perspective on prayer has changed?

3. Commit to praying through the Lord's Prayer every day for a week. As you do, focus on the things you wrote down in question 2 of today's lesson.

---

i. Answer: True: c, d; False: a, b.

Day Four

HOW GOD ANSWERS PRAYER

GETTING STARTED

Do you ever wonder if God is even listening to your prayers? Today we will talk about the different ways God might answer and how to look for them in your life.

> *Lord Jesus: Help me see what You want me to see today. Expose any lies I may believe and lead me to Your truth. Help me trust and obey You and walk out what I'm learning in every sphere of my life.*

One day, when I asked my fifteen-year-old son, Will, how he was doing with the Lord, he bluntly said, "I am not talking to Him right now."

"Why not?" I asked.

He told me that he had prayed many times that God would take his depression away. Will was angry at God for not answering him.

I told Will that God had answered him: God's seeming silence meant that his answer was *no* or *wait*. "No is an answer," I said.

At this Will exclaimed, "Why? Why would God say no?"

I reflected a moment, and then I said, "It seems to me that those who God has called, He trains through trials. There is nothing worse than trying to do a big job with little character." God humbles us and allows us to experience struggles so that we will proclaim the greatness of God rather than our own greatness.

Then I shared that God tends to allow us to deal with certain things as a way of preparing us to deal with other things. Jesus came down and became one of us so that He could be a faithful High Priest who will intercede for us with the Father. In the same way, God gives us an understanding of the pain others will go through by letting us go through it with His help—if we will abide in Him.

I told Will that perhaps God was getting him ready for ministry in a society that is increasingly anxious and depressed. The fact that God was allowing him to go through depression did not mean God was unfaithful or that God did not care.

God can say *yes, now*; *yes, but later*; or *no*. As we begin abiding in Jesus, allowing the Holy Spirit to guide us toward the Scriptures and prayer, we will struggle at times to understand why God sometimes does not answer us the way we would like or in the timing we think He should. When this happens, we may feel the devil tempting us to step away from abiding in Christ. We will sometimes decide to take matters into our own hands to get what we think we want.

But we can handle hard things much better if we can understand why God might allow them and how He might use them for eternal good. Considering God's perspective and purpose helps us fight the enemy, who seeks to get us to question God and no longer remain in Him.

God humbles us and allows us to experience struggles so that we will proclaim the greatness of God rather than our own greatness.

1. Read this passage to discover what abiding looked like in the life of Paul, and then fill in the blanks in the following statements.

> Even if I should choose to boast, I would not be a fool, because I would be speaking the truth. But I refrain, so no one will think more of me than is warranted by what I do or say, or because of these surpassingly great revelations. Therefore, in order to keep me from becoming conceited, I was given a thorn in my flesh, a messenger of Satan, to torment me. Three times I pleaded with the Lord to take it away from me. But he said to me, "My grace is sufficient for you, for my power is made perfect in weakness." Therefore I will boast all the more gladly about my weaknesses, so that Christ's power may rest on me. That is why, for Christ's sake, I delight in weaknesses, in insults, in hardships, in persecutions, in difficulties. For when I am weak, then I am strong.
>
> 2 CORINTHIANS 12:6-10

   a. Paul prayed _____ times that God would remove the thorn in his flesh that was given him by the devil because God allowed it.[i]

   b. God's answer to Paul was that His grace was _____ for him, for His power is made perfect in _____.[ii]

Most scholars think Paul was going blind and would be dependent on others to help him in ministry.[1] Paul made it clear that because of what he had seen and experienced, the potential to become proud was present. So God allowed him to have weaknesses that would keep him humble and dependent on God. God's promise was that He would give Paul grace to overcome the thorn in the flesh.

We often think that we cannot obey God, or even do ministry at all, when we can't do it the way we want to. We give up and refuse to abide in Him. When we do that, we miss the experiences we would receive by working in the areas of our weaknesses instead of our strengths.

2. Mark whether you agree with the following statements.

   a. Yes/No: When I work within my natural ability, I tend to trust my experience and strength rather than God.

   b. Yes/No: When I succeed, I am tempted to take credit rather than give credit to God. I tend to downplay that He is the important one, not me.

   c. Yes/No: When I work within my spiritual giftings, I get joy from the fact that God has given me work to do that is significant.

   d. Yes/No: I know it is God working in spite of me when good things happen even though I am not great at what I am doing for Him.

   e. Yes/No: When I work in areas of my weakness, God brings people to my team who can fill in where I am weak, which means I get to enjoy being a part of a team.

   f. Yes/No: Serving in an area that is difficult builds my character so that I can take on even bigger things later on.

3. How could Paul have chosen to respond when God told him no?

_____

4. In tormenting Paul, how would the devil have hoped for Paul to respond? Why?

_____

DAY FOUR REVIEW

1. What stood out to you or convicted you from today?

_____

2. Has God ever said no to something you have asked Him for? How did you respond to His answer?

_____

3. Share some reasons you think God may answer a prayer with *no* or *not now*.

_____

4. Do you trust God to give you the best answer when you ask Him for something?

_____

5. Have you been praying for something but not received a yes or no answer? What might God be saying?

_____

---

1. See, for example, https://christianhistoryinstitute.org/magazine/article/bald-blind-and-single and https://questions.org/attq/what-was-pauls-%E2%80%9Cthorn%E2%80%9D.
  i. Answer: Three.
  ii. Answer: sufficient; weakness.

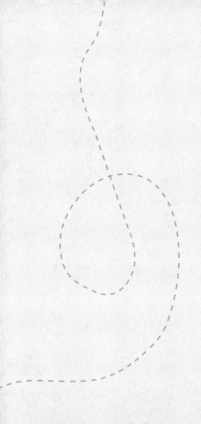

Day Five

THE JOURNEY

GETTING STARTED

Discipleship is a relational journey that takes us through the Share → Connect → Minister → Disciple (SCMD) process toward maturity. On this journey we go through the stages of spiritual growth. More specifically, we grow spiritually in every separate area of our lives—we call these areas the Five Spheres. We have been dealing with the Abiding Sphere, taken from Paul's explanation in Ephesians 1 and 2. As we go further into Ephesians, we will see him writing about the other four spheres, but the foundation of the house (the architectural plans) is most important.

Lord Jesus: Help me see what You want me to see today. Expose any lies I may believe and lead me to Your truth. Help me trust and obey You and walk out what I'm learning in every sphere of my life.

Apart from Christ we can do nothing—and our enemy knows this. When we are in the middle of a trial, the enemy tries to separate us from abiding with God. To revisit our journey metaphor, the enemy wants us to step out of the relational vehicle.

Outside the relational vehicle, we are more vulnerable to the damage sin and suffering can inflict. To prevent us from getting back in, the enemy will tell us we can't prevent the pain we're experiencing. After all, the world is painful! Since pain is inevitable, the enemy claims there is no hope and no point in trusting God; you're better off trusting yourself or some other human to lead and sustain you.

Read Romans 8:22-28 (see sidebar).

In Romans 8, Paul makes the point that all creation is groaning—which includes each of us.

1. Think back to the creation story in Genesis. Why do you think the world is groaning?

Even those of us who have the Holy Spirit still groan because we were created for a perfect relationship with God and one another in a perfect environment. Because of sin, we are stuck in a world where there is a huge gap between what we were made for and what we are living with.

However, in this space of time we are in before God returns and makes all things new again, we understand why things are the way they are and what God has done to help us.

ROMANS 8:22-28, NLT

We know that all creation has been groaning as in the pains of childbirth right up to the present time. And we believers also groan, even though we have the Holy Spirit within us as a foretaste of future glory, for we long for our bodies to be released from sin and suffering. We, too, wait with eager hope for the day when God will give us our full rights as his adopted children, including the new bodies he has promised us. We were given this hope when we were saved. (If we already have something, we don't need to hope for it. But if we look forward to something we don't yet have, we must wait patiently and confidently.)

And the Holy Spirit helps us in our weakness. For example, we don't know what God wants us to pray for. But the Holy Spirit prays for us with groanings that cannot be expressed in words. And the Father who knows all hearts knows what the Spirit is saying, for the Spirit pleads for us believers in harmony with God's own will. And we know that God causes everything to work together for the good of those who love God and are called according to his purpose for them.

Abiding means we spend time looking at the bigger story of the world. Many people around us recognize that something is wrong with the world, but they don't know what it is or how to fix it. So they rearrange the chairs on the Titanic (a useless task on a sinking boat!), little knowing that what they spend their life trying to fix won't really be the solution. We believers feel this too sometimes, but we know why the world is broken and who is going to ultimately fix it. With God's help through the Holy Spirit, we understand that even in the brokenness we are not alone. God tells us that we have hope in eternity and that He will redeem all things and fill in the empty place within us that sin has created. He tells us what will actually make this life better to keep us from wasting our time on things that don't.

Abiding doesn't take away all the trouble—although it does take away the trouble we intentionally caused ourselves and others when we lived for sin and suffered the consequences. Abiding means God helps us within our struggle and gives us joy in life. We have a relationship with Him and others to help us through this broken world until the world will be broken no more.

THE GRASS IS GREENER

Some people think the grass is greener somewhere else—that if they can find a new job or a new relationship, or just a fresh start somewhere else, they can have what they always wanted and will feel satisfied. They fail to recognize that wherever they go on planet Earth, there they are. We are living in the gap between Earth and heaven.

2. Read the promise of God in Romans 8:28. Who does God say has hope and help?

   a. Every human can have hope that all things will turn out for good.
   b. Those who believe in God can know all things will work out for good.
   c. Those who love God (versus just believing He exists) and are called according to His purpose (doing what He has purposed in our lives) will have things work out for good.[i]

Some people take this promise to mean that because God is in control of all things, He causes bad things to happen. However, Scripture tells us that God does not sin and does not tempt us to sin (James 1:13). God may allow hard things to happen, but He does not cause sin.

When evil happens, the enemy thinks he has won the final battle—but that is untrue. If you are a believer and are walking in God's purposes, God promises He will work out whatever happens for your eternal good. This promise gives us hope: No matter what hard things happen in our life, all will pale in comparison to an eternity where God will make all things right. Even when God does allow hard things to happen, He always uses the hard things for His glory and our eternal good.

THAT'S NOT FAIR!

Sometimes disciples get frustrated because they feel like nonbelievers have it easier than they do. Abiding helps us understand what's really going on. When we spend time in God's

No matter what hard things happen in our life, all will pale in comparison to an eternity where God will make all things right.

PSALM 73:1-24, NLT

Truly God is good to Israel,
   to those whose hearts
      are pure.
But as for me, I almost lost my
   footing.
   My feet were slipping,
      and I was almost
         gone.
For I envied the proud
   when I saw them
      prosper despite their
         wickedness.
They seem to live such painless
   lives;
   their bodies are so
      healthy and strong.
They don't have troubles like
   other people;
   they're not plagued with
      problems like everyone
         else.
They wear pride like a jeweled
   necklace
   and clothe themselves
      with cruelty.
These fat cats have everything
   their hearts could ever
      wish for!
They scoff and speak only evil;
   in their pride they seek
      to crush others.
They boast against the very
   heavens,
   and their words strut
      throughout the earth.
And so the people are dismayed
   and confused,
   drinking in all their
      words.
"What does God know?" they
   ask.
   "Does the Most High
      even know what's
         happening?"
Look at these wicked people—
   enjoying a life of ease
      while their riches
         multiply.

PSALM 73:1-24, NLT (CONTINUED)

Did I keep my heart pure for
nothing?
Did I keep myself
innocent for no
reason?
I get nothing but trouble all
day long;
every morning brings
me pain.

If I had really spoken this way
to others,
I would have been a
traitor to your people.
So I tried to understand why the
wicked prosper.
But what a difficult task
it is!
Then I went into your sanctuary,
O God,
and I finally understood
the destiny of the
wicked.
Truly, you put them on a
slippery path
and send them sliding
over the cliff to
destruction.
In an instant they are
destroyed,
completely swept away
by terrors.
When you arise, O Lord,
you will laugh at their
silly ideas
as a person laughs
at dreams in the
morning.

Then I realized that my heart
was bitter,
and I was all torn up
inside.
I was so foolish and ignorant—
I must have seemed like
a senseless animal
to you.

Yet I still belong to you;
you hold my right hand.
You guide me with your
counsel,
leading me to a glorious
destiny.

Word, we see what is really happening from God's perspective. When we pray, we invite God to change our hearts and allow us to be part of His Kingdom here on earth. As He gives us His perspective, we see the truth and ask God for opportunities to share the Good News, what God has done in our life, and what He has planned for the universe with the lost and spiritually dead.

Psalm 73 shows us that when the psalmist felt envy for unbelievers, he turned to abide in the Father in worship. Worship is seeing God for who He is and eternity for what He says it is. We worship when we pray for insight and strength.

Read Psalm 73:1-24 (see sidebar).

3. Based on Psalm 73, let's examine the process the author took to deal with frustration and envy from comparing his circumstances with those of unbelievers.

   a. In the first half of this chapter, does the writer seem to be looking at things through God's eyes or from his own perspective?

   b. In the New Living Translation, verse 4 reads "they seem to live such painless lives." What does that phrase reveal about the conclusions the writer was drawing as to what was really going on?

   c. It can appear that those who disobey God are popular and have no struggles. Does this seeming reality ever make you wonder if what you have been taught isn't true? Why?

   d. What did the writer do that gave him a different perspective?

   e. In King David's time, what was the sanctuary? (Do an online search or go to BibleHub.com to research the concept.)

   f. How does going into a place where the Word of God is spoken and where prayer and worship take place change our perspective?

   g. What did the writer remember after being in the sanctuary, and how did it change his view going forward?

When believers come together to study God's Word and to pray and worship, our attitudes and perspectives change. This is abiding.

Remember, the devil will seek to tempt us away from God, encouraging us to seek our own answers and purposes or to numb our pain with some form of escape. But because we trust in God, we continue our journey with Him—and we continue to abide, no matter what.

DAY FIVE REVIEW

Notes and Thoughts

1. What stood out to you or convicted you from today?

2. What are some things the enemy has used to prevent you from abiding?

3. What are some things or people in your life that you might be placing your hope in instead of Jesus?

4. What do you do when you feel discouraged? Do you turn to someone? Do you isolate yourself?

5. When are you most tempted to stop abiding with Jesus—when things are going well or when things are a struggle?

6. Share about a time or circumstance in your life when God worked difficult things out for good. Is there someone in your life right now who is going through a struggle and might be encouraged by your experience?

i. Answer: c.

Week 6

THE CHURCH SPHERE

Day One

YOUR IDENTITY, OUR IDENTITY

GETTING STARTED

The book of Ephesians helps us discover God's spiritual architectural plans for our lives by taking us through the Five Spheres. The Five Spheres illustrate that spiritual maturity, from God's perspective, affects every part of our lives. We don't have the option to say, "God, You can have my Sunday morning, but I'm in charge of my business life." God, as our spiritual Architect, has plans for every area of our lives. He bought every part of our lives for a very high price.

Lord Jesus: Help me see what You want me to see today. Expose any lies I may believe and lead me to Your truth. Help me trust and obey You and walk out what I'm learning in every sphere of my life.

As we go further with God on this journey of discipleship, we have come to believe that He is right and good. We have also come to believe that God only asks from us what is best for us. Our abiding relationship with God moves into our Church Sphere, then feeds into our Home and Family Sphere, then the World Sphere, and finally the Spiritual Sphere.

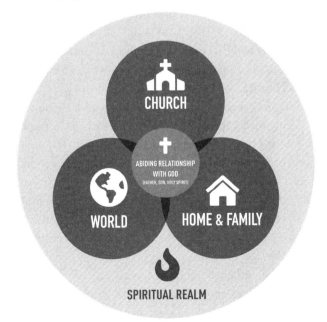

 Scan QR code to access video podcasts and other content that accompanies this week's session.

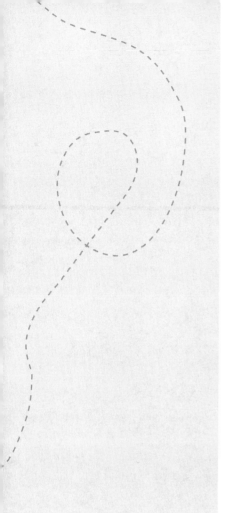

Notice that the Abiding Sphere and the Church Sphere overlap on the diagram. This is because abiding is not only personal, but relationship with God's people is also a source of abiding. The book of Ephesians reveals that those of us who have accepted Christ have become part of the body of Christ, which is also known as the church. The church is not a building where we go once a week; it is a body that requires us to function in harmony with the other parts. This doesn't mean we don't go to the weekend service—it just means that that is not the only thing we do as a body. (For example, we are also in home groups together and talking with each other periodically during the rest of the week.)

If we are to abide in Christ, we also need to be abiding in the body of Christ, which means that relationship with God leads to relationship with others. God has placed Christians in our lives who are more mature spiritually than we are, who can give us strength through spiritual words (Scripture) and wisdom from God. God's plan has always been to use people to disciple people.

> *God's Spirit*
>
> + *God's Word*
>
> + *God's people (the church)*
>
> = *abiding in Christ and growing spiritually toward maturity*

So many people claim a form of Christianity that says, "It's just me and Jesus! I don't like people, I don't need them, and I don't have time for them!" Often where I am from in northern Idaho, people will say their church is on the lake or in the woods. Others will acknowledge that they "go" to church, but that is not the same thing as being *part* of the church as Jesus designed it.

The church is Jesus' idea, so He is the one who defines it. Many like to take the word *church* and redefine it to fit their preferences or life, rather than accepting Jesus' version of church as their own.

In Matthew 16:18, Jesus said that He would build His church and that the gates of hell would never prevail against it. One of the things Jesus was communicating in saying this was that the church is His idea.

When Jesus sent His disciples out into the world, they understood that making disciples would lead to a gathering of disciples: the church. We see this in the book of Acts as the church was started, just as Jesus had intended (Acts 2:36-47). Throughout the rest of the book of Acts, we get a picture of what Jesus' church looked like: several different kinds of environments and relationships where discipleship would be able to happen.

My friend Brandon Guindon often says, "If we want to see the church succeed, it's not our job to innovate the church—but rather to imitate Jesus and His methods." Often we develop our views of the church from listening to someone else, rather looking back to the disciples and the Scriptures for a definition. But overall, most people only know what they *don't* want the church to be, rather than having a clear idea of what it *should* be.

Disciplemakers (spiritual parents) create and work within spiritual environments that reflect Jesus' definition of *church*. We facilitate experiences in these environments so people can grow. Jesus used different kinds of environments for different purposes:

- He spoke with Peter one-on-one.
- He took three of His disciples up the mountain to have an experience with Moses and Elijah.
- He worked with the twelve disciples most of the time.
- He took the disciples to the synagogue and the Temple consistently.
- He worked with one hundred and twenty other followers who were outside His most immediate discipleship focus.
- He taught thousands on many occasions.

When the disciples formed the church, they met in several environments for different purposes as well.

Some believe that because people are all different, we should design churches that make everybody feel comfortable. However, our call as disciples is to follow Jesus rather than trying to make Jesus follow us. Jesus' example shows us that the spiritual environment isn't about creating comfort but about addressing discipleship needs.

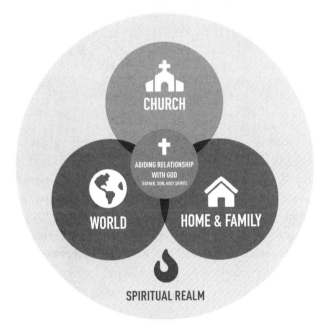

WHY DOES THE CHURCH COME NEXT?

When I teach through the book of Ephesians, people often ask me why I go from the Abiding Sphere straight into the Church Sphere. My answer is simple: because Paul did it in Ephesians.

The key verse that transitions us from the Abiding Sphere to the Church Sphere is Ephesians 2:10, where we read that God saved us by grace for good works He planned—before time began—for us to do. Next, we read that those good works start in the church. Paul then writes about the Church Sphere for almost three chapters.

EPHESIANS 2:10

We are God's handiwork, created in Christ Jesus to do good works, which God prepared in advance for us to do.

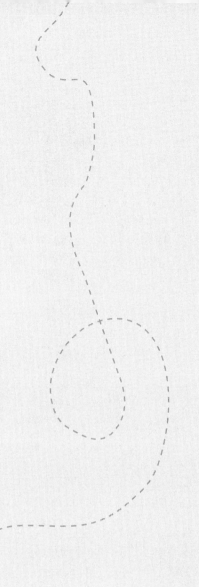

But why did Paul have this focus on the church? There are a few likely reasons:

- The Ephesians had not grown up in a culture that knew the Jewish Scripture or Jesus' teaching. Their families would not have taught them God's Word, so it would have fallen on the church's disciplemaking efforts to teach these people biblical truth.

- Living in relationship with other disciples in the church equips us to recapture or reconcile words and ideas the culture has misdefined. For example, the world uses the word *love* all the time but doesn't define it or live it out in the right way. Within the church's organized and individualized work of discipleship, however, love is active, sacrificial, and rooted in the love we have received from Christ.

- Many in the early church would have been kicked out of their physical family because of Jesus. The church would be their only family.

- In the church, mature disciples taught and modeled spiritual fatherhood and motherhood and siblinghood so that those being discipled could reform their own contexts into disciplemaking homes where Christ's love was lived out.

Just as the Church Sphere grows out of the Abiding Sphere, the Home and Family Sphere must be rooted in the larger family of God. As we study the Church Sphere these next two weeks, ask yourself, *What am I seeing in God's family, the church, that I need to take to the Home and Family Sphere when we get there?*

THE CHURCH AND OUR IDENTITY

On our journey to maturity, we are following Jesus and He is changing us. As we reflect on who He is, we will want Him to change us in accordance with His will, because He knows all things, including what will happen on planet Earth and in eternity. The changes He makes will be in accordance with what He knows we will need in the future.

As we are changed, we begin to love God and others more. Because we are abiding with Him, we see what He sees. He gives us a new identity in Christ, which changes our mindset in every part of our lives. Abiding in Christ means spending time in God's Word and in prayer, remembering who God is—His identity, our own identity in Christ—and then asking God to help us do what He would have us do (James 1:22-25).

1. Fill in the blank what is true of your new identity "in Christ":

   a. You are adopted into God's _____, which means you are a son or daughter.
   b. Your sins are _____ away and you are spotless, without stain in God's sight.
   c. You are a _____, created anew in Christ Jesus for good works God _____— before time began—for you to do.
   d. You are _____ of the Kingdom of heaven.
   e. You are part of the _____ of Christ.[i]

JAMES 1:22-23

Do not merely listen to the word, and so deceive yourselves. Do what it says. Anyone who listens to the word but does not do what it says is like someone who looks at his face in a mirror.

Abiding in Jesus reminds us who we are—and who others are in the Church Sphere. As we start looking into this sphere, we must remember that other believers also have a new identity "in Christ." Because of what God the Father and Jesus the Son have done for us, we want to honor Him and His love for others as well. When we were born again, we became sons or daughters of God—and we were born into a family with brothers and sisters. The Father loves them, too. As we abide, we . . .

- see others through God's eyes: They have been given a new identity too;

- remember that though we each have a new identity, we are in different stages of growth (infant, child, young adult, parent), and the less mature may not know or may forget their new identity, leading to "old Adam" identity behaviors; and

- understand that abiding is something we must do daily as the enemy regularly tempts us to see our circumstances through the eyes of our old nature.

WHY CAN'T IT BE JUST ME AND JESUS?

When I first became a Christian, I said I wanted a relationship with God but did not want to be part of the church. My disciplemaker—my father—let my frustration go for a while because he was aware of how the church had hurt me in the past. Eventually, though, he began to share more about why the church is a vital part of discipleship.

One day, he called me with an issue he said he wanted help with. In addition to being my disciplemaker, my father was a pastor. He told me he needed some advice on a church issue: There was a new family at church who really liked my dad but didn't like my mom. This shocked me, but he went on. He said they wanted to hang out with him but didn't want him to bring my mom along when they did get together. He asked me what he should do.

I said: "You are married, and if they want one of you, they have to have both." My dad paused for a moment, which is what he always did when he had cornered me in conversation. Then he said, "Jim, this is how God feels about His bride, the church." At the time I was unfamiliar with the phrase *bride of Christ*, and I challenged the thought that I was in any sense a bride rather than a groom. My dad shared that it was a metaphor in Scripture for the relationship Jesus has with the church.

Read Revelation 18:23; 19:7; 21:2, 9 (see sidebar).

Husbands, love your wives, just as Christ loved the church and gave himself up for her to make her holy, cleansing her by the washing with water through the word, and to present her to himself as a radiant church, without stain or wrinkle or any other blemish, but holy and blameless.

EPHESIANS 5:25-27

REVELATION 18:23
The light of a lamp will never shine in you again. The voice of bridegroom and bride will never be heard in you again. Your merchants were the world's important people. By your magic spell all the nations were led astray.

REVELATION 19:7
"Let us rejoice and be glad and give him glory! For the wedding of the Lamb has come, and his bride has made herself ready."

REVELATION 21:2
I saw the Holy City, the new Jerusalem, coming down out of heaven from God, prepared as a bride beautifully dressed for her husband.

REVELATION 21:9
One of the seven angels who had the seven bowls full of the seven last plagues came and said to me, "Come, I will show you the bride, the wife of the Lamb."

As disciples of Jesus, we are called on to be people who help others be reconciled to God, and to help those who know Jesus be reconciled to one another.

DEFINITION

reconciliation: "the restoration of friendly relations"[1]

Part of abiding in Christ is remembering who you are in Christ. It is also remembering who others are "in Christ"—and that you *together* are the bride of Christ. As you look at God's perspective of yourself and other believers, how you see other believers changes as well.

2. Based on what you have learned so far about your relationship with God and others, mark the following statements *True* or *False*.

   a. True/False: God loves me and forgives me over and over.
   b. True/False: When we were unreconciled with God, God went first to reconcile us.
   c. True/False: God loves other believers and forgives them only when they show they are truly repentant and stop sinning altogether.
   d. True/False: God is okay with me loving Him but not loving other believers.
   e. True/False: God is okay with me acting as though I am a spiritual only child.[ii]

   From now on we regard no one from a worldly point of view. Though we once regarded Christ in this way, we do so no longer. Therefore, if anyone is in Christ, the new creation has come: The old has gone, the new is here! All this is from God, who reconciled us to himself through Christ and gave us the ministry of reconciliation.

   2 CORINTHIANS 5:16-18

Others in the world may not allow people to get past their past. Others may continue to see you as one who acted in "the old Adam" identity that hurt others (and, for that matter, yourself). As believers, though, we see ourselves and others through God's eyes—in our "in Christ" identity.

Reconciliation is a picture of two opposing parties coming back together. We were separated and now have taken steps to be together. As disciples of Jesus, we are called to be people who help others be reconciled to God, and to help those who know Jesus be reconciled to one another. Jesus said it this way: "Blessed are the peacemakers, for they will be called children of God" (Matthew 5:9). For this to happen, we must value other people the way God values us. He pursued us to reconcile with us. He forgave us. He valued us. As a disciple of Jesus with a new identity, we remember that God wants to save those who are lost and that He loves other believers too.

3. What are the traits of a reconciler? Mark the following statements *True* or *False*.

   a. True/False: We help people reconcile with God by sharing the gospel with them and asking them to become a disciple.
   b. True/False: We help people reconcile the difference between who they were and who they are now "in Christ."
   c. True/False: We reconcile with other believers when there are differences.
   d. True/False: We help other believers close the gap between a disciple's goal for themselves and their achievement of it.
   e. True/False: We help those who are Christians become reconciled to those they hurt before they became one who is "in Christ" rather than "in Adam."
   f. True/False: When we are unreconciled with others, we go first to reconcile with them.[iii]

DAY ONE REVIEW

1. What stood out to you or convicted you from today?

2. When you look through the "in Adam" glasses, how do you see people who are believers?

3. How do you see people when you put on the "in Christ" glasses?

4. Is there anything you learned in today's study that you need to apply in your home?

5. Are you currently part of a church body? Why or why not?

6. Have you ever had the attitude of "it's just 'me and Jesus' and I don't need to go to church"? Why?

7. If someone tracked your church attendance, would they think that church is a priority in your life?

1. *Oxford Dictionary*, Android ed., v. 15.5.1105 (Oxford Languages, 2024), s.v. "reconciliation (*n.*)."

    i. Answer: a. family; b. washed; c. masterpiece, planned; d. citizens; e. body.

    ii. Answer: True: a, b; False: c, d, e.

    iii. Answer: True: a, b, c, e, f; False: d.

Day Two

JESUS AS OUR HEAD (KING)

GETTING STARTED

Did you look at your church attendance and attitudes toward the church to determine if church is a priority in your life? What did you discover? Today we are going to talk about what it looks like to give Jesus authority over your life as Lord.

> *Lord Jesus: Help me see what You want me to see today. Expose any lies I may believe and lead me to Your truth. Help me trust and obey You and walk out what I'm learning in every sphere of my life.*

Ephesians 2:10–5:20 describes the importance of the church and how it's supposed to work. In these passages we see some things that bind God's church together in unity.

1. a unified purpose;
2. unified beliefs;
3. an organizational structure with leadership that creates unity; and
4. relationships within the church that connect hearts.

WHO WE ARE

The Jews had been God's chosen people but had forgotten what they were chosen for.

> [God told Abraham,] "I will certainly bless you. I will multiply your descendants beyond number, like the stars in the sky and the sand on the seashore. Your descendants will conquer the cities of their enemies. And through your descendants all the nations of the earth will be blessed—all because you have obeyed me."
> GENESIS 22:17-18, NLT

> "I, the LORD, have called you in righteousness; I will take hold of your hand. I will keep you and will make you to be a covenant for the people and a light for the Gentiles, to open eyes that are blind, to free captives from prison and to release from the dungeon those who sit in darkness."
> ISAIAH 42:6-7

Because of Jesus' death and resurrection, Gentiles (non-Jews) are now also included in the Kingdom of Christ if they choose to be "in Christ." In this Kingdom, under the authority of our King, we are given identities and roles to play—both individually and together. This is what it means to be the church. God's goal was to lead us toward the salvation of all. The Scriptures reveal His purpose for His church: to join Him in seeking and saving the lost.

EPHESIANS 2:10-18

We are God's handiwork, created in Christ Jesus to do good works, which God prepared in advance for us to do.

Therefore, remember that formerly you who are Gentiles by birth and called "uncircumcised" by those who call themselves "the circumcision" (which is done in the body by human hands)—remember that at that time you were separate from Christ, excluded from citizenship in Israel and foreigners to the covenants of the promise, without hope and without God in the world. But now in Christ Jesus you who once were far away have been brought near by the blood of Christ.

For he himself is our peace, who has made the two groups one and has destroyed the barrier, the dividing wall of hostility, by setting aside in his flesh the law with its commands and regulations. His purpose was to create in himself one new humanity out of the two, thus making peace, and in one body to reconcile both of them to God through the cross, by which he put to death their hostility. He came and preached peace to you who were far away and peace to those who were near. For through him we both have access to the Father by one Spirit.

READ EPHESIANS 2:19-22 IN YOUR PERSONAL BIBLE.

He came and preached peace to you who were far away and peace to those who were near. For through him we both have access to the Father by one Spirit.

Consequently, you are no longer foreigners and strangers, but fellow citizens with God's people and also members of his household, built on the foundation of the apostles and prophets, with Christ Jesus himself as the chief cornerstone. In him the whole building is joined together and rises to become a holy temple in the Lord. And in him you too are being built together to become a dwelling in which God lives by his Spirit.

EPHESIANS 2:17-22

Citizens and Family

Read 1 Peter 2:9-10 and Revelation 5:9-10 (see sidebar).

Jesus came to unite Jews and Gentiles into a new spiritual nation. And we are not just citizens of the same Kingdom—we are also fellow princes and princesses, members of Jesus' household (Ephesians 2:19).

A Living Temple

Read Haggai 1.

Ephesians 2:20 goes on to tell us another aspect of our identity: We are a living temple for our God. In Jesus' time, the temple was a physical building that people worshiped at. The amount of time, energy, and expense it took to build the temple reflected people's devotion and love for the God of the temple.

In the New Testament, God is building a new kind of temple with living stones joined together by the Holy Spirit. The church is also described as a spiritual temple built on the apostles and prophets (their teachings), with Christ Jesus as the chief cornerstone (1 Peter 2:4-6). As God's temple, we the church are to live in such a way that we reflect our devotion and love for God.

The Light of the World

Jesus told His disciples that His people are to bring Him glory through how we live together. We are the light of the world—like a lamp placed on a table in a dark room. But we are also a city on a hill: a collection of lights that shine brighter together than we can alone (Matthew 5:14).

His intent was that now, through the church, the manifold wisdom of God should be made known to the rulers and authorities in the heavenly realms.

EPHESIANS 3:10

1. What correlation do you see between Jesus' descriptions of a city on a hill, a house built on a rock, and a living building joined together on the foundation of the apostles?

---

1 PETER 2:9-10

You are a chosen people, a royal priesthood, a holy nation, God's special possession, that you may declare the praises of him who called you out of darkness into his wonderful light. Once you were not a people, but now you are the people of God; once you had not received mercy, but now you have received mercy.

REVELATION 5:9-10

They sang a new song, saying: "You are worthy to take the scroll and to open its seals, because you were slain, and with your blood you purchased for God persons from every tribe and language and people and nation. You have made them to be a kingdom and priests to serve our God, and they will reign on the earth."

1 PETER 2:4-5

As you come to him, the living Stone—rejected by humans but chosen by God and precious to him—you also, like living stones, are being built into a spiritual house to be a holy priesthood, offering spiritual sacrifices acceptable to God through Jesus Christ.

MATTHEW 5:14

[Jesus said,] "You are the light of the world. A town built on a hill cannot be hidden."

EZEKIEL 36:19-21

"I dispersed them among the nations, and they were scattered through the countries; I judged them according to their conduct and their actions. And wherever they went among the nations they profaned my holy name, for it was said of them, 'These are the LORD's people, and yet they had to leave his land.' I had concern for my holy name, which the people of Israel profaned among the nations where they had gone."

2. Reflecting on the passages about the church you've read today, mark the following statements *True* or *False*.

    a. True/False: The purpose of God's church was to reveal to the world the wisdom of God, demonstrated by how we live according to His plans and in relationship.

    b. True/False: The church was supposed to be built on the foundation of the apostles—their teachings and writings, which we call Scripture.

    c. True/False: God doesn't care which church we are in as long as we are in a church.

    d. True/False: God's church is built on His plans and led by His leaders.

    e. True/False: The people of the early church were known as the disciples.

    f. True/False: Our behavior has no effect on God's reputation even when we are living outside God's design.[i]

THE REPUTATION OF GOD AT STAKE

Read Ezekiel 36:19-21 (see sidebar).

Years ago, my son (who is now a pastor) was rebellious beyond words. Eventually, even though he was under age eighteen, I could no longer let him stay in my home. He was breaking our rules, doing illegal things, and drawing his younger brothers into his lifestyle. After that, he began to sleep on couches in the homes of kids he hung out with. When they would ask him why he wasn't at home, he told some horrible stories about me to justify his need for a couch to sleep on. I didn't know it at the time, but those words spread. People I knew and even people who went to our church started to avoid me and leave the congregation. Some judged me because of my son's behavior, thinking I must be a terrible father. Others left or avoided me because they believed what my son told them.

After my son got saved and his life changed, he shared with me what he had said to others. Of course it was painful to hear, but he was very repentant. He agreed to go to those he had lied to and ask for forgiveness.

Embedded in this story is a lesson. When my son portrayed me in a way that was not truthful, I was judged for his portrayal of me. In fact, many others saw his behavior and thought I was an unfit father merely by the way he acted. In the same way, when we take on the name of Jesus as His representatives and speak and act inappropriately, we impact Jesus' reputation.

As we forget our identity in Christ or just refuse to take it on, and yet continue to represent Him as His disciples, we hurt those He loves within the church and those He would like to reach outside it.

3. Have you ever misrepresented someone's character to someone else? Is there anyone you may need to talk to, as my son did, to clear up any confusion?

DAY TWO REVIEW

1. What stood out to you or convicted you from today?

    _____

    _____

2. Is there anything you learned in today's study that you need to apply in your home?

    _____

    _____

    _____

3. Think about the way you are representing God in the other spheres of your life. Do you see any changes you may need to make in your Home and Family Sphere? What about your World Sphere?

    _____

    _____

---

i. Answer: True: a, b, d, e; False: c, f.

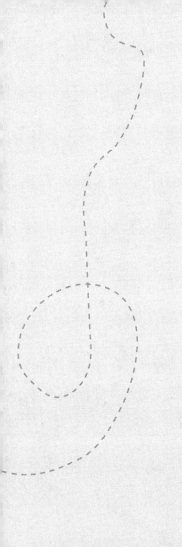

Day Three

JESUS AFFECTS OUR HEAD (THINKING)

GETTING STARTED

Yesterday we talked about some ways we may damage the reputation of Jesus by our words and behavior. Today we are going to look at what it means to strive for unity and peace with each other.

> *Lord Jesus: Help me see what You want me to see today. Expose any lies I may believe and lead me to Your truth. Help me trust and obey You and walk out what I'm learning in every sphere of my life.*

As we abide in Christ, seeking to be obedient to His Word, we begin to live our life according to the way He intended for disciples, which includes being unified around a shared belief system: the faith.

> As a prisoner for the Lord, then, I urge you to live a life worthy of the calling you have received. Be completely humble and gentle; be patient, bearing with one another in love. Make every effort to keep the unity of the Spirit through the bond of peace. There is one body and one Spirit, just as you were called to one hope when you were called; one Lord, one faith, one baptism; one God and Father of all, who is over all and through all and in all.
> EPHESIANS 4:1-6

What, then, makes the many "one" in Christ? Ephesians 4:1-6 demonstrates the essentials of our faith that lead us to unity.

- *One body*: There is one universal church from Jesus' perspective.

- *One Spirit (the Holy Spirit)*: The Spirit does His work through the Scriptures and in our hearts.

- *One hope*: We have an eternal home waiting for us (Revelation 21) and a present hope. God is for us and cares for us and will work all things out for the good of those who love Him and are called according to His purpose (Romans 8:28).

- *One Lord*: Christ is the head of His body (1 Corinthians 1:10-16) and the Lord of heaven and earth.

- *One faith*: We share one body of knowledge or affirmed truths of the faith as defined by the early church (Jude 1:3).

1 CORINTHIANS 1:10-16

I appeal to you, brothers and sisters, in the name of our Lord Jesus Christ, that all of you agree with one another in what you say and that there be no divisions among you, but that you be perfectly united in mind and thought. My brothers and sisters, some from Chloe's household have informed me that there are quarrels among you. What I mean is this: One of you says, "I follow Paul"; another, "I follow Apollos"; another, "I follow Cephas"; still another, "I follow Christ."

Is Christ divided? Was Paul crucified for you? Were you baptized in the name of Paul? I thank God that I did not baptize any of you except Crispus and Gaius, so no one can say that you were baptized in my name. (Yes, I also baptized the household of Stephanas; beyond that, I don't remember if I baptized anyone else.)

- *One baptism*: Baptism is a physical experience we all share as a spiritual family; a physical picture of the faith that solidifies allegiance to the Lord, His family, and His way of life; and an ongoing practice of the normative example in the New Testament (immersion in water—see, for example, Acts 8:34-39).

- *One God and Father of us all*: There are no other gods except the one who is described in the Bible (the triune God—Matthew 28:19-21).

1. Which of these "one" statements are you most confused about right now? Be honest.

_____

_____

UNITY OR DISUNITY?

Read Matthew 12:25 (see sidebar).

> I appeal to you, brothers and sisters, in the name of our Lord Jesus Christ, that all of you agree with one another in what you say and that there be no divisions among you, but that you be perfectly united in mind and thought.
>
> I CORINTHIANS 1:10

MATTHEW 12:25
Jesus knew their thoughts and said to them, "Every kingdom divided against itself will be ruined, and every city or household divided against itself will not stand."

In Scripture, unity is a consistent command for God's church. Disunity on the essentials of our faith suggests that our faith itself is shaky and unreliable.

2. Reflecting on the impact of disunity, mark the following statements *True* or *False*.

   a. True/False: Disunity affects how we are seen by unbelievers.
   b. True/False: Disunity affects how much we can get done on our mission.
   c. True/False: God doesn't look wise if His people can't work together.
   d. True/False: God's Spirit can't contradict God's Word.
   e. True/False: If you are a mature disciple of Jesus, then you care about working for unity with other believers.
   f. True/False: As soon as you become a disciple, the Holy Spirit moves into your life and makes clear the truth about how to be unified in all circumstances and relationships.
   g. True/False: God's Spirit, alongside God's Word and God's mature disciplemakers, helps you grow into one who will be unified with other believers.[i]

Unity takes time because it takes time for each of us to grow up as believers. When I was first saved, I had so many questions. Every time I heard something I didn't understand or was confused by what I read in Scripture, a little seed of doubt came into my heart. I would then wonder if I was even a Christian.

One day I told my father I didn't think I was a Christian, and he asked, "Why not?" I told him I had questions that made me doubt, and I will never forget what he said: "Me too."

I was surprised at his answer. He shared that over the years he had studied so hard because he had doubts. But as he studied and asked questions, he discovered answers for all the questions he had. Now when he finds something he doesn't understand or that causes him doubt (which he still deals with occasionally), he works to find an answer.

It takes time to grow, and we need to wrestle at times with the things of the faith. Doubt becomes a problem because we have a sinful nature and a mind that can only perceive so much—and a devil who uses doubt as a weapon to get us to walk away from God. That's why being surrounded by a community committed to unity in our faith is so important. There are still things that we are not sure about in Scripture, but what we do know enables us to get through our doubts. Please, please share your doubts with someone rather than hiding them. Let more mature believers help you. And please do not make someone else feel guilty for doubting. This will cause them to go underground and isolate themselves with their doubts. The devil loves us to play in the dark because he owns us there. Our unity is strengthened when we bring our doubts into the light and encourage others to do the same (Jude 1:22).

DAY THREE REVIEW

1. What stood out to you or convicted you from today?

   _____

   _____

2. Who will you talk to about the subject or subjects you are confused about?

   _____

   _____

3. Do you struggle with any of the "one" statements from today? Are there any that you don't understand?

   _____

4. Have you taken the step of baptism yet in your journey? Why or why not?

   _____

---

i. Answer: True: a, b, c, d, e, g; False: f.

Day Four

WE ARE HIS BODY

GETTING STARTED

Unity is essential to our success as we represent Jesus to the world and as we go through life as fellow disciples. Because we have sinful natures and a culture created by people with sinful natures, as well as a spiritual enemy, unity is anything but easy. There are so many things that can separate us: our preferences, our races, our languages, our ages, and more. However, the most important things can bind us together.

> *Lord Jesus: Help me see what You want me to see today. Expose any lies I may believe and lead me to Your truth. Help me trust and obey You, and to walk out what I'm learning in every sphere of my life.*

Now that we understand the importance of unity in the church, let's look at how Paul teaches believers to view the church:

> Christ himself gave the apostles, the prophets, the evangelists, the pastors and teachers, to equip his people for works of service, so that the body of Christ may be built up.
>
> EPHESIANS 4:11-12

> From him the whole body, joined and held together by every supporting ligament, grows and builds itself up in love, as each part does its work.
>
> EPHESIANS 4:16

> Just as a body, though one, has many parts, but all its many parts form one body, so it is with Christ. For we were all baptized by one Spirit so as to form one body—whether Jews or Gentiles, slave or free—and we were all given the one Spirit to drink. Even so the body is not made up of one part but of many.
>
> Now if the foot should say, "Because I am not a hand, I do not belong to the body," it would not for that reason stop being part of the body. And if the ear should say, "Because I am not an eye, I do not belong to the body," it would not for that reason stop being part of the body. If the whole body were an eye, where would the sense of hearing be? If the whole body were an ear, where would the sense of smell be? But in fact God has placed the parts in the body, every one of them, just as he wanted them to be. If they were all one part, where would the body be? As it is, there are many parts, but one body.
>
> The eye cannot say to the hand, "I don't need you!" And the head cannot say to the feet, "I don't need you!" On the contrary, those parts of the body that seem to be weaker are indispensable, and the parts that we think are less honorable we treat with special honor. And the parts that are unpresentable are treated with

special modesty, while our presentable parts need no special treatment. But God has put the body together, giving greater honor to the parts that lacked it, so that there should be no division in the body, but that its parts should have equal concern for each other. If one part suffers, every part suffers with it; if one part is honored, every part rejoices with it.

Now you are the body of Christ, and each one of you is a part of it.

1 CORINTHIANS 12:12-27

The Son is the image of the invisible God, the firstborn over all creation. For in him all things were created: things in heaven and on earth, visible and invisible, whether thrones or powers or rulers or authorities; all things have been created through him and for him. He is before all things, and in him all things hold together. And he is the head of the body, the church; he is the beginning and the firstborn from among the dead, so that in everything he might have the supremacy.

COLOSSIANS 1:15-18

In these passages, we learn to think about the church as a body, with all its different parts and functions. Christ is the head of this body.

1. With the Scripture passages about the body in mind, answer the following questions:

    a. Who is the head (brain) of the church?

    _____

    b. What does the head do in the body?

    _____

    c. What do the other parts of the body do in response to the direction of the head?

    _____

    d. What can a hand do if it is not connected to the shoulder that is getting direction from the head?

    _____

The Holy Spirit is connected to the head and to those of us who are believers. The Lord sends His directions—via the Holy Spirit—to all of us so that we can work together and do what He commands.

WHEN JESUS' CHURCH WORKS TOGETHER

His intent was that now, through the church, the manifold wisdom of God should be made known to the rulers and authorities in the heavenly realms.

EPHESIANS 3:10

The Lord sends His directions—via the Holy Spirit—to all of us so that we can work together and do what He commands.

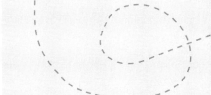

2. Do you think that the people in your community would look at your church and how it functions and say that God is wise? Why or why not?

3. If your church doesn't reflect God's wisdom, what do you think God wants you to do? Select your answer:

   ☐ leave the church
   ☐ criticize the church
   ☐ look past the faults of others
   ☐ be part of the solution

Humility is a key characteristic of a mature disciple. As we follow Jesus, our authority, we each are being changed by Him and are becoming better lovers of God and lovers of others. Humility is the heart of love because biblical love lays down its rights for the good of the other. The Ephesians passage tells us that we are equipped for acts of service and that we each have work to do. This is all about humility before God and others.

DAY FOUR REVIEW

1. What stood out to you or convicted you from today?

2. What, if anything, did you encounter in this study today that you did not know?

3. Knowing something and doing something are two different things. What do you need to do differently in your life as a result of what the Lord is showing you in Scripture? Share it with your group.

4. Where in your life right now do you need to humble yourself and serve someone else? Put that person's name below and begin praying about how God wants to use you in their life.

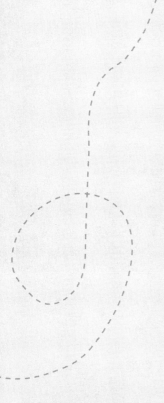

Day Five

THE CHURCH AND ITS LEADERSHIP

GETTING STARTED

God had the church in mind when He sent out His disciples to start His church. God intended the church to have mature spiritual leaders within it to act as spiritual parents.

Lord Jesus: Help me see what You want me to see today. Expose any lies I may believe and lead me to Your truth. Help me trust and obey You and walk out what I'm learning in every sphere of my life.

1 CORINTHIANS 12:28, NASB

God has appointed in the church, first apostles, second prophets, third teachers, then miracles, then gifts of healings, helps, administrations, various kinds of tongues.

EPHESIANS 4:11-16

Christ himself gave the apostles, the prophets, the evangelists, the pastors and teachers, to equip his people for works of service, so that the body of Christ may be built up until we all reach unity in the faith and in the knowledge of the Son of God and become mature, attaining to the whole measure of the fullness of Christ.

Then we will no longer be infants, tossed back and forth by the waves, and blown here and there by every wind of teaching and by the cunning and craftiness of people in their deceitful scheming. Instead, speaking the truth in love, we will grow to become in every respect the mature body of him who is the head, that is, Christ. From him the whole body, joined and held together by every supporting ligament, grows and builds itself up in love, as each part does its work.

We see order in every part of God's creation. Remember, God is a God of order (1 Corinthians 14:33). In Scripture we see guidelines for homes and workplaces, as well as the church. God gave the early church spiritual giftings that would help the church become organized in such a way that it worked as a team (1 Corinthians 12:28). According to Ephesians 4:11-16, the gift of leadership, or administration, equips the church to be orderly in the way we act.

The book of Ephesians tells us that spiritual leadership has a purpose and a responsibility. And the people within the church have a purpose and a responsibility to God's delegated authority. Many people carry the attitude that the qualities of organization and leadership are somehow nonspiritual. However, Scripture reveals that Jesus appointed leaders to do a job: to go and make disciples. He told them to lead His church, and they did (Acts 2:42-47).

Read Ephesians 4:11-16 (see sidebar).

It's important to read Ephesians 4:11-16 in context. Jesus gave gifts to His followers when He rose from the dead and ascended into heaven. He appointed different kinds of leaders: first the apostles (the Twelve, who began the church), then prophets who spoke directly from the Lord as outlined in Acts. Then He gave the gift of evangelism to those who traveled (and still travel) throughout the world to share the gospel. While all of us are evangelists in that we share our faith and make disciples, God gave some a special gifting to share the faith in uniquely powerful ways. Then He gave the role of pastors (elders who oversee the church and take care of God's people) and teachers, who teach the Word as leaders.

Scripture reveals that every church was to have elders (leaders) in every town (Titus 1:5). These leaders had qualifications that they were to meet before they were given the responsibility of eldership (1 Timothy 3:2; Titus 1:9). The early church was not a democracy; rather, the spiritual fathers of the church (elders) appointed men who met the qualifications described in Scripture.

According to Ephesians 4, leaders had a specific role. Mark the answers you see in the text:

a. Their job was to do all the work for those who were part of the church they led.

b. Their job was to work like a coach does—train the people to use their gifts for the work of the team.

c. The job of a church leader is to gather a crowd who listens to them speak about the truth.

d. Every person is saved for a purpose in the church, and a leader's job is to help everyone learn to serve with their gifts.

e. Each part of the body has work to do.

f. When we function like a team, we mature as believers.

g. The body of Christ reflects the greatness of God when we play well as a team.[i]

BEING A SPIRITUAL LEADER

A leader who serves God's church must take that calling seriously. Leadership is a sacred responsibility, not a privilege to be abused. Jesus made this clear when He said that anyone who desires to be first must become last and a servant to all (Matthew 10:42).

While a simple others-focused mindset should be true of all leaders, our leadership model is Jesus (Philippians 2:3-11). That means the motives, actions, and measures of success for Christian leaders reflect Jesus' heart and mission alone:

• The responsibility of leaders is to seek the will of God and then model going first to do it, whether other people do the same . . . or not.

• As leaders go first in forgiving, reconciling when there is conflict, and serving, they help create a culture that produces more and more disciples who do the same.

• Leaders equip Christians for works of service so the body of Christ (the church) is built up.

• Leaders work to bring the different parts of the body of Christ together in unity, knowing that as each part works together for God's glory, we become mature.

• Leaders help people identify a place to serve and equip them to do it.

• Leaders guide the church to represent Jesus (who is the head—authority) as they do His tangible work in the world.

• Success for a spiritual leader is bringing glory to Jesus (1 Corinthians 3:5-9).

DAY FIVE REVIEW

1. What stood out to you or convicted you from today?

_____

_____

_____

PHILIPPIANS 2:3-11

Do nothing out of selfish ambition or vain conceit. Rather, in humility value others above yourselves, not looking to your own interests but each of you to the interests of the others.

In your relationships with one another, have the same mindset as Christ Jesus:

Who, being in very nature God, did not consider equality with God something to be used to his own advantage; rather, he made himself nothing by taking the very nature of a servant, being made in human likeness. And being found in appearance as a man, he humbled himself by becoming obedient to death—even death on a cross!

Therefore God exalted him to the highest place and gave him the name that is above every name, that at the name of Jesus every knee should bow, in heaven and on earth and under the earth, and every tongue acknowledge that Jesus Christ is Lord, to the glory of God the Father.

1 TIMOTHY 3:1-12, NLT

This is a trustworthy saying: "If someone aspires to be a church leader, he desires an honorable position." So a church leader must be a man whose life is above reproach. He must be faithful to his wife. He must exercise self-control, live wisely, and have a good reputation. He must enjoy having guests in his home, and he must be able to teach. He must not be a heavy drinker or be violent. He must be gentle, not quarrelsome, and not love money. He must manage his own family well, having children who respect and obey him. For if a man cannot manage his own household, how can he take care of God's church? A church leader must not be a new believer, because he might become proud, and the devil would cause him to fall. Also, people outside the church must speak well of him so that he will not be disgraced and fall into the devil's trap. In the same way, deacons must be well respected and have integrity. They must not be heavy drinkers or dishonest with money. They must be committed to the mystery of the faith now revealed and must live with a clear conscience. Before they are appointed as deacons, let them be closely examined. If they pass the test, then let them serve as deacons. In the same way, their wives must be respected and must not slander others. They must exercise self-control and be faithful in everything they do. A deacon must be faithful to his wife, and he must manage his children and household well.

HEBREWS 13:17

Have confidence in your leaders and submit to their authority, because they keep watch over you as those who must give an account. Do this so that their work will be a joy, not a burden, for that would be of no benefit to you.

2. Read 1 Timothy 3:1-12; Titus 1:5-9; 1 Peter 5:1-6; and Hebrews 13:17. What further expectations of leaders in the church do you observe in these passages?

3. Is there anything you learned in today's study that you need to apply in your home?

4. What in today's study surprised or challenged your view of leadership in the church?

5. Knowing that God's view of leadership includes humility and that God's meaning of success looks different from how the world views it, how will you respond differently to your church leaders after today's study?

i. Answer: a and c are not found in the text.

THE CHURCH SPHERE (CONTINUED)

Day One

THE CHURCH AND ITS MEMBERSHIP

GETTING STARTED

God is a God of order, and He meant for the church to be a body whose parts all work together. Ephesians 4:11-13 tells us that the church has pastors (this is the same word used for elders), who are to equip the saints (all of us who are disciples).

Lord Jesus: Help me see what You want me to see today. Expose any lies I may believe and lead me to Your truth. Help me trust and obey You and walk out what I'm learning in every sphere of my life.

EPHESIANS 4:11-13

Christ himself gave the apostles, the prophets, the evangelists, the pastors and teachers, to equip his people for works of service, so that the body of Christ may be built up until we all reach unity in the faith and in the knowledge of the Son of God and become mature, attaining to the whole measure of the fullness of Christ.

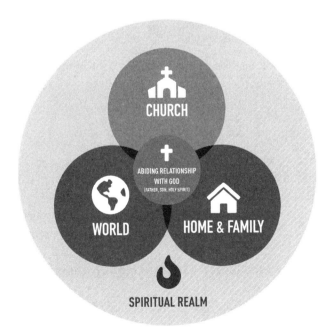

Scan QR code to access video podcasts and other content that accompanies this week's session.

HEBREWS 13:17

Have confidence in your leaders and submit to their authority, because they keep watch over you as those who must give an account. Do this so that their work will be a joy, not a burden, for that would be of no benefit to you.

1 CORINTHIANS 12:12-21

Just as a body, though one, has many parts, but all its many parts form one body, so it is with Christ. For we were all baptized by one Spirit so as to form one body—whether Jews or Gentiles, slave or free—and we were all given the one Spirit to drink. Even so the body is not made up of one part but of many.

Now if the foot should say, "Because I am not a hand, I do not belong to the body," it would not for that reason stop being part of the body. And if the ear should say, "Because I am not an eye, I do not belong to the body," it would not for that reason stop being part of the body. If the whole body were an eye, where would the sense of hearing be? If the whole body were an ear, where would the sense of smell be? But in fact God has placed the parts in the body, every one of them, just as he wanted them to be. If they were all one part, where would the body be? As it is, there are many parts, but one body.

The eye cannot say to the hand, "I don't need you!" And the head cannot say to the feet, "I don't need you!"

The church is a body, but another way to think about that is that the church is a team. Every teammate has a role, and the coach (pastor/elder) prepares members of the team for works of service (Ephesians 4:12). A leadership role is not so much a privilege as it is a responsibility given to us by the Lord. Leaders answer to the Lord for the work that they do with His team, the church.

Today, we're going to consider a question that many people in the church do not think about: What is our God-given obligation to the human leaders who lead us in the church?

Read Hebrews 13:17 (see sidebar).

1. Read through 1 Timothy in your devotions and answer the following questions in context.

    a. Who is Timothy?

    _____

    b. Who is Paul? What authority has Jesus given Paul?

    _____

    c. What authority has Paul given Timothy?

    _____

    d. If you were part of the church Timothy led and you read this letter from Paul to Timothy (remember, it is God-breathed Scripture), how would Paul's words have influenced your understanding of Timothy's authority in your life?

    _____

2. What does success look like for a member of the Lord's church?

    _____

In Ephesians 2:19, we are told we are members of God's household. Then in Ephesians 3:6, we are told that we are members of one body. Paul tells us elsewhere (1 Corinthians 12:12-21) that we are all like members of one body that are supposed to work together. When we each do our part, we contribute to the body functioning correctly.

SPIRITUAL PARALYSIS

We learned in previous weeks how few Christians regularly engage in church community:

- Only 32 percent of Christians between the ages of 23 and 75 attend church weekly.[1]
- In my experience, few Christians are involved in some kind of discipleship community.

- Around 20 percent of churchgoers serve in any way in the church.[2]
- Only 21 percent follow the biblical practice of tithing.[3]

Most Christians go to a church based on whether it offers what they *want* in a church. This is spiritual consumerism—all "take" and no "give."

If only a limited portion of our physical body worked, we would still be valuable and useful to the Lord, but we would likely be considered paralyzed. We could not do many things that we would love to do and would be able to do if our body were whole. In the same way, if only a limited portion of God's people play their part, we as the body of Christ cannot do what God intended for us.

3. When a pastor seeks to guide people in their church to serve in an organized, God-honoring way, the answer they get most often is no. Why do you think that is?

   ☐ The pastor has not taught the people that they are supposed to serve in the church body.

   ☐ The members reject what God's Word says because they don't care or it's inconvenient.

   ☐ The members decide that because they are saved and have their "hell insurance," the rest of the Christian life is just a suggestion rather than a command from God.

   ☐ The members don't make time because they have other priorities.

   ☐ The members believe that the church is just the personal relationship they have with Jesus and they don't need to be involved in what the leaders of a church say.

   ☐ The members don't know that they are disciples and that discipleship is incomplete without allowing God to tell them what the Church Sphere is supposed to look like.

4. Consider your own involvement in church. Do you seek to obey your leaders in the church as they obey Christ?

   ☐ Yes.

   ☐ No.

   ☐ With conditions (e.g., I obey when they teach me what the Bible says about my personal life, but not when they ask me to change my priorities so I can serve with other believers.).

   ☐ Other: _____

5. If your answer was something other than "yes," why is that the case?

6. Are you currently serving in the church (e.g., in a life group, in children's ministry, on the worship team, or in another organized way)? If so, how? If not, why not?

ACTS 8:15-19

When they arrived, they prayed for the new believers there that they might receive the Holy Spirit, because the Holy Spirit had not yet come on any of them; they had simply been baptized in the name of the Lord Jesus. Then Peter and John placed their hands on them, and they received the Holy Spirit.

When Simon saw that the Spirit was given at the laying on of the apostles' hands, he offered them money and said, "Give me also this ability so that everyone on whom I lay my hands may receive the Holy Spirit."

HEBREWS 2:1-4

We must pay the most careful attention, therefore, to what we have heard, so that we do not drift away. For since the message spoken through angels was binding, and every violation and disobedience received its just punishment, how shall we escape if we ignore so great a salvation? This salvation, which was first announced by the Lord, was confirmed to us by those who heard him. God also testified to it by signs, wonders and various miracles, and by gifts of the Holy Spirit distributed according to his will.

1 PETER 4:7-11

The end of all things is near. Therefore be alert and of sober mind so that you may pray. Above all, love each other deeply, because love covers over a multitude of sins. Offer hospitality to one another without grumbling. Each of you should use whatever gift you have received to serve others, as faithful stewards of God's grace in its various forms. If anyone speaks, they should do so as one who speaks the very words of God. If anyone serves, they should do so with the strength God provides, so that in all things God may be praised through Jesus Christ. To him be the glory and the power for ever and ever. Amen.

Jesus tells us that if we abide in Him we will bear fruit, and Paul furthers this teaching, telling us that abiding leads to a change in how we live. As we are becoming submitted to the teachings of Jesus, we are becoming like Him in the way we love God and others. We commit to the mission of Christ within the spheres He has designated for us—which includes the church.

Through the gospel, God purposed to give us grace and salvation—but His grace is not a onetime dose. He continues to give us grace in various ways, and His church (the people of the church) is an ongoing conduit of that grace.

DEFINING A GIFT

A spiritual gift is an ability meant to be used for God's glory and other people's good. It can be a natural ability that God knit within you in your mother's womb but that the Holy Spirit now empowers because you are a disciple of Jesus. A spiritual gift can also be an ability you were not born with but received when you followed Christ. (For example, you understand spiritual things because God has helped you understand His Word, and you are able to make practical use of it as you teach others.)

God gave the prophets and apostles of old particular supernatural spiritual gifts as a means to prove that what they were saying came from God; these particular gifts validated their message (Acts 8:15-19; Hebrews 2:1-4). At times God may still give these particular intense gifts—such as a miraculous healing in conjunction with prayer—to confirm His presence when He deems it is needed. These more miraculously expressed gifts are not generally the normative experience.

Our human inclination is to use our gifts only for earthly purposes, but God intends us to use those gifts for His purposes as well. We use our gifts to minister to other believers and reach the lost.

Read 1 Peter 4:7-11 and 2 Corinthians 9:11 (see sidebars on this page and the next page).

7. God has given us gifts. What kind of gifts has the Lord given you?

_____

_____

_____

8. God gave us spiritual gifts because He loves us and we need them. What other reason does 2 Corinthians 9:11 give us?

_____

_____

_____

9. What happens if we don't use God's gifts to us for the reasons He intended them?

_____

_____

_____

10. When people don't obey Christ concerning the church, how does this affect the believers within the church? Jesus' reputation with outsiders? The other spheres of your life?

11. How mature can we become spiritually if we don't submit to the Lord's will? What are the ramifications to us, our family, and our work life?

12. If you serve individually but won't serve in an organized way with other believers, are you truly bringing glory to God in every way He would have you do it?

DAY ONE REVIEW

1. What stood out to you or convicted you from today?

2. How does today's lesson change how you see others in the church?

3. When others in the church see things differently or have a different bent than you do, is that a good or bad thing? Why or why not?

4. What from today's study do you need to apply in your engagement with the local church?

2 CORINTHIANS 9:11
You will be enriched in every way so that you can be generous on every occasion, and through us your generosity will result in thanksgiving to God.

Notes and Thoughts

God has a place for us to serve as part of His body.

1. "A New Chapter in Millennial Church Attendance," Barna, August 4, 2022, https://www.barna.com/research/church-attendance-2022. This percentage is the average of the weekly church attendance of Millennials (39 percent), Gen Xers (31 percent), and Boomers (25 percent) according to a 2022 study.
2. Shari Finnell, "Declining Volunteerism Is Changing the Church Experience," Faith & Leadership, March 7, 2023, https://faithandleadership.com/declining-volunteerism-changing-the-church-experience. This statistic is as of March 2022, according to a study of the effect of the global COVID-19 pandemic on church involvement.
3. "What Is a Tithe?: New Data on Perceptions of the 10 Percent," Barna, September 7, 2022, https://www.barna.com/research/what-is-a-tithe.

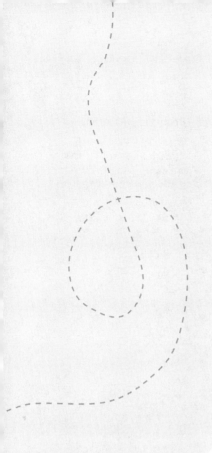

Day Two

THE CHURCH AND ITS RELATIONAL ENVIRONMENTS

GETTING STARTED

God has a place for us to serve as part of His body. We have a purpose and a function that is important. We also know that God has a purpose for others as well. God's leaders for the church have a purpose and a function too.

Lord Jesus: Help me see what You want me to see today. Expose any lies I may believe and lead me to Your truth. Help me trust and obey You and walk out what I'm learning in every sphere of my life.

I often hear people say things like "I don't like the organized church." My question to those who say this is "Does God like an organized church?" Because you have been on this journey of discipleship, you will know the answer: absolutely, yes. God is a God of order, and that order supports His values.

Jesus sent the disciples to make disciples who would form His church (Matthew 16:18). The book of Acts describes how the apostles understood Jesus' version of the church. Acts 2 shows how the gospel was preached for the first time and what the required response to it is (Acts 2:38), as well as how the church was organized.

Read Acts 2.

1. What kind of environments (sizes of groups) can you see in this passage?

_____

_____

Some of us want to downplay the purpose of environments we don't feel comfortable in—we might say large groups are impersonal or small groups are draining. But remember: The church is God's idea, and it is not based on our preferences or comfort level.

The relational vehicle on our journey of discipleship is the relational environment where discipleship happens with a more mature, intentional leader. The physical environments and contexts in which discipleship happens will necessarily look different depending on where we need to grow. No one changes through being comfortable.

How did the early church in Acts create environments for discipleship? They just replicated what Jesus had done. As we've looked at before, Jesus modeled using several kinds of environments to help His disciples grow—from one-on-one talks to small groups to huge crowds, in places ranging from towns to synagogues to mountains. Jesus had a purpose for each environment, and that included the larger events, which He used as an opportunity to explain further and press deeper afterward. A larger gathering such as a church service has always fit into the journey of discipleship.

MATTHEW 16:18

[Jesus said,] "I tell you that you are Peter, and on this rock I will build my church, and the gates of Hades will not overcome it."

ACTS 2:38

Peter replied, "Repent and be baptized, every one of you, in the name of Jesus Christ for the forgiveness of your sins. And you will receive the gift of the Holy Spirit."

UNDERSTANDING THE VEHICLES

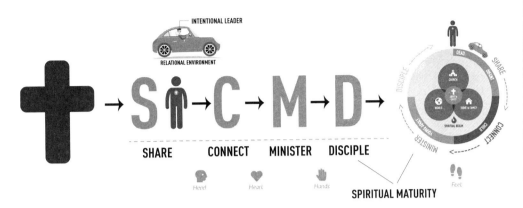

Remember our journey graphic? Jesus shared who He was and invited His disciples to go on a journey with Him, then He connected with His disciples in a relational vehicle.

So far, we've mostly talked about relationship as the vehicle in which discipleship happens. Real Life Ministries' international missions pastor, Dave Campbell, took our original analogy a step further to unpack the ways relational environments influence our discipleship.

Dave travels all over the world, and in the countries he visits, he sees all kinds of vehicles. As he trains disciples in other countries, he tries to use visuals that connect with their daily lives. To do that, he explains that on our journey of discipleship we will take a variety of relational vehicles—and most of the time we will be in more than one at the same time. Each relational vehicle has different things we can learn while in it and different things we can offer to others.

Here are the relational vehicles for discipleship that Dave has identified:

- *motorcycle*: a one-on-one environment;
- *car*: a one-on-few environment (fewer than twelve people);
- *van*: a mid-size group (twelve to eighteen people);
- *bus*: a ministry or event of the local church; and
- *train*: the local church.

2. Recall a place in the New Testament where Jesus used a one-on-one (motorcycle) environment. What are some of the benefits of this environment? What are some downsides?

3. What is an example of Jesus using a small group (car) environment in Scripture? What are some of the benefits and downsides of this environment?

Jesus modeled using several kinds of environments to help His disciples grow—from one-on-one talks to small groups to huge crowds, in places ranging from towns to synagogues to mountains.

As part of our journey toward spiritual maturity, we are told by Jesus to deny ourselves and take up our cross and follow Him.

HEBREWS 10:25
Let us consider how we may spur one another on toward love and good deeds, not giving up meeting together, as some are in the habit of doing, but encouraging one another—and all the more as you see the Day approaching.

ACTS 2:42-47
They devoted themselves to the apostles' teaching and to fellowship, to the breaking of bread and to prayer. Everyone was filled with awe at the many wonders and signs performed by the apostles. All the believers were together and had everything in common. They sold property and possessions to give to anyone who had need. Every day they continued to meet together in the temple courts. They broke bread in their homes and ate together with glad and sincere hearts, praising God and enjoying the favor of all the people. And the Lord added to their number daily those who were being saved.

4. Share an example of Jesus using a ministry or a group meeting (van) environment. What are some of the benefits and downsides of this environment?

5. Can you think of a time when Jesus used the train (large-group environment)? What are some of the benefits and downsides of this environment?

As we travel on our journey toward spiritual maturity, Jesus tells us to deny ourselves, take up our cross, and follow Him (Matthew 16:24). This means we need to be willing to go wherever He leads us. Part of that willingness means saying yes to whatever environment He asks us to be in—to think of what we can give, rather than what we want to get.

6. What are disciples learning to do? Mark the following statements *True* or *False*.

   a. True/False: Disciples decide what environment they feel most comfortable in and shape their faith life around that.
   b. True/False: A disciple of Jesus asks and answers the question *Where do I learn best?* and then builds their schedule around that.
   c. True/False: A disciple of Jesus disciples another person to create their faith life around the practices and environments that God has decided work well.
   d. True/False: A disciple will learn better in some environments than others, but learning is not the only thing a disciple does.
   e. True/False: Some environments are better than others for reaching the lost.
   f. True/False: If a disciple's heart is open to the Holy Spirit's leading in a relational environment, they can learn something.
   g. True/False: Each kind of environment provides a benefit that God wants His disciples to receive.
   h. True/False: As a disciple, part of following Jesus is learning to deny one's own desires and obey Jesus no matter how it makes them feel or what they like.
   i. True/False: No one environment meets every need of a disciple.
   j. True/False: Disciples cannot say they are in the Lord's version of church if they try to fit their whole faith walk into one church service per week.[i]

As we look through Scripture, we see the Lord commanding us to not neglect meeting together as believers (Hebrews 10:25). What kind of gatherings are disciples being commanded not to neglect? When you remember what the early church did as a normal course of action (Acts 2:42-47), then you know that we should not neglect any one environment.

7. My life verse is Hebrews 3:12-13. Why do you think the Holy Spirit led the author to write that we need to encourage one another daily?

_____

_____

8. What could happen if we neglect the gathering of believers?

_____

_____

DAY TWO REVIEW

1. What stood out to you or convicted you from today?

_____

_____

2. Was there anything you read today that you disagreed with? Why?

_____

_____

3. Which environment is the hardest for you to want to be in? Why?

_____

_____

4. What relational environments are you currently involved in with your church body? How do they correspond with the list of relational environment vehicles?

_____

_____

HEBREWS 3:12-13

See to it, brothers and sisters, that none of you has a sinful, unbelieving heart that turns away from the living God. But encourage one another daily, as long as it is called "Today," so that none of you may be hardened by sin's deceitfulness.

Notes and Thoughts

---

i. Answer: True: c–j; False: a, b.

Day Three

THE FAMILY OF GOD

GETTING STARTED

God designed the church to look like a family. Ideally the church will fill in the relational gaps we have in our lives as God uses the body as His hands and feet to care for His children.

Lord Jesus: Help me see what You want me to see today. Expose any lies I may believe and lead me to Your truth. Help me trust and obey You and walk out what I'm learning in every sphere of my life.

In the book of Ephesians, Paul makes it clear that we are not only citizens of Christ's Kingdom but also members of God's household—a new family. We can see the use of family terms throughout the rest of Scripture as well. For instance, many of the apostles and writers of the New Testament refer to themselves as a father, or parent, of those they were discipling.

Within the church, we will encounter and be in relationship with people in each of the spiritual stages of growth—infant, child, young adult, and parent (Ephesians 3:17-18). With that in mind, what should our love for one another look like?

Read Ephesians 4:1-3 (see sidebar).

Paul tells us exactly what it looks like when we love each other the way God defines it. Love requires an attitude of humility to . . .

- consider others as valuable to the Lord as we are;
- believe others have something to offer, just as we do;
- be patient as we work through differences;
- go first to make peace when brothers or sisters are unreconciled, as Jesus did;
- show gentleness toward others as we deal with their struggles; and
- look past (bear with) others' faults, just as the Lord looks past ours.

1. Which of the aspects of love from Ephesians 4:1-3 would you say is hardest for you? Why?

_____

_____

The old "Adam" identity still struggles to pull us backward, and the enemy seeks to pull us back toward a lesser identity as well. We as disciples, children of God, new creatures, and part of His Kingdom and family are called on to help one another remain in our new identity.

EPHESIANS 3:16-18

I pray that out of his glorious riches he may strengthen you with power through his Spirit in your inner being, so that Christ may dwell in your hearts through faith. And I pray that you, being rooted and established in love, may have power, together with all the Lord's holy people, to grasp how wide and long and high and deep is the love of Christ.

EPHESIANS 4:1-3

As a prisoner for the Lord, then, I urge you to live a life worthy of the calling you have received. Be completely humble and gentle; be patient, bearing with one another in love. Make every effort to keep the unity of the Spirit through the bond of peace.

Read Ephesians 4:25–5:21.

2. Based on Ephesians 4:25-32, match the verse number with the appropriate statement below.

EPHESIANS 4:25

Each of you must put off falsehood and speak truthfully to your neighbor, for we are all members of one body.

i. Tell each other the truth.	a. verse 27
ii. Only say what builds others up.	b. verse 28
iii. The devil is looking for a foothold so he can gain a stronghold in your life.	c. verse 32
iv. Do not allow any bitterness, anger, and fighting.	d. verse 25
v. Share with one another rather than being a taker all the time.	e. verse 31
vi. Forgive one another from the heart.	f. verse 29*

As humans we are still struggling with sin, and we make many mistakes. As disciples, we can't expect the people in our church to be perfect because they are saved. The devil is still trying to divide and conquer us from within. He hopes we will exhaust ourselves fighting internally rather than externally fighting him for the souls of human beings. He wants us to believe the lie that because people are so hard to deal with, and because we can get hurt and hurt others, we have the option to make church a "just me and Jesus" thing. This is far from the truth.

CALLED TO RELATIONSHIP

As Christians we are called to love others, and God calls us to be open to allowing others to love us as well. So often believers commit to loving others as Jesus defines it, but they keep people at arm's length, avoiding real, honest, vulnerable relationships. Real relationships are reciprocal, not one-sided.

We all need support, and it's humbling to accept it—but when we bring this kind of humility to relationships, we can carry burdens together. Pretending to have it all together and hiding (putting on a face) so we can look good to others or isolating ourselves spiritually and relationally because of shame is not what it means to be a believer (Ephesians 4:25; James 5:16).

Being transparent with one another is essential to winning the spiritual battle warring in our own minds. When we allow others to know our struggles and help us with them, we experience the safety of an environment of honesty, accountability, and support (Galatians 6:2; Jude 1:22). The devil hates this. If he can cut us off from the family, he can overpower us—but transparency creates deep family bonds he can't break. I love what Ecclesiastes 4:9-12 says: that when we truly know each other and walk together, there is strength. *This is what the family of God is supposed to look like.*

JAMES 5:16

Confess your sins to each other and pray for each other so that you may be healed. The prayer of a righteous person is powerful and effective.

ECCLESIASTES 4:9-12, NLT

Two people are better off than one, for they can help each other succeed. If one person falls, the other can reach out and help. But someone who falls alone is in real trouble. Likewise, two people lying close together can keep each other warm. But how can one be warm alone? A person standing alone can be attacked and defeated, but two can stand back-to-back and conquer. Three are even better, for a triple-braided cord is not easily broken.

---

* Answers: i=d; ii=f; iii=a; iv=e; v=b; vi=c.

3. Who in your life knows what you really struggle with?

4. If you feel alone spiritually, why haven't you shared and received the help God wants you to have through others?

5. Mark one or more of the statements below if they apply to you:

☐ I have been hurt before because I was honest.
☐ I know if people knew my real struggles, they would reject me.
☐ I have to look good to others to be considered mature.
☐ I don't have time for relationships, and since I don't have deep relationships, I am not sharing.
☐ I don't want anyone to know what I struggle with because I don't want to be held accountable to quit.

Here we are again, facing another step of faith: *Will I do what God's Word tells me I should, or will I hold on to my own perspective?* Humility and trust say that even though we have past hurts and the world is a tough place, we will obey Jesus and trust Him to change us even though it's scary (Proverbs 3:5).

In a few days, we will be looking at the Home and Family Sphere, which comes next in Paul's progression in Ephesians. Just as our Abiding Sphere impacts our Church Sphere, our Abiding Sphere and Church Sphere affect our Home and Family Sphere. As we learn what leadership looks like from a spiritual perspective, those of us who are parents are better equipped to lead our home. As we learn how to work together in the church, we discover how to relate as a spouse, family member, or friend in healthier ways. And as we learn how to forgive one another and encourage each other in the church, our home becomes a place where we seek to serve and are quick to forgive wrongs.

DAY THREE REVIEW

1. What stood out to you or convicted you from today?

2. As you think about what we are learning within the Abiding Sphere and Church Sphere, what do you want to carry into your relationships at home?

3. Of the attitudes listed in Ephesians 4:1-3, which do you struggle with the most when it comes to the family of God? Why?

Notes and Thoughts

Day Four

WHERE THERE ARE PEOPLE, THERE IS CONFLICT

GETTING STARTED

Conflict with others may be inevitable, but working through it is not. Many people either run from conflict or toward it—and neither way ensures a good outcome! If God calls us to unity, we will need to make an intentional choice to work through conflict with others. God's Word gives us some insight on how to do that.

> *Lord Jesus: Help me see what You want me to see today. Expose any lies I may believe and lead me to Your truth. Help me trust and obey You and walk out what I'm learning in every sphere of my life.*

When we are dealing with humans on this side of heaven, conflict is inevitable. We were designed for a perfect relationship with God and others, but we lost that status when sin entered the world and tainted everything. Now we have the Holy Spirit working in us, and the Scriptures give us God's directions for how to live—including how to interact with other believers.

An older couple once visited our church and then set up a meeting with me to discuss whether they would make our church their spiritual home. As we talked, I realized I was being interviewed as part of their decision-making process.

Over the course of the conversation, I also asked them many questions. I discovered they had been married for more than fifty years and that they had been part of many, many churches in our area. When I asked them why they had changed churches so often, they gave me a variety of reasons: personality problems, stylistic issues, and so on.

That's when I asked them how they had stayed married for so long. They shared that 1 Corinthians 13 (God's architectural plans, if you will) had been their blueprint for love, and they had used that along with other verses like Ephesians 4:26 ("Do not let the sun go down while you are still angry") to create a relationship that endured.

After listening for a while, I asked this question: "Why have you applied those verses to your marriage but not used them for the main purpose they were intended for?" In context, Paul is writing to churches that were supposed to be acting like family and were not. Yes, those verses work for marriage, too—in fact, they were supposed to be part of discipleship that teaches us what love is. But this couple had decided not to use those verses for their main context, the church. (Remember, to understand Scripture correctly, we must understand who is writing and to whom.)

People often tell me they want to know God's will for their lives, and what they often mean by that is they want to know where to move or what job to take. But God wants us to live every day in His will, in every situation, with His Word as our guide.

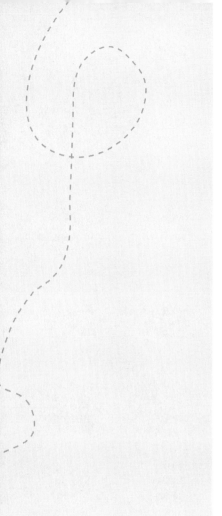

1. We are meant to live in God's will as we . . .

   ☐ live, love, and work in the family of God (His church).
   ☐ forgive others (looking past faults).
   ☐ encourage others with our words.
   ☐ speak honestly with others.
   ☐ share our physical possessions with others.[i]

   In the family of God, as well as in the Home and Family Sphere, God wants us to treat each other in accordance with His will and His words in Scripture.

   We are the bride of Christ. If God hates divorce in marriage, then He must also hate division and relational breakdown in His bride. He desires that we love well, forgive well, and be united.

2. If the church is a spiritual family as Jesus intended it to be, how should we deal with conflicts and disagreements? Mark the correct answer.

   ☐ I should go to a different church.
   ☐ I should demonstrate my opinions with my attendance and giving.
   ☐ I should go humbly to a leader in the church and ask some questions.
   ☐ I should keep quiet and just go along with the leaders, even when I secretly disagree.
   ☐ I should talk about my frustrations with someone else in the church who is not a leader and see if they agree with me.
   ☐ I should stop going to church in person and only watch church online.
   ☐ I should stop going to church at all.
   ☐ Other: _____[ii]

Read Ephesians 4:26-27 (see sidebar).

Getting angry and not dealing with it can give the devil a foothold (something to grab on as he climbs the walls of our churches and lives to get in). The reality is, in the church we will at times get angry. Misunderstandings happen, people fail us, and we fail others. When that occurs, the devil is seeking to thwart us in our task to bring glory to God in this life. Thankfully, Jesus gave us a way to resolve issues of conflict and discord with other believers if we obey Him.

Read Matthew 18:15-17 (see sidebar).

3. What is the purpose of going to a person when they are in sin? (This applies to issues of conflict as well.) Mark the right answer.

   ☐ To vent your anger on them.
   ☐ To make them repent.
   ☐ To resolve the issue so you can be at peace.
   ☐ To make them leave the church so that they won't be a problem anymore.[iii]

EPHESIANS 4:26-27

"In your anger do not sin": Do not let the sun go down while you are still angry. Do not give the devil a foothold.

MATTHEW 18:15-17

If your brother or sister sins, go and point out their fault, just between the two of you. If they listen to you, you have won them over. But if they will not listen, take one or two others along, so that "every matter may be established by the testimony of two or three witnesses." If they still refuse to listen, tell it to the church; and if they refuse to listen even to the church, treat them as you would a pagan or a tax collector.

4. According to Jesus, what do you do first when trying to resolve a broken relationship in the church?

☐ Go get "wise counsel" from someone else about the situation, telling them who hurt you and what they did.

☐ Go to a leader to get their help.

☐ Go to the person alone.[iv]

Paul tells us that we should seek resolution and reconciliation when, not if, an offense occurs (Ephesians 4:25-27).

5. Which of these things is hardest for you to do?

☐ Speak the truth in love to the person who has hurt you.

☐ Go to them quickly so that bitterness does not take root in your life.

☐ Keep it between you and them until you have had the conversation.

☐ Forgive them as Jesus has forgiven you.

Read Hebrews 12:15 (see sidebar).

Resolving conflict and reconciling broken relationships are vital to the health of the church. Neither can happen without forgiveness. That's why the author of Hebrews warns about the root of bitterness.

- A lack of forgiveness is like drinking a poison and hoping it will kill someone else.

- A lack of forgiveness is like driving forward in your car while looking in your rearview mirror. You pass by things that were meant for your good—and run over things you shouldn't have because your focus is on the past.

- The devil defiles you with a lack of forgiveness. And he uses your lack of forgiveness to defile your church and family, too.

Jesus came to resolve the conflict between us and God. More than that, Jesus came to give us His Holy Spirit, who would help us resolve conflict among one another. God knew what this large-scale reconciliation would take, so He made the first move (John 3:16; Romans 5:5-8; 1 John 4:16). Because of what God has done for us already, we respond and obey Him. When others hurt us, we forgive because He first forgave us.

DAY FOUR REVIEW

1. What stood out to you or convicted you from today?

_____

_____

HEBREWS 12:15

See to it that no one falls short of the grace of God and that no bitter root grows up to cause trouble and defile many.

JOHN 3:16

God so loved the world that he gave his one and only Son, that whoever believes in him shall not perish but have eternal life.

ROMANS 5:5-8, NLT

This hope will not lead to disappointment. For we know how dearly God loves us, because he has given us the Holy Spirit to fill our hearts with his love.

When we were utterly helpless, Christ came at just the right time and died for us sinners. Now, most people would not be willing to die for an upright person, though someone might perhaps be willing to die for a person who is especially good. But God showed his great love for us by sending Christ to die for us while we were still sinners.

1 JOHN 4:16

We know and rely on the love God has for us.

God is love. Whoever lives in love lives in God, and God in them.

Notes and Thoughts

2. Did this section cause you to look at 1 Corinthians 13 in a different light? If so, how?

_____

_____

_____

3. Share a situation in which you felt offended. What was your response to the person who offended you? How did your reaction help or hinder the relationship?

_____

_____

_____

4. Who is someone in your life you have had a hard time forgiving? Is the Holy Spirit saying anything to you about that situation right now?

_____

_____

_____

---

i.   Answer: All these answers are correct.
ii. Answer: The third response is correct.
iii. Answer: The third response is correct.
iv. Answer: The third response is correct.

Day Five

TRUSTWORTHINESS

GETTING STARTED

As individuals, we have a new identity, but so do other disciples in our church.

- You are blameless in the Lord's sight because you are "in Christ," and so are they.
- You are a child of God "in Christ," and so are other disciples.
- You are a citizen of the Kingdom, and so are other disciples.
- You are part of the body of Christ (you have a position on His team), and so are others in God's family.

In God's family, conflict is inevitable. We are to forgive one another and resolve to work through conflict.

> *Lord Jesus: Help me see what You want me to see today. Expose any lies I may believe and lead me to Your truth. Help me trust and obey You and walk out what I'm learning in every sphere of my life.*

As we fight for relationship in the church, we are being changed by Christ to become more like Him. This means we are becoming more loving, which makes us easier to bear with and more trustworthy. Trustworthiness is central to healthy relationships in the church. Why?

- We are made for relationships, but the depth of our relationships will be determined by our trustworthiness.
- Where sin and pride reign, so does untrustworthiness.
- Trustworthiness in relationship creates a safe place to reveal who you really are.
- Abiding in Jesus determines your trustworthiness. Jesus is a perfect picture of trustworthiness, and He roots you in trustworthiness.

What makes a person safe and trustworthy to be in relationship with?

- They love well.
- They are grace-filled and empathetic.
- They listen well, put themselves in your place, and share your pain.
- They are not trying to fix you or give you easy answers.
- They are not seeking to make you feel stupid for how you feel.
- They do not lie (Proverbs 12:22).
- They keep a confidence and don't share what you have said with anyone (Proverbs 11:13). (However, there are boundaries to this; if someone is going to hurt themselves or someone else, share it with people who can help.)

PROVERBS 12:22, NLT
The LORD detests lying lips, but he delights in those who tell the truth.

PROVERBS 11:13, NLT

A gossip goes around telling secrets, but those who are trustworthy can keep a confidence.

PSALM 141:5, NLT

Let the godly strike me! It will be a kindness! If they correct me, it is soothing medicine.

PROVERBS 27:6, NLT

Wounds from a sincere friend are better than many kisses from an enemy.

EPHESIANS 4:29

Do not let any unwholesome talk come out of your mouths, but only what is helpful for building others up according to their needs, that it may benefit those who listen.

EPHESIANS 4:15

Instead, speaking the truth in love, we will grow to become in every respect the mature body of him who is the head, that is, Christ.

EPHESIANS 4:9-12

(What does "he ascended" mean except that he also descended to the lower, earthly regions? He who descended is the very one who ascended higher than all the heavens, in order to fill the whole universe.) So Christ himself gave the apostles, the prophets, the evangelists, the pastors and teachers, to equip his people for works of service, so that the body of Christ may be built up.

- They tell the truth (Psalm 141:5; Proverbs 27:6). Because they love you, they tell you what you need to hear for your good (after listening well and empathizing with you).
- They are encouraging and want the best for you (Ephesians 4:29).
- They are honest (Ephesians 4:15, 25).
- They tell you the truth about themselves, too. The relationship is open and vulnerable for both people.
- They help and allow themselves to be helped. The relationship is characterized by give-and-take (Ecclesiastes 4:9-12).

1. These characteristics are not meant to be a comprehensive list, but they provide a good starting point. What are others that should be on the list? Why?

_____

_____

At this point, many of you will be asking, "Whom do I trust?" But instead, I would ask you to consider, "Who can trust me?" Sometimes we think others can trust us, but if people are not sharing details of their real life with us, then it may be that we are wrong about whether they trust us.

2. Do you think people feel safe being open about their lives and struggles with you? What indicates that to you? If not, why do you think that is?

_____

_____

Here are some ideas to create a safe environment for others to tell you how they really feel about being honest with you:

- Rather than being defensive when someone shares something you could change, thank them for having the courage to be honest and loving.
- When you don't agree with another's opinion, rather than just rejecting the idea, tell them you will pray about it and think it over.
- Admit you make mistakes and be humble and coachable as a person. Remember that your identity is not in being perfect but in being forgiven.

Ask your friends how they see you in this area of your spiritual walk. Remember, if you have been unsafe, they won't feel safe to tell you. See that as an invitation to grow in trustworthiness.

Awareness of what it means to be trustworthy equips us to grow in trustworthiness. As a disciple of Jesus, we are called to discern what Jesus would have us be and then to live in that way. Because Jesus went first, we now go first for His sake, to be what He would have us be. Sometimes, things will not go as we wish they would. But we follow through anyway because of what Jesus has already done for us.

3. Based on what you have learned today about trustworthiness, mark the following statements *True* or *False*.

    a. True/False: A mature disciple serves those they do life with.
    b. True/False: A mature disciple discerns the will of God in any situation and goes first to do it.
    c. True/False: A mature disciple has people in their life who are real with them.
    d. True/False: A mature disciple is real and honest in general but reveals more of themselves to those who have been trustworthy.
    e. True/False: A mature disciple is more aware of those who are struggling and helps them.
    f. True/False: A mature disciple allows others into their private world so they can receive help too.
    g. True/False: A mature disciple will not necessarily share their deepest thoughts and feelings with those who are not trustworthy.[i]

DAY FIVE REVIEW

1. What stood out to you or convicted you from today?

2. Do you typically identify yourself more as a leader or a follower? Why?

3. Which do you find harder: sharing the truth with others, or hearing the truth from others? Why?

---

i. Answer: All these statements are true.

THE HOME AND FAMILY SPHERE

Day One

DISCIPLESHIP IN THE HOME

GETTING STARTED

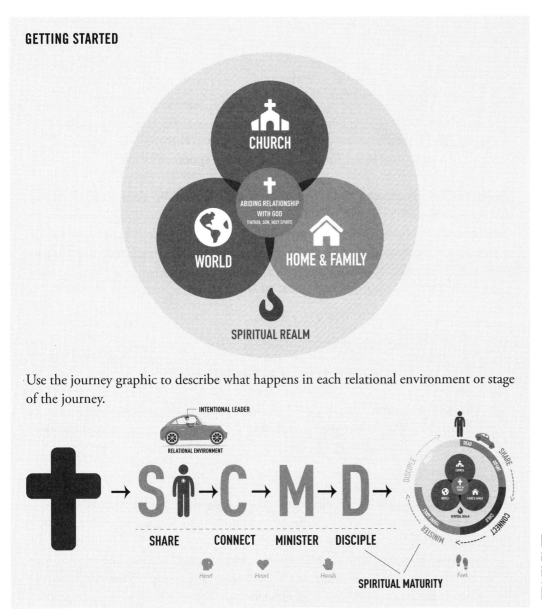

Use the journey graphic to describe what happens in each relational environment or stage of the journey.

Scan QR code to access video podcasts and other content that accompanies this week's session.

Relational vehicle:

_____

The intentional leader (vehicle driver):

_____

Share:

_____

Connect:

_____

Minister (train for ministry):

_____

Disciple (make disciples):

_____

Five Spheres:

_____

Lord Jesus: Help me see what You want me to see today. Expose any lies I may believe and lead me to Your truth. Help me trust and obey You and walk out what I'm learning in every sphere of my life.

Abiding in Christ produces spiritual fruit and gives us direction. We understand God's will, which provides us with the energy and strength to live our life according to it. Abiding in Christ equips us to abide within the body of Christ. Relationships in the church play a part in our abiding. We hear God through others when they encourage, challenge, or teach us.

> *the Holy Spirit of God*
>
> + *the Word of God*
>
> + *the people of God*
>
> = *the direction and strength God provides*

Similarly, our relationships in the Home and Family Sphere help shape us in our discipleship. God designed marriage, love, sex, and the family for our good and His glory. However, because of sin, this sphere and all it contains has moved far away from the Architect's design.

Our culture rebels against what Scripture tells us in every sphere. To live for and with God and others, rather than for self, is antithetical (directly opposed) to what this world produces. Submitting to God and His delegated authority is not something most are willing to do. We see the fallout of this especially in the Home and Family Sphere, in things like self-centered decision-making, broken marriages, and estranged parent-child relationships.

We could talk at length about any number of issues related to our relationships and our discipleship in the Home and Family Sphere. However, because this workbook is intended

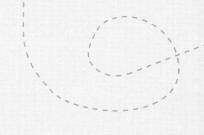

to serve as a starting point, we will stick with the foundational topics Paul discusses in Ephesians. Discipleship is a lifelong journey, and we will learn much over the years as we spend time with the Lord in His Word and with His people. This is why we continue to need to grow in our study of the Word and get wise counsel from more mature believers.

Paul's words to the Ephesians are helpful for us today because he shows us God's intent for the Home and Family Sphere. The Ephesian church was made up primarily of Gentiles, who did not know the Old Testament Scriptures, so they passed along to their children whatever version of home they had been given (1 Peter 1:18). But now God, through the Old and New Testaments, was teaching His architectural plans for the home to the Gentiles, too. As this new community of believers taught and modeled love, purpose, and order, their homes would move toward God's plans as well.

We have learned what love looks like from Jesus, and in the local church we are learning what this looks like through preaching and teaching and seeing it lived out in relationships. As we learn through our spiritual family what the words God used were originally supposed to mean (rather than what they have come to mean in our culture), we're equipped to bring God's perspective and plans into the home as well.

> **1 PETER 1:18**
> You know that it was not with perishable things such as silver or gold that you were redeemed from the empty way of life handed down to you from your ancestors.
>
> **1 CORINTHIANS 3:19**
> The wisdom of this world is foolishness in God's sight. As it is written: "He catches the wise in their craftiness."

1. Based on what you have learned about God's perspective and plans so far, match each term to the correct statement:

i. Love	a. Following Jesus' example of going first
ii. Leadership	b. Loving others and letting them love you, too
iii. Submission to authority	c. Sharing God's perspective accurately with love
iv. Relationship	d. Doing your part quickly to close the gap
v. Servant	e. Humbling yourself before God-given authority
vi. Conflict resolution	f. Giving what people need rather than deserve
vii. Telling the truth	g. Meeting the needs of others at your own expense*

GOD'S PLAN FOR MARRIAGE

Read Ephesians 5:21-33.

Paul spends time in Ephesians 5 talking about a central aspect of God's architectural plans for the home: marriage in a Christian family. For both the woman and the man, Jesus is the example we follow. As a leader, Jesus is our example. As a follower of His Father, Jesus is our example. Part of how we learn what marriage should look like is through what Scripture reveals about Jesus' relationship with His bride, the church:

---

* Answers: i=f; ii=a; iii=e; iv=b; v=g; vi=d; vii=c.

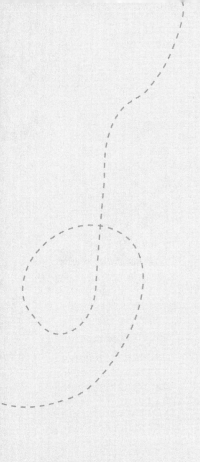

- Jesus is like the groom and the church is His bride (John 3:29; Revelation 19:7). Jesus answered to God the Father, and the church answers to Jesus (Philippians 2:3-9).

- We also see in Ephesians 5:21 that we are to submit (humble ourselves) to one another. Once again, humility is a characteristic of Jesus and should be a growing characteristic in our lives as well.

- Women are told that they (out of reverence for Christ) should submit to their husbands (Ephesians 5:22-24). In our world today, *submission* has become a dirty word. However, in God's Kingdom it is one of the most valuable things you can possess.

Paul, led by the Spirit, starts with directions for the wives. Why? Well, Jesus and Paul often point to the story of creation to help us understand what was supposed to be and what went wrong (Matthew 19:5-8; 2 Corinthians 11:3; 1 Timothy 2:14). In the Garden, Eve was the first to eat the fruit, giving in to Satan's temptation. Now, let's be clear: Both Adam and Eve took part in the sin (Genesis 3:1-7). Satan came to deceive Eve, but Adam was right there with her, watching it happen.

Adam's behavior reminds me of how in my younger years, I would watch my little sisters go first on something I thought might be risky, just so I could see how it affected them. When they made it all right, I would follow. Only when Eve saw that the fruit was good—and did not die right away from her disobedience—did Adam decide to try it too. Adam played a full part in this story: by standing back silently while his created helper was tempted and joining when he felt there wouldn't be consequences.

We'll look at the consequences for Adam tomorrow, but we'll start with the first person addressed in the aftermath of the fall: the woman. Let's look at the curse that was levied against her:

> Then [God] said to the woman, "I will sharpen the pain of your pregnancy, and in pain you will give birth. And you will desire to control your husband, but he will rule over you."
> GENESIS 3:16, NLT

Birth was originally meant to be beautiful and pain-free! I would also suggest that because of the sinful nature every human is born with, not only is birth now painful but child-raising can be painful too.

Note the second half of verse 16. According to the Hebrew language here, God is really saying that now you "will desire to control your husband, but he will rule over you."[1] According to the Hebrew language here, he is really saying that "now you will desire to rule over him, but he will rule over you." The curse of sin between husband and wife is the desire to control the other. Rather than humble and sacrificial love, the sinful nature in marriage leads to mistrust, fear, anger, and competition for control. Left unchecked, sin makes for hard relationships.

Now let's go back to Paul's directions to wives, as given by the Holy Spirit of God.

GENESIS 3:1-7, NLT

The serpent was the shrewdest of all the wild animals the LORD God had made. One day he asked the woman, "Did God really say you must not eat the fruit from any of the trees in the garden?"

"Of course we may eat fruit from the trees in the garden," the woman replied. "It's only the fruit from the tree in the middle of the garden that we are not allowed to eat. God said, 'You must not eat it or even touch it; if you do, you will die.'"

"You won't die!" the serpent replied to the woman. "God knows that your eyes will be opened as soon as you eat it, and you will be like God, knowing both good and evil."

The woman was convinced. She saw that the tree was beautiful and its fruit looked delicious, and she wanted the wisdom it would give her. So she took some of the fruit and ate it. Then she gave some to her husband, who was with her, and he ate it, too. At that moment their eyes were opened, and they suddenly felt shame at their nakedness. So they sewed fig leaves together to cover themselves.

In a direct counter to the Curse and men and women's competing desire to control the other, Paul starts his teaching on the family by telling the woman what God desires for her good. In a sense he says, "Out of reverence for Christ, put down your desire for control, and submit to your husband as to the Lord." This submission is not the action or attitude of a doormat or a weak person—it takes the same strength and humility that Jesus demonstrated when He was here on Earth.

Read Colossians 3:18; Titus 2:4; and 1 Peter 3:1 (see sidebar).

Submission does not mean that a woman is less than her husband. Scripture tells us that men and women are of equal value (Galatians 3:28). As equal parts, we just play different roles.

2. Are you bothered by the word *submission*? If so, what do you think it means?

    ☐ It means women are less valuable.

    ☐ It means a wife has to be a doormat.

    ☐ It means the husband gets to treat the wife like a slave.

    ☐ It means that a wife can't have a leadership gifting.[i]

The Bible never defines *submission* as a statement of a person's value, right to assert themselves, or leadership gifting. Jesus submitted to the Father, which means our Savior Himself is our model for what submission looks like.

Submitting does not mean you don't have an opinion. In fact, Paul's commands to the husband in Ephesians (which we will look at tomorrow) demonstrate that the man's role is to seek the wisdom that God gives the woman and include it in his view and direction for their family. God commands husbands to understand their wives and care about their hearts.

However, wives need to remember that if their husband rejects their counsel, the wife must follow Jesus' will. Even if her husband makes a poor decision, the wife can take comfort in the many examples of how, when women obeyed God, He intervened to protect them even when their husbands didn't. If you are a wife, remember that God has control so you don't have to.

I have heard some women say, "I don't respect my husband because he doesn't deserve my respect." But Ephesians 5:33 says women are to respect their husbands—full stop. Our respect should not hinge on whether the recipient deserves it. Respect is a choice that we make out of reverence for Christ. We follow His directions because of who He is and what He has done for us, even when we don't believe that the other person deserves it.

This passage in Ephesians does not mean that wives must submit to their husbands no matter what. If a husband asks his wife to disobey God, she must say no out of reverence for Christ. She should seek godly counsel from godly women to determine if and when she must reject her husband's authority. Ultimately, the husband is responsible before God as the head of the household.

Marriage is a partnership, and each person has valid perspectives and gifts that come together in the partnership. Partnership and shared leadership are the keys to marriage as God designed it.

DAY ONE REVIEW

1. What stood out to you or convicted you from today?

2. Has the word *submissive* ever had a negative connotation in your life? Why or why not?

3. How have you seen this word defined by the culture around you?

4. If you are married, have you ever experienced the struggle for control, which dates back to creation? If so, what has that struggle looked like for you?

5. Have you ever experienced the partnership and shared leadership that can occur when both people involved are following God's plan? Share an example.

6. If you are married, choose one attitude or action you can implement this week with your spouse that will demonstrate love or respect and write it below. If you are unmarried but plan to marry one day, write down one truth from what we read today that you will set in your mind as a relationship goal with a future spouse. Begin praying that God will start shaping you and your future spouse to build your marriage on His foundation. If you are unmarried and remain unmarried, commit to giving godly counsel to others in your church family.

1. See, for example, https://www.gotquestions.org/desire-husband-rule.html.
i. Answer: None of the statements are correct.

Day Two

LEADERSHIP IN THE HOME

GETTING STARTED

The battle of the sexes started in the Garden as a result of a shared disobedience to God. After the Fall, Adam and Eve used fig leaves to hide from God and one another. If the person you are with seeks their own good first, then you cannot trust them to consider your needs. If your spouse seeks their own good first, then you have reason to fear. People try to avoid or control things that can hurt them. There is nothing more painful than a relationship that should be safe but isn't.

Scripture makes it clear that God has designed the relationship between men and women to follow an order that is for the good of all. That order is for the good of all. We have equal value but differing roles in the church, home, and world.

Lord Jesus: Help me see what You want me to see today. Expose any lies I may believe and lead me to Your truth. Help me trust and obey You and walk out what I'm learning in every sphere of my life.

When Paul begins speaking to the husband in Ephesians 5, he again points to Jesus as our model. Jesus gave up His life for His bride, the church. In Ephesians 5:21, Paul writes that we submit ourselves to one another "out of reverence for Christ"—because we honor Him. In a sense, a husband discerns the real needs a wife has and then gives himself up for her by giving her what she needs at the expense of himself. In this way we are submitting to one another.

THE PRIVILEGE OF LEADERSHIP

Many men think of leadership as a privilege to be used and abused, but leadership in Scripture (and in the model Jesus gave us) is defined as a responsibility to serve others for their good. Remember that Jesus is our model for good leadership. He saw the conflict He had with us and went first to resolve it at the ultimate expense to Himself (John 3:16).

Let's look at some of the other Scriptures that describe a husband's role:

- Colossians 3:19
- 1 Peter 3:7

Notice the key words in these passages. Husbands are to love their wives just as Christ loves His church (Ephesians 5:25). As we learned in the Church Sphere, love is not a feeling but an act of the will to lay down your life for another, to give them what they need rather than what you think they deserve or what makes you comfortable.

EPHESIANS 5:21
Submit to one another out of reverence for Christ.

COLOSSIANS 3:19, NLT
Husbands, love your wives and never treat them harshly.

1 PETER 3:7
Husbands, in the same way be considerate as you live with your wives, and treat them with respect as the weaker partner and as heirs with you of the gracious gift of life, so that nothing will hinder your prayers.

1 CORINTHIANS 13:4
Love is patient, love is kind. It does not envy, it does not boast, it is not proud.

PROVERBS 13:20, NLT

Walk with the wise and become wise; associate with fools and get in trouble.

In 1 Peter 3:7, we find that if men do not deal with their wives in an understanding way, their prayers are hindered. Why is that?

My father-in-law loved my wife (his daughter) intensely. If I wanted a good relationship with him, I could not treat his daughter poorly. In the same way, your wife is a daughter of the Most High God, and He loves His daughter intensely. If you treat His daughter wrongly, your connection with God through prayer suffers.

1. Paul states that the husband is the head (the authority), but what does that mean? Mark the following statements *True* or *False*:

   a. True/False: A husband seeks God's will for his family and then goes first to do what needs to be done for those he leads.
   b. True/False: A husband discerns what he thinks his family needs without asking them their thoughts and then proceeds as "the leader."
   c. True/False: The husband facilitates good decisions by seeking and listening to the wise counsel of his wife.
   d. True/False: The husband listens to the wife and then does what she wants.
   e. True/False: The husband and wife are partners in their goal to be a godly family.
   f. True/False: The husband leads by example in humility as \he serves the needs of others in the family.
   g. True/False: The husband's job is to make the others in the family do what they think God wants them to do.[i]

As the spiritual leader of a family, a husband's first aim is to be the kind of man God wants him to be. Husbands do this by abiding in Christ and walking with other godly men, who can help them discern the truth in the various nuanced situations they will encounter (Proverbs 13:20).

The husband's role is not to force God's will (or his own) on others. We are seeking to become more like Jesus, and He does not do this to us in our lives.

With their spouse, husbands are to seek to become the kind of person who is easier to follow. When husbands love like Jesus does and seek to understand their wives—their needs and perspectives—this leads to better outcomes.

Remember, we all fail at loving perfectly. Humility requires that we seek forgiveness when—not if—we blow it. Expecting another human being to do their part perfectly is unreasonable, and humility leads us to accept others' mistakes as well. For husbands, doing your part does not guarantee that your wife will allow you to lead, but it does mean that God will walk closely with you through whatever situations you face.

PARTNERSHIP

Remember, partnership and shared leadership is the key. Husbands, your wife has abilities and insights that contribute to the family's direction and purposes. God gave us marriage as a way to fulfill us relationally and to help us achieve the Lord's purposes in life. We are called on to partner in the discipleship process with our children as we raise them in the

Lord. God wants children to have all their relational needs fulfilled in a relationship with Himself and with others in a family (which extends to a spiritual family within the church). This is spiritual community. It takes a team to pull off life as God intended.

DAY TWO REVIEW

1. What stood out to you or convicted you from today?

2. Name some ways Jesus' relationship with the church is similar to a marriage.

3. Have you ever experienced the effects of someone else trying to force God's will on you? If so, how did you respond?

4. What makes a person easy to follow?

5. If you are a married woman, what causes you to resist being led? What areas of your life may need to be submitted to Christ for the sake of God's design in marriage?

6. If you are single, what are some reasons why God would have you choose wisely about whom you would marry?

---

i. Answer: True: a, c, e, f; False: b, d, g.

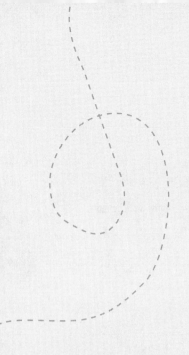

Day Three

THE PURPOSE OF PARTNERSHIP

GETTING STARTED

We were all deserving of God's wrath because of our sin, but God was merciful and gave us access to salvation by faith in Jesus. Ephesians 2:10 tells us we were saved from God's wrath for His service. We moved from living for self to living for Christ (Galatians 2:20). Now that we understand where we came from and what reality really is, we understand true and lasting value:

- eternity over the temporary;
- people over things;
- others over me;
- God's approval over peoples';
- following God's heart rather than my own;
- trusting not in my own understanding but trusting in and acknowledging Him so He can make my paths straight (Proverbs 3:5-6); and
- seeing true worth in others from God's perspective (1 Samuel 16:7).

We start to understand that storing up money and possessions for this life is essentially unwise and shortsighted. Every gift we have (physical gifts, positions or honors, financial capability) was given to us for a purpose.

Lord Jesus: Help me see what You want me to see today. Expose any lies I may believe and lead me to Your truth. Help me trust and obey You and walk out what I'm learning in every sphere of my life.

The role of parents is to raise children to know God and equip them to live in relationship with Him. If we are truly Jesus' disciples, we are committed to His mission, serving as His ambassadors to the world with the message that there is so much more than what we currently have (2 Corinthians 5:18-21). We cannot neglect that mission in our own homes. Raising children is a stewardship responsibility that God has given to parents.

Jesus told His disciples a parable to illustrate what He wanted from them until His final return, and His instructions to them show us how to view our calling as disciples not only in the world but also in our home.

Read Matthew 25:14-30.

As you read this parable, your version of the Bible may use the word *talent*. Today, a talent means a personal ability, but in Jesus' day it was an amount of money. Talents—gifts and abilities—are indeed given to us for His purposes, as we see elsewhere in Scripture.

GALATIANS 2:20

I have been crucified with Christ and I no longer live, but Christ lives in me. The life I now live in the body, I live by faith in the Son of God, who loved me and gave himself for me.

EPHESIANS 2:10

We are God's handiwork, created in Christ Jesus to do good works, which God prepared in advance for us to do.

1 SAMUEL 16:7

The Lord said to Samuel, "Do not consider his appearance or his height, for I have rejected him. The Lord does not look at the things people look at. People look at the outward appearance, but the Lord looks at the heart."

2 CORINTHIANS 5:18-21

All this is from God, who reconciled us to himself through Christ and gave us the ministry of reconciliation: that God was reconciling the world to himself in Christ, not counting people's sins against them. And he has committed to us the message of reconciliation. We are therefore Christ's ambassadors, as though God were making his appeal through us. We implore you on Christ's behalf: Be reconciled to God. God made him who had no sin to be sin for us, so that in him we might become the righteousness of God.

1. Whose wealth was it that was given to the master's servants?

2. Who does God think owns everything? (Psalm 24:1)

3. Who determines how much each servant gets?

4. What does the story reveal about what the Master wanted when He returned?

5. What are the consequences of doing nothing with what a servant is given?

6. Read Matthew 6:25-33. Does the Lord want us to store up money while He is away? What does He want us to do with what He has given us?

7. Based on what you've learned from Jesus' parable, mark the following statements *True* or *False*.

   a. True/False: What we do with what we have been given reveals what we believe about who we are—the owner or a steward/manager of what we have.

   b. True/False: The fact that the Master said the same things to the two faithful servants means that He cares not about the amount, but rather their faithfulness to serve with whatever was given them.

   c. True/False: The Master heard how the unfaithful servant saw the Master and then in effect said, "Fine, if this is how you see me and it's the reason you did nothing with what I gave you, then I will treat you as you believe."

   d. True/False: We can't take this parable too seriously because we are saved by grace, not by works.

   e. True/False: This parable reveals that Jesus knew He would go away for a while and would again come to judge the world for what they did with His things and time.

   f. True/False: True faith (trusting God and obeying Him) leads to obedience.[i]

The false statement in this list is a bit tricky. It's true that we are not saved by works but by faith, but true faith has a changed and repentant heart toward the Lord and leads to practical obedience.

PARENTING AS STEWARDSHIP

Following Jesus means that we learn His commands (Matthew 28:19) and we obey them. Children were knit together in their mother's womb for a reason (Psalm 139:13), and parents get to help guide them toward the Father, who made them for a purpose. Because of sin, we are a marred masterpiece, but through Christ we have been reclaimed and restored

MATTHEW 6:25-33

[Jesus said,] "Therefore I tell you, do not worry about your life, what you will eat or drink; or about your body, what you will wear. Is not life more than food, and the body more than clothes? Look at the birds of the air; they do not sow or reap or store away in barns, and yet your heavenly Father feeds them. Are you not much more valuable than they? Can any one of you by worrying add a single hour to your life?

"And why do you worry about clothes? See how the flowers of the field grow. They do not labor or spin. Yet I tell you that not even Solomon in all his splendor was dressed like one of these. If that is how God clothes the grass of the field, which is here today and tomorrow is thrown into the fire, will he not much more clothe you—you of little faith? So do not worry, saying, "What shall we eat?" or "What shall we drink?" or "What shall we wear?" For the pagans run after all these things, and your heavenly Father knows that you need them. But seek first his kingdom and his righteousness, and all these things will be given to you as well."

MATTHEW 28:19

"Therefore go and make disciples of all nations, baptizing them in the name of the Father and of the Son and of the Holy Spirit."

PSALM 139:13, NLT

You made all the delicate, inner parts of my body and knit me together in my mother's womb.

Notes and Thoughts

(Ephesians 2:8-10) to do the work we were saved to do while we wait for our Master's return.

This means that as parents, God has placed our children in our care so we can raise them to know Him and His mission in the world. We do this through demonstrating our own relationship with God as well as using our abilities and resources within every sphere for the Lord's mission. Parents model how they use their time, abilities, and money for the Lord's work. As our children watch us reach out to lost image bearers, make disciples, and minister to the needs of those who are on their discipleship journey, they learn what it looks like to follow God and participate in His work in the world.

DAY THREE REVIEW

1. What stood out to you or convicted you from today?

   _____

   _____

2. Does how you use your talents (abilities) and finances show others that you are following Jesus? If so, how?

   _____

   _____

3. If you are a parent, do your kids know God's mission is your priority? If so, how?

   ☐ I tell them how we set up our finances.
   ☐ They see me give at the offering time at church.
   ☐ They see me help people around me who are hurting.
   ☐ They hear me (and our family) pray about opportunities to bless others.
   ☐ Other: _____

4. Is God asking you to do something differently with your time, talents, or money for the sake of His Kingdom?

   _____

   _____

5. Who can hold you accountable for your stewardship of what God has given you?

   _____

   _____

---

i. Answer: True: a, b, c, e, f; False: d.

Day Four

DISCIPLESHIP AND FINANCES

GETTING STARTED

Today we are going to talk about giving back to God from what He has given us when it comes to finances. Tithing consistently indicates a heart position—it shows we acknowledge that all we have comes from Him and that we believe He will take care of our needs. The way we steward our finances is tangible evidence of our spiritual maturity.

Lord Jesus: Help me see what You want me to see today. Expose any lies I may believe and lead me to Your truth. Help me trust and obey You and walk out what I'm learning in every sphere of my life.

As we go through Scripture, it's hard to miss that our relationship with money matters to God. He knows that serving any other "god"—anything we put before Him—keeps us from the abundant life He offers us. While money on its own is neutral, it can easily become a source of temptation in this regard—and not just because of greed. As fallen creatures with a sinful nature, we seek to serve ourselves and avoid discomfort in the temporary, taking matters into our own hands for relief. More money allows us to rely on ourselves rather than on God, thus making us our own god.

Think back to the Garden and how the devil sought to undermine our trust in God. Satan can also use money to lie to us: to promise security, safety, and control of our own lives. Scripture shows that the devil will try to lure us away from trusting in God by giving us worldly wealth (Luke 4:3-13).

Read Acts 20:35; Colossians 3:5; and 1 Corinthians 6:9-11 (see sidebar).

God, as the Architect of our lives, gives us a way to live with money that safeguards our souls. Not only is giving more spiritually satisfying than receiving, but it is also an antidote to our temptation to make money an idol.

Read Leviticus 27:30; Matthew 23:23; and 1 Corinthians 16:1-2.

In the Old Testament, God gave His people a way to have not just enough for their own needs but also for playing their part in the mission of God as well: through a tithe.

Look up the word *tithe* and write down what it means.

_____

_____

_____

ACTS 20:35

"In everything I did, I showed you that by this kind of hard work we must help the weak, remembering the words the Lord Jesus himself said: 'It is more blessed to give than to receive.'"

COLOSSIANS 3:5, NLT

Put to death the sinful, earthly things lurking within you. Have nothing to do with sexual immorality, impurity, lust, and evil desires. Don't be greedy, for a greedy person is an idolater, worshiping the things of this world.

1 CORINTHIANS 6:9-11

Or do you not know that wrongdoers will not inherit the kingdom of God? Do not be deceived: Neither the sexually immoral nor idolaters nor adulterers nor men who have sex with men nor thieves nor the greedy nor drunkards nor slanderers nor swindlers will inherit the kingdom of God. And that is what some of you were. But you were washed, you were sanctified, you were justified in the name of the Lord Jesus Christ and by the Spirit of our God.

Notes and Thoughts

The word *tithe* in Hebrew means the "tenth part,"[1] indicating that a tenth of a person's resources—whether crops, animals, or money—was to be given to God. The tithe was not optional because it was an act of worship and obedience that God would use for His purposes in the world. In the Old Testament, a tithe was required to be given to the Temple, and an offering was what you could give freely above that.

Read Malachi 3:6-12.

We know tithing was important because God became angry when His people disobeyed. Why was God angry? He did not need their money, but tithing was the way in which God reminded the people that He was the source of all they had. Their money and resources had specific, important purposes. The tithe . . .

- fed the fatherless and the widow;
- provided for the priests, who were not given a parcel of land of their own to work; and
- was the means through which the Temple was cared for. When the tithe didn't come in, the Temple fell into disrepair (read Haggai 1:4).

The priests were to teach God's Word and offer sacrifices for the people in the Temple. Because the tithe had not come in, the priests had no living and had to go back to a different form of work. The teaching of the Word and the sacrifices were not happening. It's as if the people were saying, "We don't care about God's Word, and we don't care about our sin."

Other countries had poured their wealth into their false gods, but the true God was not being honored by His own people. God's people were supposed to live for Him and others as a testimony to the whole world about how great the true God was. But if God's own people did not honor or appreciate Him, then why would anyone else?

1. Because people used what they had (time, talents, money) for themselves rather than for the Lord, what do you think was left undone in God's mission?

_____

_____

2. Reference Malachi 3:6-12 and put a checkmark next to the statements that seem correct to you.

   ☐ The Jews were not bringing the whole tithe to the storehouse (the Temple), which implies they were only giving a partial amount.

   ☐ The Jews were not bringing the money to the storehouse.

   ☐ God warned them that if they didn't give in God's prescribed way rather than in the way they wanted to give, there would be consequences.

   ☐ God promised He would supply their needs if His people would be obedient.

Giving a portion of our resources to the Lord is not an outdated practice. Just as the Temple was God's place in Old Testament Jerusalem, the church is the living temple in the New Testament era. We also have a job to do, and that job requires our resources to move forward.

3. Why do you think many Christians today do not support the Lord's church with their resources?

☐ They are spending their money on themselves.

☐ They don't want to give it to the church, so they give it wherever they want when they do give.

☐ They give whatever amount they have in their wallet, rather than what Scripture prescribes.

☐ They don't trust churches because of what they have heard about how churches spend money.

☐ Other: _____

4. What effect do you think Christians not obeying God's command to tithe has had on the church's ability to fulfill His mission?

DAY FOUR REVIEW

1. What stood out to you or convicted you from today?

2. Is tithing a new concept to you, or is it something you have already been practicing?

3. Have you ever disagreed with the way a church has handled their finances? If so, have you spoken with any of the leaders about your concerns? Why or why not?

4. Has there ever been a time you gave an offering (amount above your tithe) to someone or something? Write about how that experience made you feel.

5. Is there something God is showing you or convicting you of today? What might He be calling you to change about your current finances and budget?

1. Blue Letter Bible, "Lexicon: Strong's H4643—*ma'ăśēr*," accessed April 5, 2024, https://www.blueletterbible.org/lexicon/h4643/niv/wlc/0-1.

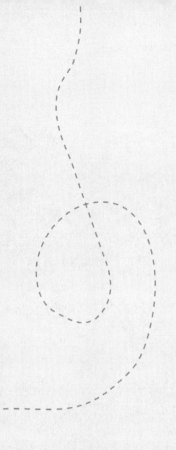

Day Five

PARENTS AND CHILDREN

GETTING STARTED

If you are walking through this discipleship journey as a parent, you need to know that your credibility in your children's lives is directly affected by your desire and commitment to follow Jesus faithfully. Bear that in mind as you read through today's lesson.

Lord Jesus: Help me see what You want me to see today. Expose any lies I may believe and lead me to Your truth. Help me trust and obey You and walk out what I'm learning in every sphere of my life.

Paul now goes on to speak to children and parents about God's architectural plans that refer to them.

Read Ephesians 6:1-4 (see sidebar).

Notice that in these verses Paul points the children back to the Ten Commandments to show them God's plan for the family. Children are told they must obey their parents. He is talking here to children who live at home. God's plan is that parents will become the main teachers of their children concerning God's truth. He promises that if children will obey their parents, then they will enjoy a long life.

HUMILITY (AGAIN!)

God commands every person in the human family to live in humility. A father loves, laying down his own life for the good of another. Husbands are to lay down their life as Christ laid down His life for the church. Men must submit their very being so that they can meet needs in their family. Wives are to submit to their husbands, and children are to obey their parents.

Of course, as we've mentioned before, obedience and submission to other humans comes with an important boundary: If we are asked to sin against God, then we must choose to humbly say no. But this is always a serious matter requiring wise counsel.

DISCIPLESHIP IN THE FAMILY

Let's look again at Ephesians 6:4, where Paul directs us toward the goal of Christian parents—especially the father—in raising children. Paul is telling the parents that they must instruct their children in the Lord. This is reminiscent of Matthew 28:19, which says we must make disciples, baptizing them and teaching them to obey all that Jesus commanded. You see, parents are to disciple their kids.

EPHESIANS 6:1-4

Children, obey your parents in the Lord, for this is right. "Honor your father and mother"—which is the first commandment with a promise—"so that it may go well with you and that you may enjoy long life on the earth."

Fathers, do not exasperate your children; instead, bring them up in the training and instruction of the Lord.

Often when people read or reference Ephesians 6:4, they forget that this verse is part of an overall letter and is built on things that have come before it:

- We are saved by grace through faith (Ephesians 2:8). Now we have a relationship with God, and we abide in Him and in His Word.

- God's Spirit indwells us, and we now also abide within the community of believers.

- God has told us that we are saved for good works in the church, our homes, and our work lives.

- We are part of a new spiritual nation, and our allegiance is to the King and the spiritual nation that He oversees.

- The community of believers has the same beliefs (one faith, one Lord, one baptism; Ephesians 4:5).

- In the church, we have a different kind of relationship with other believers: We love each other, we exhort one another, and we support one another.

Parents in the Christian home are fellow believers in Christ who are learning to obey Jesus and live unselfish lives together in partnership. Children living in this context are told to obey and honor their parents.

With this family structure in mind, fathers are now told to teach their kids. If parents are living the kind of life Paul describes in the first part of Ephesians, there is no hypocrisy in what they teach. Failure and humble confession, yes—but not hypocrisy (acting or game playing). Because the family lives within a community of relationships in the church, the children are seeing and hearing a consistent message. Children are learning where they came from and what life is about—they are understanding their purpose.

The goal of discipleship for children, as with all others, is that they learn to grow in spiritual maturity. As the child gets older and the relational environment changes, so does the command. Grown children who leave their parents' home are told to honor their father and mother. This means that we respect our parents and care for them, but not that we must obey them. (For further study on dealing with your parents when you no longer live in their home, see Jesus' teaching in Matthew 15.)

HOW TO DISCIPLE YOUR CHILDREN

In the Old Testament, God tells us what discipleship at home looks like. You will see that Jesus, as the spiritual parent in His discipleship group, used this approach with His disciples.

Read Deuteronomy 6:1-12 (see sidebar).

1. To whom is Moses writing?

DEUTERONOMY 6:1-12, NLT

[Moses said,] "These are the commands, decrees, and regulations that the LORD your God commanded me to teach you. You must obey them in the land you are about to enter and occupy, and you and your children and grandchildren must fear the LORD your God as long as you live. If you obey all his decrees and commands, you will enjoy a long life. Listen closely, Israel, and be careful to obey. Then all will go well with you, and you will have many children in the land flowing with milk and honey, just as the LORD, the God of your ancestors, promised you.

"Listen, O Israel! The LORD is our God, the LORD alone. And you must love the LORD your God with all your heart, all your soul, and all your strength. And you commit yourselves wholeheartedly to these commands that I am giving you today. Repeat them again and again to your children. Talk about them when you are at home and when you are on the road, when you are going to bed and when you are getting up. Tie them to your hands and wear them on your foreheads as symbols. Write them on the doorposts of your house and on your gates.

"The LORD your God will soon bring you into the land he swore to give you when he made a vow to your ancestors Abraham, Isaac, and Jacob. It is a land with large, prosperous cities that you did not build. The houses will be richly stocked with goods you did not produce. You will draw water from cisterns you did not dig, and you will eat from vineyards and olive trees you did not plant. When you have eaten your fill in this land, be careful not to forget the LORD, who rescued you from slavery in the land of Egypt."

2. What was the environment like for the people who received this?

3. What had to come first in the heart of the parents?

4. What were they to teach their kids?

5. How were they to teach their kids?

6. What were they to guard against?

As parents, we must remember that our example and our partnership with our spouse affects our children's spiritual lives. Our sincere commitment to follow God faithfully is our credibility as parents in a world with false gods and differing views.

For example, if we say we love God and expect our kids to know and obey Him too but don't model that, our children become confused. If relationship is the key, and God's Spirit gives us the ability to love, and yet we don't do that well—then our children will wonder about the truth of our beliefs.

Read Malachi 2:13-15 (see sidebar).

Divorce between believers is a severe blow to our spiritual lives, our church's unity, and our children's ability to believe there is something different about us as Christians. God absolutely forgives and can even get involved in our lives and help us deal with consequences, but there is still a price to pay for not obeying Jesus and not loving people the way He commands. Whether we divorce ourselves from His community, the church, or we divorce ourselves from our spouse, that separation grieves God and affects our children spiritually.

Similarly, many have married unbelievers and suffered as a result. They may have married someone who claimed to be a believer, but over the years that person has demonstrated little fruit of their faith. As a result, being in a godly partnership has been very hard. These people will need God's help from wise counsel to know how to deal with the issues that result. This is why the community of believers and spiritual fathers and mothers and brothers and sisters are so important.

Some Pharisees came to him to test him. They asked, "Is it lawful for a man to divorce his wife for any and every reason?"

"Haven't you read," he replied, "that at the beginning the Creator 'made them male and female,' and said, 'For this reason a man will leave his father and mother and be united to his wife, and the two will become one flesh'? So they are no longer two, but one flesh. Therefore what God has joined together, let no one separate."

"Why then," they asked, "did Moses command that a man give his wife a certificate of divorce and send her away?"

MALACHI 2:13-15

Another thing you do: You flood the LORD's altar with tears. You weep and wail because he no longer looks with favor on your offerings or accepts them with pleasure from your hands. You ask, "Why?" It is because the LORD is the witness between you and the wife of your youth. You have been unfaithful to her, though she is your partner, the wife of your marriage covenant.

Has not the one God made you? You belong to him in body and spirit. And what does the one God seek? Godly offspring. So be on your guard, and do not be unfaithful to the wife of your youth.

Jesus replied, "Moses permitted you to divorce your wives because your hearts were hard. But it was not this way from the beginning. I tell you that anyone who divorces his wife, except for sexual immorality, and marries another woman commits adultery."

The disciples said to him, "If this is the situation between a husband and wife, it is better not to marry."

MATTHEW 19:3-10

Remember, God forgives if there is true repentance, but there are still real consequences to sin in this life. Ask for God's help through His Holy Spirit (who never contradicts God's Word) and His people to figure out how to deal with past mistakes.

DAY FIVE REVIEW

1. What stood out to you or convicted you from today?

2. Where does God expect children to receive their teaching about Him?

3. According to Deuteronomy 6, what is discipleship in the family supposed to look like?

4. Share an occasion as a parent or spouse when you have had to humble or submit yourself to another.

5. Is there something in your past or current situation that makes these principles hard for you? Relationships are hard because people are messy. If there is some family bitterness or trauma you are dealing with, past or present, find someone you can share it with and ask for prayer and accountability from them as God leads you toward healing.

THE HOME AND FAMILY SPHERE (CONTINUED)

Day One

YOUR FAMILY + GOD'S FAMILY

GETTING STARTED

On our spiritual road trip we accepted Christ when the gospel was shared with us, and then we got connected in a spiritual relational vehicle and the Holy Spirit started to change the way we thought and lived. As time went by, our lives became a ministry to God and others, rather than a vacuum to suck the life out of others. As we changed, our mission became clearer and clearer within the Five Spheres Paul describes in Ephesians and Colossians.

Lord Jesus: Help me see what You want me to see today. Expose any lies I may believe and lead me to Your truth. Help me trust and obey You and walk out what I'm learning in every sphere of my life.

Abiding in Christ affects our relationship with those in His spiritual family and body. God's desire is that as we live in relationship with Him and with others in His family, we will experience life as He intended it this side of heaven. (This world will never be heaven no matter what we do, but we will experience how good it can be when we follow His architectural plans.)

Just as our abiding life affects every other sphere, our church life is supposed to affect our Home and Family Sphere. Within the community of believers we find a place to live out our true, God-given identities. We find encouragement, teaching, support, accountability, and lifelong relationships.

Within the community of believers we find a place to be our true God-given identities. We find encouragement, teaching, support, accountability, and life-long relationships.

- Men find encouragement and honest accountability from older men, receive wise counsel when difficult situations arise, and become true friends who do life together.

- Women develop godly relationships with other women who pray with them, encourage them, and help them live wisely by holding them accountable when they are off course.

- Children are raised in a community that helps support the biblical truths we see in Scripture. They develop relationships with other Christian kids whom they can do life with. Other adults reinforce what their parents say, so that truth doesn't only come from the parents. When they're grown, children can find godly spouses among the other young people in the church.

 Scan QR code to access video podcasts and other content that accompanies this week's session.

Because we are part of God's family, we have godly spiritual grandparents and uncles and aunts and brothers and sisters. The church is meant to be this kind of spiritual community!

1. Why do you think that the church often doesn't look like this?

   ☐ Churches I have attended have not been set up like that.
   ☐ I haven't committed myself to being in that kind of community because I didn't know I was supposed to—I wasn't discipled.
   ☐ I have refused to commit the time needed to have this kind of spiritual family.
   ☐ I don't have time to make godly friends; I spend most of my time with people who are not part of God's family.
   ☐ Other: _____

GOD'S FAMILY AS A PRIORITY

There have been so many times God's family has helped me in the Home and Family Sphere:

- When I was angry at my wife, godly men listened to my frustration and prayed with me. They gave me Scripture to read about my part of the problem and asked me to do what God would have me do no matter who was in the wrong.
- Godly women listened to my wife's frustrations and prayed with my wife, pointing her back to honoring God by doing what He asked her to do, rather than doing what I deserved.
- I got godly counsel from friends when my rebellious son was dealing with a drug addiction.
- Other men spoke into my sons' lives when my sons were over at their houses with their kids, and my sons were able to hear them even when they wouldn't listen to me.
- My sons had relationships with godly kids, who provided positive influences that steered them away from things that would destroy them.
- My sons met and married godly women from our youth groups.
- My sons have men pouring into them in the small groups they are in.
- My sons were given the opportunity to serve in the church and mature into their roles as spiritual leaders.
- When Lori and I were struggling with tragedy, our spiritual family cried with us and encouraged us.
- When we had a victory with our son's addiction, so many who had prayed and reached out during that time joined us in a huge victory party.
- I have great friends to play games with, to fish and hunt with, to talk to and hang out with when it is time to just have fun.
- I have lifelong friends who know when I am getting off course and challenge me to refocus on Jesus.

- My wife and I have friends we can hang out together with for fun.
- My family went on mission trips together and formed relationships with others as a result.
- My kids went on mission trips with the youth group and built relationships that they will have the rest of their lives.

To have this kind of spiritual community, I had to be committed to making it a priority in my life. Many people may want that kind of community but will not do what it takes to have it. Yes, we've sometimes had difficulties with relationships and had to choose whether we would take our ball and go home (move to another town or church) or fight for the relationship. I've had a struggle with almost every friend I have, and through fighting to resolve things I've developed stronger relationships and deeper trust than I ever thought possible.

2. If you were in this kind of spiritual community, how would you live out the following verses?

Do not be misled: "Bad company corrupts good character."
1 CORINTHIANS 15:33

Do not be yoked together with unbelievers. For what do righteousness and wickedness have in common? Or what fellowship can light have with darkness? What harmony is there between Christ and Belial? Or what does a believer have in common with an unbeliever? What agreement is there between the temple of God and idols? For we are the temple of the living God. As God has said: "I will live with them and walk among them, and I will be their God, and they will be my people." Therefore, "Come out from them and be separate, says the Lord. Touch no unclean thing, and I will receive you." And, "I will be a Father to you, and you will be my sons and daughters, says the Lord Almighty."
2 CORINTHIANS 6:14-18

The godly give good advice to their friends; the wicked lead them astray.
PROVERBS 12:26, NLT

Plans succeed through good counsel; don't go to war without wise advice.
PROVERBS 20:18, NLT

In Deuteronomy 6, which we read yesterday, we discovered that the Israelites were going into a country with false gods where they would face aggressive attacks on their faith. God was telling them through Moses to get their children ready.

Relationship with God and relationships with other believers built around faith are like the ropes that hold us fast and strong when the waves of the culture crash in on us. If you have no ropes, you have no stability. People who are abiding in Christ and in relationship with a spiritual community and who are working as a family centered on God's architectural plans and purposes hold fast and thrive in a broken world.

DAY ONE REVIEW

1. What stood out to you or convicted you from today?

2. Consider the characteristics of the spiritual community you read about in this section. Do you believe you have these kinds of friendships and community within your church? Why or why not?

3. What steps do you think you need to take to ensure this kind of community is available for you and your family? What might you need to give up?

4. Write down below how much time you as an individual and your family spend each week in community with God's people. How do you think God would view the amount? What do you think the fruit of spending enough time in community looks like?

Day Two

SINGLE BUT NOT ALONE

GETTING STARTED

If you are currently on this disciple's journey as a single person, I want you to know that the principles in the Home and Family Sphere still apply to you. We all have a home in the body of Christ. You may be single, but as a child of God you are never alone. God's plan is for His body, the church, to help fill in the gaps.

Lord Jesus: Help me see what You want me to see today. Expose any lies I may believe and lead me to Your truth. Help me trust and obey You and walk out what I'm learning in every sphere of my life.

Many who accepted Jesus during His time on Earth would lose their family when they chose to follow Him. Some were cast aside by their spouses, and because of that some lost their children too. Jesus told us that if we chose our families over Him, then we could not be His disciples (Matthew 10:37). The church became the only family some would have at that time. This is also true today in many countries where Christianity is illegal or looked down upon by other religious cultures.

At the same time in the early church, some had no family for a variety of other reasons. Maybe a woman became a widow and had no children. Maybe someone lost their parents and never married. In fact, Paul makes it clear that he was not married and that he felt it was better not to be married in some cases.

Whether you are married or single, you are an equally valuable part of God's family and have a Home and Family Sphere. God's plan is for us all to have relationships in every sphere of our lives.

Read 1 Corinthians 7:1-15 (see sidebar).

We may be called to be single, but we are never called to be alone! A biological family is not our only or even our primary home. We are citizens of the Kingdom of heaven, children of God, brothers and sisters in Christ! The church is our spiritual home, and we have each been given gifts, abilities, time, and more to help with being a grandmother, grandfather, mentor, friend, uncle, or aunt to those within the church.

Within this spiritual family, people who are single have unique wisdom and perspective to offer, and they often have more energy and flexible time to devote to serving God and connecting with other believers. In 1 Corinthians 7, Paul tells us that he can be totally committed to serving the Lord without the responsibility of a wife. In 1 Timothy 5:3-16 we read that widows can serve the Lord and their family without being married again. According to Paul, being single can be the best for some people—it is even called a gift.

The church is also a place where single people can experience the support and care of a family. There are so many single moms or struggling parents that need the help of the available

MATTHEW 10:37

"Anyone who loves their father or mother more than me is not worthy of me; anyone who loves their son or daughter more than me is not worthy of me."

1 CORINTHIANS 7:1-15

Now for the matters you wrote about: "It is good for a man not to have sexual relations with a woman." But since sexual immorality is occurring, each man should have sexual relations with his own wife, and each woman with her own husband. The husband should fulfill his marital duty to his wife, and likewise the wife to her husband. The wife does not have authority over her own body but yields it to her husband. In the same way, the husband does not have authority over his own body but yields it to his wife. Do not deprive each other except perhaps by mutual consent and for a time, so that you may devote yourselves to prayer. Then come together again so that Satan will not tempt you because of your lack of self-control. I say this as a concession, not as a command. I wish that all of you were as I am. But each of you has your own gift from God; one has this gift, another has that.

1 CORINTHIANS 7:1-15
(CONTINUED)

Now to the unmarried and the widows I say: It is good for them to stay unmarried, as I do. But if they cannot control themselves, they should marry, for it is better to marry than to burn with passion.

To the married I give this command (not I, but the Lord): A wife must not separate from her husband. But if she does, she must remain unmarried or else be reconciled to her husband. And a husband must not divorce his wife.

To the rest I say this (I, not the Lord): If any brother has a wife who is not a believer and she is willing to live with him, he must not divorce her. And if a woman has a husband who is not a believer and he is willing to live with her, she must not divorce him. For the unbelieving husband has been sanctified through his wife, and the unbelieving wife has been sanctified through her believing husband. Otherwise your children would be unclean, but as it is, they are holy.

But if the unbeliever leaves, let it be so. The brother or the sister is not bound in such circumstances; God has called us to live in peace.

body of Christ. They need the family of God to help them raise godly children and be with them as they go through life.

When I think of the church working together as a family, I think of a couple of people I know. One is a widow who lost her husband many years ago. She later lost her son. This woman has helped so many other women in our church, and my wife is one of them. She has been a source of friendship, comfort, and wisdom to so many. She has been single but never alone, and God has used her to save many marriages, families, and children. I have another friend who is a single older man who uses his handyman skills to help many struggling young families in our church. He makes himself available not only to serve but also to lead a men's Bible study that includes other single men and widowers. He, too, is single but never alone (Psalm 68:6).

LIFE TOGETHER

Whether single people are divorced, single by choice, or waiting for the right person, they are part of God's family, with gifts and abilities to offer the community and needs to care for.

1. There are many ways the church can come alongside single brothers and sisters. Mark the following statements *True* or *False*.

    a. True/False: A single mom needs godly male figures in her children's lives so that the children can learn the importance of fatherhood.
    b. True/False: A single parent does not need any help financially.
    c. True/False: A single parent needs help with the kids so that they can get some time to themselves.
    d. True/False: A single dad doesn't need any help from a godly woman who can show his children what womanhood should look like.
    e. True/False: Just as someone needs a physical family around them in a home to support them and help them grow, a single person needs a spiritual family around them to help them grow and support them through both good and bad times.
    f. True/False: Single parents need spiritual grandparents and uncles and aunts to create a spiritual community.[i]

Oftentimes, singles feel like they are out of place in the church. Because they are divorced, widowed, or have never been married, they feel they are too different and have nothing to contribute. Many with families are so busy that they don't think beyond the immediate demands of life, and the enemy likes to use this to pit us against each other in God's family. He wants married couples or families to feel like they shouldn't have to give up their time, and he wants singles to feel excluded. People in families need to ask for the Lord's help to see those who are single around them as potential valuable friends, and they need to take intentional steps to build relationships with single people. And, if you are single, notice when the enemy is lying to you about who you are and the value you bring to a friendship. Ask God to lead you to spiritual family.

Our understanding of the role of single people in God's family is often limited: Often we do not recognize and learn from their unique spiritual contributions to the community.

God does not see married people or people who are parents as more useful or valuable to His Kingdom than single people are. He desires to use all of us for His glory.

2. Consider the following statements about the role of single people in the church. Mark your answers *True* or *False*:

   a. True/False: Married people don't want to hang out with single people.
   b. True/False: There is nothing that a single person can do to help a married family.
   c. True/False: Life groups are great places where married and single people can do life together.
   d. True/False: Single people can be spiritual parents and help others along their discipleship journey.
   e. True/False: If you are single, you can't learn anything from a group with married people in it.
   f. True/False: The devil loves to isolate people, and one of the ways he does this is by making singles feel excluded in the church.
   g. True/False: A single person can help with a single-parent home in huge ways.[ii]

The apostle Paul was single, and God used him to give us our framework for a godly home! He became the spiritual parent of great men like Timothy, who previously had no spiritual father in his life. God's desire is that we all find a place in the family of God. We all have needs and abilities that, if shared, can make the church and the home a respite from the storms of life.

DAY TWO REVIEW

1. What stood out to you or convicted you from today?

   _____

   _____

2. Share about someone among your family or friends who is single and has had an impact on your life.

   _____

3. Consider a single person or single parent in your life whom God is calling you to help or encourage. Write down the person's name and an action you will take this week to connect with them.

   _____

4. If you are a single person, do you believe your singleness has had an impact on how you live out community in the church body? Share below and with the group both the negative and positive differences you see in church community due to singleness.

   _____

   _____

---

i. Answer: True: a, c, e, f; False: b, d.
ii. Answer: True: c, d, f, g; False: a, b, e.

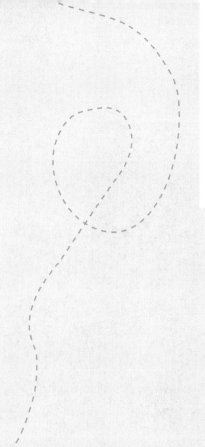

Day Three

PARENTING AS A DISCIPLE

GETTING STARTED

The whole purpose of our discipleship road trip is to become more spiritually mature along the way. We start out as spiritually dead until we hear and receive the shared message of the gospel. We are then born again and become an infant in Christ.

We are invited into a spiritual family/connection where we begin to learn God's Word (1 Peter 2:2) with spiritually mature parents who invest in us and disciple us to know and understand His Word (Hebrews 5:11-13). We also begin to understand our identity in Christ rather than the broken one we were born with.

As our understanding of God's truth and His love grows, we become more like Him—we grow into childhood and young adulthood, and finally we grow to become spiritual parents ourselves. Now we are part of a community filled with spiritual parents, infants, children, and young adults all learning to live for Christ on mission with Him in the Five Spheres.

Lord Jesus: Help me see what You want me to see today. Expose any lies I may believe and lead me to Your truth. Help me trust and obey You and walk out what I'm learning in every sphere of my life.

Discipleship is learning to follow Christ, being changed by Him and committed to His mission in every sphere of our lives. The mission of the church is to make disciples of all nations, and part of that mission is teaching parents to become mature disciplemakers in the Home and Family Sphere. When that happens, their children can become not only physical adults who can contribute to their own families but also spiritually mature disciples who can make disciples in their own homes.

1. What do you believe is the most important purpose of a physical parent?

    ☐ To raise their child to be independent, able to support themselves and eventually a family.
    ☐ To help their child become what the parent wished they themselves would have been.
    ☐ To protect their child from what hurt them in the past.
    ☐ To make sure their child gets a good college education so they can succeed in life.
    ☐ To help their child discover their dream and achieve it.
    ☐ Other: _____

Perhaps you have already raised your children and feel as though, knowing what you know now, you would have done it differently. You may be feeling that you have missed

1 PETER 2:2

Like newborn babies, crave pure spiritual milk, so that by it you may grow up in your salvation.

HEBREWS 5:11-13

We have much to say about this, but it is hard to make it clear to you because you no longer try to understand. In fact, though by this time you ought to be teachers, you need someone to teach you the elementary truths of God's word all over again. You need milk, not solid food! Anyone who lives on milk, being still an infant, is not acquainted with the teaching about righteousness.

out. But it is never too late. The place to start is by confessing and repenting before the Lord. The next step is asking forgiveness from your children.

Be honest with your Christian friends about your failure and struggle. Then seek wise counsel to help you know where to start and give you encouragement and accountability to continue, even when you face uphill battles.

My mom and dad did their best when I was growing up. They both were undisciplined believers who were trying to do their best but who often failed. But as time went on, they learned and grew, and those lessons changed the way they parented. And becoming empty nesters didn't mean that their job was done—not even close. In fact, the best teaching times come when your kids discover they don't know what they thought they did. Life can humble you, and what parents do next can affect their kids forever. My parents pursued me and loved me though I had hurt them consistently in my teenage years.

Now that Lori and I are empty nesters, we still consistently live our lives around our children (and grandchildren!). More than ever, it takes a family that works together to raise children who know Jesus. Lori watches our grandkids several days a week so our kids can work with confidence that their kids are protected. We want our kids to have date nights so that they stay connected with their spouses.

Where did we learn this from? Lori's parents and my parents modeled consistent support for us in our marriage and parenting times. Our parents moved to our area when they were in their early sixties because their idea of legacy was a family that reproduced godly offspring. I would never have gotten through the trial with my oldest son if it had not been for the support of our physical family and spiritual family (the church). For my father and mother to do this meant a great deal of sacrifice, but their priorities were set: Eternity matters most!

Of course, not all families can provide that kind of support. Many people don't have those kinds of parents. However, even in a season when my parents did not live near us, we were still sustained by God's family—the church.

I am so grateful for people who have cared for me and my family as though we were their own. Some had no family of their own and responded to our desire for them to enter ours. They were blessed, and so were we. Others were mature believers who intentionally pressed into my family because they understood God's intentions for spiritual family. Again, we were blessed and so were they.

More than ever, it takes a family that works together to raise children who know Jesus.

DAY THREE REVIEW

1. What stood out to you or convicted you from today?

_____

_____

_____

2. What part does abiding in Christ play in our ability to raise our children?

_____

_____

_____

3. What part does being part of God's family have to do with raising our children to become spiritually mature?

4. What changes do we need to make if our families are to be focused on discipleship and the things of God?

5. What is one change you can personally implement this week to help you become a more effective disciplemaker to your family?

Day Four

GOD'S DESIGN FOR ADULT CHILDREN AND THEIR PARENTS

GETTING STARTED

The charge God gives us to honor our parents does not go away when we grow out of childhood and are no longer living under their roof. Honoring our parents is a posture that we are called to continue to hold throughout our lives—it just looks differently once we are adults. And once again, God in His Word shows us how to live out the things He calls us to do.

Lord Jesus: Help me see what You want me to see today. Expose any lies I may believe and lead me to Your truth. Help me trust and obey You and walk out what I'm learning in every sphere of my life.

In the Old Testament and in Jesus' day, those who no longer could support themselves through work didn't have a social security or retirement plan in place to take care of them. Their retirement program was their children. This is why it was so heartbreaking for people who could not have children in ancient times. Just as parents raised, protected, and supplied for their children, the children cared for their parents later on.

While this is not how our culture today usually functions, we as believers have surrendered to the Lord's directions given in His Word. The family is not built on our cultural situations or the times we live in, but rather upon God's design:

"Honor your father and your mother, so that you may live long in the land the LORD your God is giving you."

EXODUS 20:12

Children, obey your parents in the Lord, for this is right. "Honor your father and mother"—which is the first commandment with a promise—"so that it may go well with you and that you may enjoy long life on the earth."

EPHESIANS 6:1-3

And [Jesus] continued, "You have a fine way of setting aside the commands of God in order to observe your own traditions! For Moses said, 'Honor your father and mother,' and, 'Anyone who curses their father or mother is to be put to death.' But you say that if anyone declares that what might have been used to help their father or mother is Corban (that is, devoted to God)—then you no longer let them do anything for their father or mother. Thus you nullify the word of God by your tradition that you have handed down. And you do many things like that."

MARK 7:9-13

When you are older and no longer under your parents' supervision, you are called on to honor them by having a respectful and helpful relationship with them.

Jesus was frustrated with the religious leaders of His day because they had taught and modeled a disobedience to what God had commanded. You see, in Jesus' time Pharisees (religious leaders) would give money in public so that they could gain praise from their higher-ups. The more they showed their supposed righteousness through physical appearance, the higher their standing was in the religious community. So rather than take care of their parents, they would declare that they had given to the Temple instead. Not because they loved God but because it gained them a better life for themselves. They were honoring God with their lips, but their hearts were far from Him.

It's not so different today. Many today don't care for their aging parents or even visit them in a nursing home regularly. Sometimes it's because the adult children feel overwhelmed; sometimes they simply don't want the hassle. As a result, the elderly are all too often missed, dismissed, and forgotten.

God's design for the family as seen in Scripture is meant to take care of the real needs of people. That's why Jesus declared to the Pharisees on more than one occasion that obedience is better than sacrifice. Honoring your father and mother when you are a child living in their home would be obeying them. When you are older and no longer under your parents' supervision, you are called on to honor them by having a respectful and helpful relationship with them.

> Take care of any widow who has no one else to care for her. But if she has children or grandchildren, their first responsibility is to show godliness at home and repay their parents by taking care of them. This is something that pleases God.
>
> Now a true widow, a woman who is truly alone in this world, has placed her hope in God. She prays night and day, asking God for his help.
>
> I TIMOTHY 5:3-5, NLT

The early church worked together to help those who had no family to help them. Christians were also commanded to care for their own family (their aging parents and grandparents).

Today, we live in a world that separates people in different houses and far-off geographical locations. If that's the case for you, that doesn't mean you miss out on God's plan for His people to live in relationship with one another, to be a community of nurturers who work together to raise godly children. You may not be able to be part of that kind of life because of the choices of others in your past, but you can start to build your life now based on these plans for your family's future.

Consider the following statements about caring for your parents as they age, and mark them *True* or *False*.

a. True/False: Caring for your parents in their old age has no practical benefits for your family.

b. True/False: Caring for your parents enables your children to be loved by an extra set of hands and watched with an extra pair of eyes.

c. True/False: Caring for your parents when they are unable to care for themselves should always be done in your own house.

d. True/False: Caring for your parents means that you must learn to forgive them for their past failings and you must seek forgiveness for yours as well.

e. True/False: Caring for widows and orphans is the responsibility of the church.

f. True/False: Honoring our parents means we do what they want us to do.[i]

Read James 1:2.

Caring for your parents in their old age can have many benefits, including that they may help you raise your family. Your own children get the benefit of their wisdom and care, and if your parents are committed followers of Jesus, your children learn from their relationship with Christ as well as yours. My parents invested in my children when my kids didn't want to listen to their parents. They took them fishing and camping, as well as helped them with homework. They gave Lori and me the ability to have a date night every week. My mother-in-law lives with Lori and me, and she and Lori watch our grandkids together during the week so that our children can work.

In some cases we do not have the ability to care for our parents physically because they have health issues beyond our capability. Our parents may get to the point where we cannot take care of them in our own homes, needing care we cannot give them. Honoring them in this situation looks like ensuring they get the care they need. Even if they have saved enough for retirement and may not need money or a place to live, honoring them involves camaraderie and relationship. They may be unhappy about the decisions we make to care for them, but giving our parents what they think they want, rather than what God's Word says they need, is not real love. We honor God by putting Him first, and this may mean that people are unhappy with us. We give or withhold not because of anger or hurt but because what they want us to do is unloving from God's standpoint.

Some nuances created by sin may make it unhealthy to have our parents in our home. Sin has complicated life so much, and we must act wisely. Our parents may be a negative influence that we cannot allow in the lives of our kids without our presence. If our parents are unsafe, we cannot risk our own children, whom we are to protect. But again, in God's perfect plan, we take our parents into consideration in what we do. We must consider what Scripture teaches and apply it wisely to our circumstances. We don't do what we do because of what our parents deserve but out of reverence for Christ. We should care for our parents in a way that does not threaten our children's security. If a parent is not safe for our spouse, we must choose our spouse's safety and well-being over our parents'. In these cases, we need to help where we can without leaving our direct responsibility to our spouse and kids unmet.

Finally, if we have broken relationships with our parents, we must remember that restoring relationships is what Jesus is all about, so we should be about it as well. We must seek reconciliation as far as we are able to without sin (Romans 12:18). This may mean we must forgive our family members when they seek it. We may need to ask for forgiveness from our parents for what we have done. We may need to forgive them for our own sake even when they don't show remorse. Remember, a lack of forgiveness contaminates our

ROMANS 12:18, NLT
Do all that you can to live in peace with everyone.

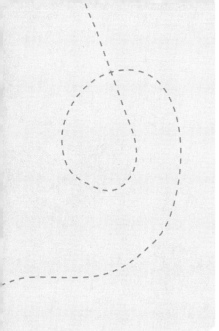

own hearts. This does not mean that we must trust people who have harmed us or that we forget the harm they caused but that we release it to the only one who can: Jesus. If you have bitterness or unforgiveness toward a parent due to past struggles, pray this week that God will show you how to resolve and heal it, and find someone to confess it to who can also pray for you.

The job of the Lord's church is to care for widows and orphans. This means that we recognize that our responsibility is both to our blood relatives and to all whom the Lord puts in our spiritual family (the church). When we see someone who has lost their family or never had one, we become to them what God has declared us to be "in Christ"—the family of God.

Notes and Thoughts

DAY FOUR REVIEW

1. What stood out to you or convicted you from today?

2. What would be some of the practical benefits you or your children might gain by spending time with your parents (or your spouse's parents)?

3. Share a couple of the ways you have honored your parents since becoming an adult.

---

i. Answer: True: b, d, e; False: a, c, f.

Day Five

RETIREMENT AS A SPIRITUAL GOAL

GETTING STARTED

Did yesterday's lesson change anything about the way you think about your parents and your relationship with them as they age? Today we are going to look at what God expects of us as we ourselves begin to age. Do you have a financial plan for your future as you get older? What about your spiritual life: Do you also have a plan for how you will serve as a disciple of Jesus as you move closer to the end of your time here on Earth?

> *Lord Jesus: Help me see what You want me to see today. Expose any lies I may believe and lead me to Your truth. Help me trust and obey You and walk out what I'm learning in every sphere of my life.*

In America, Christians are often in pursuit of the same things the rest of the world goes after: seeking their identity and satisfaction in a job title and trying to accumulate wealth and possessions (Matthew 6:25-34). Rather than putting Jesus first and living for His mission, they want God to help them pursue their own mission of getting more of what the world offers.

Most people don't serve the Lord very much in their younger years, and then in their older years they seek to enjoy themselves. Christians hope to earn enough to retire some day and live the rest of their lives for their own dreams, which they feel they have earned. At a time when they could be serving their family by helping raise up a generation who knows and serves God and His mission, they are often moving somewhere warm and away from all the "worries" of life. They may say they had to raise their kids without help, so now it's their kids' turn.

Would it surprise you that retirement is not a biblical concept? Years ago I asked my pastor father if he was going to retire when he turned sixty-five. He asked me a question in return: "When you turn sixty-five, if Jesus hasn't returned, will there still be people going to hell if they die without Jesus?"

I said yes. He said, "Then I guess I am not retiring because this isn't a job I get paid for—it's a mission given by the Lord until He returns."

My father and mother to this day still serve the Lord. My father's health is iffy at best, but he volunteers as an elder in our church, shepherding as he always has. My mom still works for the Lord in ministry as well. They both help us raise our grandkids (their great-grandkids) and pour into all our lives. They could have moved away, but the mission isn't done. They are also spiritual parents and grandparents to many in our church and model for others what a spiritual family looks like.

MATTHEW 6:25-34

[Jesus said,] "Therefore I tell you, do not worry about your life, what you will eat or drink; or about your body, what you will wear. Is not life more than food, and the body more than clothes? Look at the birds of the air; they do not sow or reap or store away in barns, and yet your heavenly Father feeds them. Are you not much more valuable than they? Can any one of you by worrying add a single hour to your life?

"And why do you worry about clothes? See how the flowers of the field grow. They do not labor or spin. Yet I tell you that not even Solomon in all his splendor was dressed like one of these. If that is how God clothes the grass of the field, which is here today and tomorrow is thrown into the fire, will he not much more clothe you—you of little faith? So do not worry, saying, 'What shall we eat?' or 'What shall we drink?' or 'What shall we wear?' For the pagans run after all these things, and your heavenly Father knows that you need them. But seek first his kingdom and his righteousness, and all these things will be given to you as well. Therefore do not worry about tomorrow, for tomorrow will worry about itself. Each day has enough trouble of its own."

LUKE 12:13-21

Someone in the crowd said to [Jesus], "Teacher, tell my brother to divide the inheritance with me."

Jesus replied, "Man, who appointed me a judge or an arbiter between you?" Then he said to them, "Watch out! Be on your guard against all kinds of greed; life does not consist in an abundance of possessions."

And he told them this parable: "The ground of a certain rich man yielded an abundant harvest. He thought to himself, 'What shall I do? I have no place to store my crops.'

"Then he said, 'This is what I'll do. I will tear down my barns and build bigger ones, and there I will store my surplus grain. And I'll say to myself, "You have plenty of grain laid up for many years. Take life easy; eat, drink and be merry."'

"But God said to him, 'You fool! This very night your life will be demanded from you. Then who will get what you have prepared for yourself?'

"This is how it will be with whoever stores up things for themselves but is not rich toward God."

Read Luke 12:13-21 (see sidebar).

1. In Jesus' parable in Luke 12, the foolish man called the grain and barns his rather than acknowledging that everything he had really belonged to God (Psalm 24:1; 1 Corinthians 4:7). What in your life do you treat as your accomplishment or possession without acknowledging God's authority and mission?

2. The fool wasn't content with what he had. He wanted more—and only then, he thought, would enough be enough (Ecclesiastes 5:10). Is there something you're seeking right now that you think would finally give you contentment? What is it?

3. The fool put off enjoyment (or perhaps doing what was right) because he thought he would have plenty of time later. Is there something you are putting off now that you shouldn't be (James 4:13)? What is it?

4. Notice Jesus' warning: We need to think of storing treasure in heaven, being rich toward God, rather than seeking pleasure or things on Earth. What do you think it means to store treasure in heaven? What might that treasure look like in your life?

We are so blessed in our church that many of those who could have decided to retire in a warmer climate and chase the great white golf ball have instead become our best spiritual grandparents and parents—both to their own families and to those without them. They have become unpaid pastors and ministers who have helped us reach the lost and care for the saved.

What if God's people pursued God's mission in their own families and the church all the days of their lives? I am not saying that our older believers do not deserve to have flexibility to work less or that they can't go golfing or boating. But this world is not heaven, and we can't make it so by fleeing meaningful service to our King and others. What we do for the Lord lasts for eternity.

DAY FIVE REVIEW

1. What stood out to you or convicted you from today?

2. Do you struggle to remember who owns what you have been entrusted with? What do you struggle with in this regard?

3. What has your view of retirement been up to this point? Has anything changed after today's lesson?

4. Look around your church community this week. Who is someone older, and perhaps wiser, whom you could ask to meet with to give you advice or wisdom for life? Who is someone younger who may need to hear wisdom from you?

Week 10

THE WORLD SPHERE

Day One

THE WORLD SPHERE

GETTING STARTED

Up to this point we have been talking about spheres, where it is fairly easy to see the boundary lines. As we come to the World Sphere, however, we will see that it encompasses many different areas. This sphere includes work, hobbies, sports, education, neighborhoods, clubs—the list goes on! In today's lesson, we see that God once again lays out a plan for us in His Word that shows us how we can reflect Him out in a world that can be filled with darkness.

> *Lord Jesus: Help me see what You want me to see today. Expose any lies I may believe and lead me to Your truth. Help me trust and obey You and walk out what I'm learning in every sphere of my life.*

Now that we are grounded in the spheres of abiding, the church, and home and family, we enter the next sphere of our lives: the World Sphere.

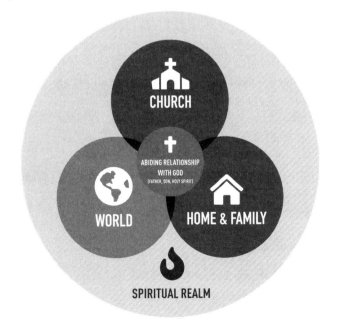

Scan QR code to access video podcasts and other content that accompanies this week's session.

EPHESIANS 4:28

Anyone who has been stealing must steal no longer, but must work, doing something useful with their own hands, that they may have something to share with those in need.

GALATIANS 5:22-25

The fruit of the Spirit is love, joy, peace, forbearance, kindness, goodness, faithfulness, gentleness and self-control. Against such things there is no law. Those who belong to Christ Jesus have crucified the flesh with its passions and desires. Since we live by the Spirit, let us keep in step with the Spirit.

2 THESSALONIANS 3:6-12, NLT

And now, dear brothers and sisters, we give you this command in the name of our Lord Jesus Christ: Stay away from all believers who live idle lives and don't follow the tradition they received from us. For you know that you ought to imitate us. We were not idle when we were with you. We never accepted food from anyone without paying for it. We worked hard day and night so we would not be a burden to any of you. We certainly had the right to ask you to feed us, but we wanted to give you an example to follow. Even while we were with you, we gave you this command: "Those unwilling to work will not get to eat."

Yet we hear that some of you are living idle lives, refusing to work and meddling in other people's business. We command such people and urge them in the name of the Lord Jesus Christ to settle down and work to earn their own living.

Paul now begins to reveal to us God's design for our interactions with the world around us. Today we understand *slaves* and *masters* in terms of ownership and deprivation of freedom; however, in Paul's day, these terms could also refer to people who would serve others in an area for a time period as a way to pay off debt. That use of the terminology can help us connect Paul's words to what we call the Work Sphere. However, our engagement with the larger world is not limited to just our work life; many of us are involved in things like sports, clubs, and hobbies, and we have neighbors all around us. We work as volunteers in our schools and out in the community.

We move into the world as people who have learned God's will for us as we journey in relationship with Jesus and His people. We are becoming humble, and when we fail, we acknowledge it rather than justify our attitudes. We are becoming people of peace (peacemakers) as the Holy Spirit does His work in us (Galatians 5:22-25). We are learning to love others as Jesus loves His people and to care about the lost still out there in the dark. We already learned that we no longer steal (take from others) but work with our hands so we have something to share (Ephesians 4:28). According to what we see in Scripture and in God's design, Christians should work if they are able. If we would rather be given a handout we don't need than do work to care for ourselves and others, we are not living in accordance with what we see in Scripture and we are not demonstrating God's design to the world.

Scripture reveals to us that God is our Savior and Lord in every area of our lives. We demonstrate this wherever we are and in whatever we do because we as God's people have been given the task to reach the lost world with the message of salvation.

Before we get into what kind of worker or boss we need to be, let's study the topic of work as it is addressed in the New Testament.

Read 1 Timothy 5:8.

1. According to Paul, we work so that we can take care of our _____ needs.

Read 2 Thessalonians 3:6-12 (see sidebar).

2. According to 2 Thessalonians 3, when we are not working and we have too much time on our hands, we are tempted to do what?

_____

_____

3. Based on Paul's rule, which of these statements is true?

   • True/False: A person who cannot work will not eat.
   • True/False: A person who is unwilling to work shall not eat.

Read Ephesians 4:28 (see sidebar).

4. We work not only to take care of our own needs but also so that we can _____ with other believers.

Read 1 Thessalonians 4:9-12.

5. We mind our own business and work hard so that our daily life _____.

Read Galatians 6:9-10.

6. We care for those who cannot care for themselves due to infirmity or loss of job, not because of laziness or pride. We especially focus on _____ first before we help those outside the family of God.

YOUR IDENTITY "IN CHRIST" IN YOUR WORK

Many believers see their job as the place to determine, achieve, or hold on to their identity. But as we abide in Christ (who we are "in Christ"), we live from an identity that has already been established by the Creator and Sustainer of the world.

Even if we keep our eyes fixed on Christ in our work, oftentimes we work for people whose identity is wrapped up in their business or pursuits. In their minds, we are working for their identity, and they try to push us in their pursuit of what they think will make them something in the eyes of the world. So they push us to work as hard as they do for what they want for themselves and place great pressure on us to conform to their idea of work. This can also happen in other contexts in the World Sphere, such as a sport or a hobby—anything where others want you to care about what they care about as much as they do.

7. Has someone ever pushed you to help them achieve their identity in life? How did they pressure you?

THE GOSPEL WORK ETHIC

Because we are believers, every part of our lives belongs to God. Something we learn from today's Scripture passages is that those who follow God are known for hard work. We are not lazy, and we are generous with others, especially other believers.

If God's Word tells us to work hard and share with believers, then we must also be willing to receive help when we are struggling. The "one another" statements in Scripture reveal that there are times when we can help and times when we need help. Maturity in Christ helps us accept the fact that we need each other to get through life to the finish line.

If God's Word tells us to work hard and share with believers, then it cannot be wrong to receive help when we are struggling.

8. Determine the spiritual maturity level behind the following statements. Score each one on a scale of 1 to 4, with 1 being the most mature and 4 being the least.

   a. _____ I will not ask for help and I will not give help—what's mine is mine, and you are not my problem.

   b. _____ I will work hard to take care of myself and my family with God's help. I will do my best to have something to share with those in need, personally and as a part of the church through tithing and offerings. When a time comes that I have done my best and I am still in need, I will humbly share my need and allow others the blessing of helping me.

c. _____ I will help others, but I need to be in a place where I don't need help from others.

d. _____ I will help those who help me, or at least those who I think would help me if I help them.[i]

Over the years many people have told me that they like to be one who helps and hate being helped themselves. This can be a subtle form of pride. Even Jesus allowed His needs to be met by others (Luke 8:1-3).

9. When you think about the Scriptures we just read, which do you think is harder to do: helping others or being helped by others? Why?

_____

_____

DAY ONE REVIEW

1. What stood out to you or convicted you from today?

_____

_____

2. Would you say you are comfortable asking for help from others when you need it? Why or why not?

_____

_____

3. Have you ever pushed someone else to work harder or be perfect so that it could feed your false identity? How did it affect your relationship with them?

_____

_____

4. Think about the people you interact with out in the world every week, whether in a job, at a school, or at a sporting event. Do you think they would be surprised to hear that your identity is "in Christ"?

_____

_____

---

i. Answer: a=4; b=1; c=3; d=2.

Day Two

A DISCIPLE'S INTEGRITY AT WORK

GETTING STARTED

Today we are going to talk about what it looks like to live as a disciple of Jesus when you are surrounded by people who are not. Many times, Christians think that their job is somehow set apart from Jesus' call and teaching on their lives when they are functioning in the secular world. They act as if the same standards of a disciple's life that apply in the Home and Church Spheres don't apply to their work environment. However, God's Word tells us something different.

Lord Jesus: Help me see what You want me to see today. Expose any lies I may believe and lead me to Your truth. Help me trust and obey You and walk out what I'm learning in every sphere of my life.

Many people put on one face at church and a completely different one at work. But a disciple should be the same person at home, at church, and at work because their motives and actions emerge from the same place: their abiding life in Christ. So what does Scripture tell us about how to bring our identity "in Christ" to our work as an employee?

Read Ephesians 6:5-9.

In week 5, we discussed that to truly understand Scripture, we must understand the context of those writing and those being written to. This is called the historicity principle. In Paul's day, a significant portion of the Roman world would have been considered slaves.[1] Slaves served in a variety of roles and industries, from taxing menial labor to more specialized service. While slavery in ancient Rome did not generally contain the level of horrors we are familiar with from slavery in the United States, the dynamic it created in the early church—where one follower of Jesus claimed ownership over another—would have been complicated. In speaking to slaves and masters, Paul was not glorifying slavery or condoning it—he was merely writing to the reality of what was happening during that time period.

However, since the employer/employee relationship as we know it did not exist in biblical times, we can find some benefit in considering Paul's words to masters and slaves in light of our relationships at work today. The parallel is contextually imperfect, but these biblical instructions can demonstrate broader principles of submission under authority and humility and gentleness in leadership.

1. Which assumptions do you see in this passage?

    ☐ Paul is implying that people must work in some form or fashion.

    ☐ Paul is assuming that either you are working for someone or someone is working for you.

    ☐ Paul is making the point that as disciples of Jesus, we must obey His commands regardless of our status in life.

> A disciple should be the same person at home, at church, and at work because their motives and actions emerge from the same place: their abiding life in Christ.

2. As believers, we obey our earthly employers with _____ and _____.

3. What kind of heart do we do this with? What does it mean to have that kind of heart? (Go to BibleHub.com and do some research.)

4. We are to do what we do for our employers because Jesus has asked us to. We do this even when employers are not looking, because _____ is looking.

Here are some other Scriptures that can shed light on the posture and heart we should have as we submit to authority in our work:

Slaves, in reverent fear of God submit yourselves to your masters, not only to those who are good and considerate, but also to those who are harsh. For it is commendable if someone bears up under the pain of unjust suffering because they are conscious of God. But how is it to your credit if you receive a beating for doing wrong and endure it? But if you suffer for doing good and you endure it, this is commendable before God. To this you were called, because Christ suffered for you, leaving you an example, that you should follow in his steps.

"He committed no sin,
and no deceit was found in his mouth."

When they hurled their insults at him, he did not retaliate; when he suffered, he made no threats. Instead, he entrusted himself to him who judges justly. "He himself bore our sins" in his body on the cross, so that we might die to sins and live for righteousness; "by his wounds you have been healed." For "you were like sheep going astray," but now you have returned to the Shepherd and Overseer of your souls.

I PETER 2:18-25

Slaves, obey your earthly masters in everything you do. Try to please them all the time, not just when they are watching you. Serve them sincerely because of your reverent fear of the Lord. Work willingly at whatever you do, as though you were working for the Lord rather than for people. Remember that the Lord will give you an inheritance as your reward, and that the Master you are serving is Christ. But if you do what is wrong, you will be paid back for the wrong you have done. For God has no favorites.

COLOSSIANS 3:22-25, NLT

All slaves should show full respect for their masters so they will not bring shame on the name of God and his teaching. If the masters are believers, that is no excuse for being disrespectful. Those slaves should work all the harder because their efforts are helping other believers who are well loved.

Teach these things, Timothy, and encourage everyone to obey them.

I TIMOTHY 6:1-2, NLT

Teach slaves to be subject to their masters in everything, to try to please them, not to talk back to them, and not to steal from them, but to show that they can be fully trusted, so that in every way they will make the teaching about God our Savior attractive.

TITUS 2:9-10

As believers, our goal is to glorify God in how we act even when we are treated poorly. Our workplace is our mission field: where we get to reveal our Christlikeness and the differences Jesus has made in us so we can draw people to Jesus for their salvation. We can also interact with other believers and partner together on how to share Christ where we work. Our workplace is where we are on mission with Christ as disciplemakers who are becoming fishers of men.

In our culture today, we don't have to work for someone if we don't want to, but we should still consider the deeper implications of Paul's exhortations. If we do work for someone, what kind of work should we do? How faithful should we be? How should we talk about our boss? What should we do even when they are not looking?

Remember, we do what we do for the Lord, and He sees us and has promised to bless us when we act with integrity.

Read 1 Corinthians 10:31; Colossians 3:17, 23 (see sidebar).

DAY TWO REVIEW

1. What stood out to you or convicted you from today?

2. How would you approach your work differently if you looked at your workplace as a mission field?

3. Have you ever worked with someone who worked harder when the boss was watching? What effect did that have on your opinion of that person?

4. Do you have a boss who doesn't seem to appreciate or value you? Pray that God will open your eyes this week to some ways you can serve or bless him or her anonymously. You may be surprised by how God blesses you for this.

1 CORINTHIANS 10:31

Whether you eat or drink or whatever you do, do it all for the glory of God.

COLOSSIANS 3:17, NLT

Whatever you do or say, do it as a representative of the Lord Jesus, giving thanks through him to God the Father.

COLOSSIANS 3:23

Whatever you do, work at it with all your heart, as working for the Lord, not for human masters.

1. "Slavery in Ancient Rome," The British Museum, accessed April 8, 2024, https://www.britishmuseum.org/exhibitions/nero-man-behind-myth/slavery-ancient-rome.

Day Three

THE HUMBLE LEADER

GETTING STARTED

Yesterday we talked about what it looks like to be a follower of Jesus as an employee in the secular world. But what does it look like if you are the employer? Today we will talk about who God calls us to be when we are leaders of other people in our secular job. How does He expect us to treat those we hold authority over?

> *Lord Jesus: Help me see what You want me to see today. Expose any lies I may believe and lead me to Your truth. Help me trust and obey You and walk out what I'm learning in every sphere of my life.*

Jesus has made it clear that leadership is not a privilege to be abused but a responsibility to be used for people's good and God's glory. Godly leaders are to be humble servants who care about others. That's true in the World Sphere just as it is in the Church Sphere. So what does it look like to be employers who seek to serve for God's glory, no matter where we work?

Let's look back at the following Scripture:

> Masters, treat your slaves in the same way. Do not threaten them, since you know that he who is both their Master and yours is in heaven, and there is no favoritism with him.
>
> Finally, be strong in the Lord and in his mighty power.
>
> EPHESIANS 6:9-10

MATTHEW 23:11-12

The greatest among you will be your servant. For those who exalt themselves will be humbled, and those who humble themselves will be exalted.

Remember: While slavery in Paul's time didn't always look like the kind of "chattel slavery" we are familiar with from American history, the master/slave metaphor requires appropriate discernment to be helpful in today's context. We can learn what our heart and posture should be toward those we have authority over from the things Paul is addressing here, but as employers, we must also understand the boundaries of our authority.

However, the context Paul is speaking into means that "[God] is both their Master and yours . . . and there is no favoritism with him" holds even more profound weight. Where we today can acknowledge equality of value between us and those we work with and for, Paul was calling masters to an unthinkably high standard: holding themselves as equal to those their culture considered lesser. The cross of Christ created a radical change in how believers of different cultural statuses related to one another. If those in the early church were commanded to this level of humility, how much more should we pursue it in our contexts today?

1. How might the recognition that they both have the same Master in heaven (according to Colossians 4:1) change the perspective of an employer toward an employee today?

Scripture tells us that when we hold authority over others, we must remember that those people are image bearers of our heavenly Father and that our Father wants to be their Father as well. If they are disciples of Jesus, then we share the same Father—and we must always be careful how we treat our Father's children.

Years ago my son got a job with someone in our church. I asked the man to please not give my son any special treatment simply because he was the pastor's child. My son needed to learn to be someone who worked hard. If he didn't dedicate himself to the role, his employer should correct him and train him. If he still didn't work hard, his employer should fire him in a way that was both honest and compassionate—saying what he needed to say without demeaning or emotionally destroying an impressionable young man. My posture essentially was, *Do what you need to do, but keep in mind that he is my son and I care deeply about his future.*

I have thought much about this concept regarding what God expects of those of us in authority. Your employees are either God's children already or people who He wants as part of His family. Do what you do with God the Father in mind. We must be careful with our Father's sons and daughters and potential children.

Here is more Scripture that helps us consider what the role of an employer should look like:

Masters, be just and fair to your slaves. Remember that you also have a Master—in heaven.

COLOSSIANS 4:1, NLT

Jesus commanded us to treat others as we would have them treat us (Luke 6:31). Scripture reveals here that if you want your Master in heaven to treat you well, you should treat those you oversee well.

2. Employers are not to take advantage of anyone but are to treat them in ways that are right and _____.

If the masters are believers, that is no excuse for being disrespectful. Those slaves should work all the harder because their efforts are helping other believers who are well loved.

Teach these things, Timothy, and encourage everyone to obey them.

1 TIMOTHY 6:2, NLT

3. This verse assumes that a Christ follower in authority is concerned about the _____ of those they oversee.

Some see people through the eyes of the world rather than through the eyes of God. We must always remember that our job does not define us (or anyone else), and any authority we have does not lend us greater value than anyone who is under that authority. If we are "in Christ," Jesus establishes and maintains our identity.

My brothers and sisters, believers in our glorious Lord Jesus Christ must not show favoritism. Suppose a man comes into your meeting wearing a gold ring and fine clothes, and a poor man in filthy old clothes also comes in. If you show special attention to the man wearing fine clothes and say, "Here's a good seat for you," but say to the poor man, "You stand there" or "Sit on the floor by my feet," have you not discriminated among yourselves and become judges with evil thoughts?

Listen, my dear brothers and sisters: Has not God chosen those who are poor in the eyes of the world to be rich in faith and to inherit the kingdom he promised those who love him?

JAMES 2:1-5

The greatest among you will be your servant. For those who exalt themselves will be humbled, and those who humble themselves will be exalted.

MATTHEW 23:11-12

1 SAMUEL 16:7

But the LORD said to Samuel, "Do not consider his appearance or his height, for I have rejected him. The LORD does not look at the things people look at. People look at the outward appearance, but the LORD looks at the heart."

We have received the truth bound up in the gospel, and we are called to live out of our identity in Christ. We live in a world that is filled with racism, classism, and other forms of partiality that tell us we are less or more based on human classifications. That is not the truth—we are part of God's holy nation, given equal worth through His choice to reveal Himself to us and our acceptance of His grace through Jesus.

The world will tell you we can find our true self and happiness through influential relationships or earthly possessions. This is not the truth. As children of the Most High God, we are princes and princesses—even if some people reject us or consider us less important. We are part of the body of Christ, bestowed with a calling of the highest significance: fighting an eternal battle for the souls of those God loves. Eternity hangs in the balance of what you do with the Lord's guidance. You are important.

As you abide in Christ, you realize that your earthly work is important because it gives you the ability to bring glory to God. Even work that seems insignificant in the world's eyes is an opportunity to be on mission with Jesus (1 Samuel 16:7).

Notes and Thoughts

DAY THREE REVIEW

1. What stood out to you or convicted you from today?

2. Have you ever experienced working for someone whom you were surprised to find out was a believer?

3. Have you ever found yourself believing that you were defined by your job or position? What brought that belief to light?

4. Describe a time when you misjudged someone because of their appearance or title. Make a point this week to ask God to reveal someone around you whom you may have overlooked or not noticed. Go out of your way to speak to and encourage that person.

Day Four

POLITICS AND RELIGION

GETTING STARTED

When it comes to controversial or explosive topics to discuss, religion and politics certainly lead the list. In today's lesson we will discover how we can address those issues with humility and peace when we find ourselves in a conversation about them, and what God says about our attitudes toward the ruling authorities around us.

Lord Jesus: Help me see what You want me to see today. Expose any lies I may believe and lead me to Your truth. Help me trust and obey You and walk out what I'm learning in every sphere of my life.

As humans who live on planet Earth, we are to live a life worthy of the gospel (Philippians 1:27), being *in* the world but not *of* it (John 17:11-17). We have a responsibility to be salt and light (Matthew 5:13-16) as we live as Christians among many nations.

Since Jesus' time on Earth, many nations have come and gone. Despite wars and changing governments, Christians are still here. The Scripture is the constitution for our spiritual government; God's Word sets the terms for our lifestyle. God's instructions are our "priority one," superseding whatever loyalty we have to any other country or person.

We know that abiding in Christ means obeying what He says, and John 17 says God will sanctify us (purify us) by His Word, which is truth. In Matthew 24:35, Jesus tells us that heaven and earth will disappear, but His Word will never disappear. Our first allegiance must be to the Kingdom of heaven, the only kingdom that will last.

There is nothing you and I can do to make this world heaven, and our true country is the restored new heaven and earth that Jesus will bring with Him when He returns (Philippians 3:20; Hebrews 11:6). In the meantime, we are filled with the Spirit, and there is no law against the fruit of the Spirit (Galatians 5:23).

One of the characteristics of the Spirit's work in us is peace. Jesus tells us, "Blessed are the peacemakers" (Matthew 5:9). As peacemakers, we love God and others and are to obey human authority unless we are asked to disobey God (which would violate our first allegiance to His Kingdom). As Christians, we are told very clearly to honor authority within the church, within our homes, within our jobs, and within the countries in which we live.

Everyone must submit to governing authorities. For all authority comes from God, and those in positions of authority have been placed there by God. So anyone who rebels against authority is rebelling against what God has instituted, and they will be punished. For the authorities do not strike fear in people who are doing right, but in those who are doing wrong. Would you like to live without fear of the authorities? Do what is right, and they will honor you. The authorities are God's servants, sent for your good. But if you are doing wrong, of course you should be

PHILIPPIANS 1:27
Whatever happens, conduct yourselves in a manner worthy of the gospel of Christ. Then, whether I come and see you or only hear about you in my absence, I will know that you stand firm in the one Spirit, striving together as one for the faith of the gospel.

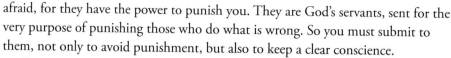

1 TIMOTHY 2:1-4, NLT

I urge you, first of all, to pray for all people. Ask God to help them; intercede on their behalf, and give thanks for them. Pray this way for kings and all who are in authority so that we can live peaceful and quiet lives marked by godliness and dignity. This is good and pleases God our Savior, who wants everyone to be saved and to understand the truth.

TITUS 3:1-2

Remind the people to be subject to rulers and authorities, to be obedient, to be ready to do whatever is good, to slander no one, to be peaceable and considerate, and always to be gentle toward everyone.

1 PETER 2:13-17

Submit yourselves for the Lord's sake to every human authority: whether to the emperor, as the supreme authority, or to governors, who are sent by him to punish those who do wrong and to commend those who do right. For it is God's will that by doing good you should silence the ignorant talk of foolish people. Live as free people, but do not use your freedom as a cover-up for evil; live as God's slaves. Show proper respect to everyone, love the family of believers, fear God, honor the emperor.

PHILIPPIANS 2:8

And being found in appearance as a man, he humbled himself by becoming obedient to death—even death on a cross!

afraid, for they have the power to punish you. They are God's servants, sent for the very purpose of punishing those who do what is wrong. So you must submit to them, not only to avoid punishment, but also to keep a clear conscience.

Pay your taxes, too, for these same reasons. For government workers need to be paid. They are serving God in what they do. Give to everyone what you owe them: Pay your taxes and government fees to those who collect them, and give respect and honor to those who are in authority.

ROMANS 13:1-7, NLT

1.   Remember, to understand Scripture we must understand the context in which it was written. Who was in charge of the government in Paul's time?

2.   Who does Paul say institutes authority in the world?

God either brings authority to power or allows it to emerge for purposes at times only He knows. This reality should remind us again of our primary allegiance to His Kingdom—because He is the King over all other kings.

When we look at a topic in Scripture, we shouldn't just look at one passage, but rather study the whole subject. To do this, we look for other direct passages with instructions, find stories that illustrate the principle, and put everything together.

Read 1 Timothy 2:1-4; Titus 3:1-2; and 1 Peter 2:13-17 (see sidebar).

3.   Based on the passages we just read, what kind of attitude should Christ followers have?

Now let's look at a passage where the disciples did not obey human authority.

Read Acts 4.

4.   The apostles chose not to obey the authorities within Jerusalem at this time. What does this tell us about when and how to follow the authority God has designed and designated?

Many times, people have a spirit of rebellion rather than a spirit of humility, and they are just looking for an opportunity to rebel. Christ humbled Himself even to the point where He went to the cross (Philippians 2:8). Yes, there is a time to say, "No, I will not obey." In fact, the disciples were killed because they would not shut up about Jesus and would not stop preaching. However, being mature means knowing when and how to stand up. We do not fight like the devil for the things of God. Spending time in prayer and with mature believers can help us discern wisdom in this area.

So often I speak with Christians who like to point out what the constitution of the United States says. They know the first and second amendments. They know the Bill of Rights and make it clear that they will fight for those rights.

Let me say that I love our constitution. I believe that it is the best version of a human-made government. I love the rights set out in our constitution, and I believe it has created the best conditions for free and moral living. However, I am concerned that these same people I speak to do not know Scripture. They do not know what Jesus says about life, liberty, the pursuit of happiness (and what His version of it looks like). For believers, Scripture should take priority in our lives over every other document. Our pledge of allegiance is first and foremost to the one who died for our salvation and who will rule a perfect, amazing Kingdom for eternity.

DAY FOUR REVIEW

1. What stood out to you or convicted you from today?

2. Have there been times in your life when you have disagreed with something the governing authorities around you have done? How did you react?

3. What do you think it means not to fight like the devil for the things of God?

4. Think about the last conversation you had about the government, either in person or on social media. Would you say your words and attitude were a good representation of the Titus 3:1-2 passage we looked at today? Why or why not?

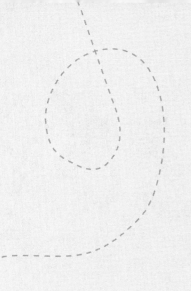

Day Five

WHO IS MY NEIGHBOR?

GETTING STARTED

We have been talking about our attitudes and encounters in the work world, but what about our relationships with nonbelievers outside of work? Today we will address the way Jesus viewed the lost around Him, and we will look at the teaching and example He laid out for us in His Word.

> *Lord Jesus: Help me see what You want me to see today. Expose any lies I may believe and lead me to Your truth. Help me trust and obey You and walk out what I'm learning in every sphere of my life.*

In the World Sphere, we live around both believers and unbelievers. Our role is to act as Jesus would have us act so we can experience Him and show others what it is like to have Him in our lives. We can learn much about Jesus' desire for us as we look at how Jesus viewed the people around Him.

Read Luke 10:25-37 (see sidebar).

1. Remember, to truly understand God's Word, we must understand the context it was written in when the story was told. Do an online search or go to BibleHub.com or GotQuestions.org to learn about the Samaritans. What is a Samaritan, and why didn't the Jews like them?

    _____

    _____

2. Jesus was asked the question "Who is my neighbor?" But then He answered a different question: "Who is being a neighbor?" How does that change things?

    _____

    _____

3. Why do you think the religious people chose to walk past the hurt man?

    ☐ Maybe they had already served at the Temple and were going on vacation, and thought they had already done their job for the week.

    ☐ They may have been on their way to serve in another town and didn't want to be late.

    ☐ Perhaps they thought the man deserved what he got and he must have sinned in some way.

    ☐ They may have decided he deserved what he got because he was unwise to travel on a dangerous road alone.

    ☐ Other: _____

LUKE 10:25-37

On one occasion an expert in the law stood up to test Jesus. "Teacher," he asked, "what must I do to inherit eternal life?"

"What is written in the Law?" he replied. "How do you read it?"

He answered, "'Love the Lord your God with all your heart and with all your soul and with all your strength and with all your mind'; and, 'Love your neighbor as yourself.'"

"You have answered correctly," Jesus replied. "Do this and you will live."

But he wanted to justify himself, so he asked Jesus, "And who is my neighbor?"

In reply Jesus said: "A man was going down from Jerusalem to Jericho, when he was attacked by robbers. They stripped him of his clothes, beat him and went away, leaving him half dead. A priest happened to be going down the same road, and when he saw the man, he passed by on the other side. So too, a Levite, when he

4. What are some reasons the Samaritan could have chosen to not help the injured Jew?

5. How does Jesus want us to see the needs of those around us?

Jesus saw the needs of others as an opportunity to help them with their perceived need so He could point them to their real need. (See the passage about the Samaritan woman at the well in John 4 as an example.)

6. What do the following passages tell us about the reason we are to be wise among unbelievers?

> Be very careful, then, how you live—not as unwise but as wise, making the most of every opportunity, because the days are evil. Therefore do not be foolish, but understand what the Lord's will is. Do not get drunk on wine, which leads to debauchery. Instead, be filled with the Spirit, speaking to one another with psalms, hymns, and songs from the Spirit. Sing and make music from your heart to the Lord, always giving thanks to God the Father for everything, in the name of our Lord Jesus Christ.
>
> EPHESIANS 5:15-20

> Live wisely among those who are not believers, and make the most of every opportunity. Let your conversation be gracious and attractive so that you will have the right response for everyone.
>
> COLOSSIANS 4:5-6, NLT

> In your hearts revere Christ as Lord. Always be prepared to give an answer to everyone who asks you to give the reason for the hope that you have. But do this with gentleness and respect, keeping a clear conscience, so that those who speak maliciously against your good behavior in Christ may be ashamed of their slander. For it is better, if it is God's will, to suffer for doing good than for doing evil.
>
> 1 PETER 3:15-17

> Live such good lives among the pagans that, though they accuse you of doing wrong, they may see your good deeds and glorify God on the day he visits us.
>
> 1 PETER 2:12

came to the place and saw him, passed by on the other side. But a Samaritan, as he traveled, came where the man was; and when he saw him, he took pity on him. He went to him and bandaged his wounds, pouring on oil and wine. Then he put the man on his own donkey, brought him to an inn and took care of him. The next day he took out two denarii and gave them to the innkeeper. 'Look after him,' he said, 'and when I return, I will reimburse you for any extra expense you may have.'

"Which of these three do you think was a neighbor to the man who fell into the hands of robbers?"

The expert in the law replied, "The one who had mercy on him."

Jesus told him, "Go and do likewise."

We live in a world that is darkened in its understanding. And in this world, we, as God's children, are the light and the city on a hill (Matthew 5:14).

DAY FIVE REVIEW

1. What stood out to you or convicted you from today?

2. What did you discover in your research about the relationship between the Samaritans and the Jews?

3. Has there ever been a time in your life when you didn't stop to help someone because of timing or other factors?

4. Has there ever been a time when you needed help and someone walked by you? What effect did that have on you?

5. As you go throughout this week, ask God to open your eyes to those around you in every sphere who may be in need. Who comes to mind? Ask God to reveal to you how He might use you to help them.

Week 11

THE SPIRITUAL SPHERE

Day One

THERE IS A BATTLE

GETTING STARTED

When we look back at our road trip analogy, we see the destination that Jesus has in mind for us. We are riding in a relational environment with Him and with believers who are more mature than we are. As we continue our journey, we are connecting with others and learning to love, which requires true humility. We are learning to use our gifts and resources individually to serve others in every sphere—as part of church, home, and the workplace. As we spend time in the relational vehicle, we are reminded that we, too, will learn to help others in their journey.

> *Lord Jesus: Help me see what You want me to see today. Expose any lies I may believe and lead me to Your truth. Help me trust and obey You and walk out what I'm learning in every sphere of my life.*

As you abide in a relationship with Jesus, He directs and empowers you in the Church Sphere, the Home and Family Sphere, and the World Sphere. The outer circle that encompasses all the other spheres represents the spiritual realm. Ephesians 6:10-19 introduces the spiritual realm and the battle that is waged there.

This sphere consists of the unseen realm, where the devil and his demons seek to distort, distract, and tempt God's people to deviate from God's design and will for their lives. It is where the devil works against God's people (and God's angels) to thwart the Lord's church and its given mission.

> Our struggle is not against flesh and blood, but against the rulers, against the authorities, against the powers of this dark world and against the spiritual forces of evil in the heavenly realms.
>
> EPHESIANS 6:12

 Scan QR code to access video podcasts and other content that accompanies this week's session.

EPHESIANS 6:10-19

Finally, be strong in the Lord and in his mighty power. Put on the full armor of God, so that you can take your stand against the devil's schemes. For our struggle is not against flesh and blood, but against the rulers, against the authorities, against the powers of this dark world and against the spiritual forces of evil in the heavenly realms. Therefore put on the full armor of God, so that when the day of evil comes, you may be able to stand your ground, and after you have done everything, to stand. Stand firm then, with the belt of truth buckled around your waist, with the breastplate of righteousness in place, and with your feet fitted with the readiness that comes from the gospel of peace. In addition to all this, take up the shield of faith, with which you can extinguish all the flaming arrows of the evil one. Take the helmet of salvation and the sword of the Spirit, which is the word of God.

And pray in the Spirit on all occasions with all kinds of prayers and requests. With this in mind, be alert and always keep on praying for all the Lord's people. Pray also for me, that whenever I speak, words may be given me so that I will fearlessly make known the mystery of the gospel.

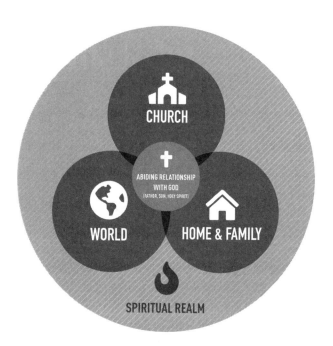

On the journey of discipleship, we are in a driver's training course led by an Intentional Leader who encourages us to help others learn to drive toward maturity. This week we are going to learn that we have an enemy who wants to get us off course.

This enemy wants to get us to take detours out in the desert, to make us run out of gas. He is trying to get our relational vehicles to break down, hoping that we will die out there—and that those with us will die too. We first encounter the enemy in Genesis, and we see his activity throughout the entire history of the world. The Old Testament gives us glimpses, and the gospel story of Jesus reveals a direct encounter with the devil.

Understanding the Spiritual Sphere is vital if we're going to oppose the enemy, who wants to thwart our progress toward obeying Jesus, being changed by Jesus, and being committed to the mission of Jesus in all the other spheres. Disciples of Jesus must know who the enemy is and how he works. When we know we have an enemy hunting us and are familiar with how he camouflages himself, he has a much harder time ambushing us. Paul is going to teach us how to defeat him and stay on course to finish the journey.

Paul is just giving us more information (as the Holy Spirit leads him) into what Jesus has already shared with the disciples. In an encounter with the religious leaders of His day, Jesus challenges those who claim to know God but are rejecting His Son, saying that they are really working for the devil:

> "You belong to your father, the devil, and you want to carry out your father's desires. He was a murderer from the beginning, not holding to the truth, for there is no truth in him. When he lies, he speaks his native language, for he is a liar and the father of lies."
>
> JOHN 8:44

1. The devil's goal is to _____ us.

2. His method of accomplishing this goal is to _____ to us.

As humans it's easy to focus on what we can see with our physical eyes, rather than what is happening in the spiritual realm. But Jesus is showing us that there is more going on than what we can see.

We live by faith, not by sight.

2 CORINTHIANS 5:7

PUTTING ON ARMOR

The Holy Spirit inspired Paul to give the Ephesian church (and all of us) directions on how to resist the enemy so we can continue to grow to maturity and pursue God's mission. Let's break down the passage here to discover what spiritual battle requires:

- Paul is writing to the church here, which means that though individuals have a part to play, they are called on to work together as one body with spiritual armor that is shared by them all.

- In Ephesians 6:10, when Paul calls on us to be strong in the Lord and in His mighty power, he is again referring to the strength that God provides when we abide in Him. As we abide, we accept and stand firm in what God in Christ has done for us as individuals and what He has done for others in His family as well. We have a new identity, and so do other believers. Abiding means walking with Jesus in relationship and standing with Him on who He says we are.

- What we learned in the Abiding Sphere we carry into the Church Sphere. As we grow in the Abiding Sphere and Church Sphere (discipleship), our Home and Family Sphere starts to look like what God would have it be. As we spend time abiding in the Church Sphere and the Home and Family Sphere, our lives spill into the World Sphere. We are being changed from the inside out. In the Spiritual Sphere, we discover that the enemy is attacking from the outside in, but that God equips us for the conflict.

- God has given us His Holy Spirit and His holy Word, as well as His holy people, to help us stand firm. Yes, as we abide in Christ as individuals, we receive the strength we need—but Paul is also saying that together as a church we are to stand as a spiritual army against the devil's schemes. So often Christians think fighting the devil is a personal battle, but Ephesians tells us that we are not alone.

3. To learn more about what is happening in the spiritual battle, read the following Scripture passages and fill in the blanks:

- *Daniel 10:12-13*: There are angels and _____ fighting that we cannot see.
- *Ephesians 4:17-19*: Their understanding is _____.

DANIEL 10:12-13

Then he continued, "Do not be afraid, Daniel. Since the first day that you set your mind to gain understanding and to humble yourself before your God, your words were heard, and I have come in response to them. But the prince of the Persian kingdom resisted me twenty-one days. Then Michael, one of the chief princes, came to help me, because I was detained there with the king of Persia."

EPHESIANS 4:17-19

I tell you this, and insist on it in the Lord, that you must no longer live as the Gentiles do, in the futility of their thinking. They are darkened in their understanding and separated from the life of God because of the ignorance that is in them due to the hardening of their hearts. Having lost all sensitivity, they have given themselves over to sensuality so as to indulge in every kind of impurity, and they are full of greed.

2 TIMOTHY 2:25-26, NLT

Gently instruct those who oppose the truth. Perhaps God will change those people's hearts, and they will learn the truth. Then they will come to their senses and escape from the devil's trap. For they have been held captive by him to do whatever he wants.

LUKE 4:1-13

Jesus, full of the Holy Spirit, left the Jordan and was led by the Spirit into the wilderness, where for forty days he was tempted by the devil. He ate nothing during those days, and at the end of them he was hungry.

The devil said to him, "If you are the Son of God, tell this stone to become bread."

Jesus answered, "It is written: 'Man shall not live on bread alone.'"

The devil led him up to a high place and showed him in an instant all the kingdoms of the world. And he said to him, "I will give you all their authority and splendor; it has been given to me, and I can give it to anyone I want to. If you worship me, it will all be yours."

Jesus answered, "It is written: 'Worship the Lord your God and serve him only.'"

The devil led him to Jerusalem and had him stand on the highest point of the temple. "If you are the Son of God," he said, "throw yourself down from here. For it is written: "'He will command his angels concerning you to guard you carefully; they will lift you up in their hands, so that you will not strike your foot against a stone.'"

Jesus answered, "It is said: 'Do not put the Lord your God to the test.'"

When the devil had finished all this tempting, he left him until an opportune time.

- *2 Timothy 2:25-26*: The devil has _____ them.
- *2 Corinthians 4:4*: The devil has _____ the minds of unbelievers.
- *2 Corinthians 10:3-5*: We have spiritual _____ against the thoughts that are placed in our minds; we take captive every thought, making it obedient to Christ.

Paul wants us to love those who are lost in the same way that Jesus did and recognize who the real enemy is.

Read Luke 4:1-13 (see sidebar).

We are given this true story to show us that Jesus understands us. He has been where we are. Through Jesus' example, we learn how the devil works, how he attacks, and how we can defeat him.

4. Look up the definition of the word *schemer*. What does it mean?

_____

5. When did the enemy come to tempt Jesus? Why did he come when he did?

_____

6. What did the enemy want Jesus to do? How did Jesus answer?

_____

7. What did the enemy want Jesus to doubt?

_____

8. What is the most important food we can have?

_____

9. How did the enemy seek to trick Jesus with the second temptation?

_____

10. Go back and read Ephesians 6:16-18 in light of Luke 4. How do you see Jesus using the weapons referenced there?

_____

DAY ONE REVIEW

1. What stood out to you or convicted you from today?

2. What are some ways you have seen the enemy attack from the inside out in your own life?

3. We read today about the spiritual armor we are to put on (Ephesians 6:10-19). If you could look into a mirror and see the spiritual armor you are wearing right now, would you feel protected? Why or why not?

4. Who in your life seems to be going through a spiritual battle right now? What are some things you could do to help them in that battle?

Day Two

WE ARE STRONGER TOGETHER

GETTING STARTED

Abiding with Jesus gives us the strength to live for Him in each sphere of our lives. How we abide in Jesus and in the church are supposed to be interconnected. We are individually called a temple of the Holy Spirit (1 Corinthians 6:18-19), but we are also called to be a collection of living stones (1 Peter 2:4-9). Together, via connection and purpose, we form a collection of beautifully made stones brought together as a mighty, living temple that represents our God. The Holy Spirit guides us into our place in the living building and places us next to other living stones God wants us to be connected to. God uses other people to hold us in our place, and He uses us to hold them as well.

God often uses His people to speak into our lives, and as we praise the Lord together, He is there (Psalm 22:3; Matthew 18:20). Of course, God is with us as individuals, but He is also with us in a special way when we come together as the church.

Lord Jesus: Help me see what You want me to see today. Expose any lies I may believe and lead me to Your truth. Help me trust and obey You and walk out what I'm learning in every sphere of my life.

The strength and direction we gain individually from walking with God also works *in us* as the church, giving us the wisdom and strength we need to fight together against the enemy, who seeks to thwart us at every turn. As we seek to be God's people, the enemy attacks us from every side. While we fight the enemy as individuals, God also intends us to fight him together as a church.

Paul uses Roman battle armor as his analogy here. Read through this passage again and do some research to find out about Roman armor and their methods of fighting during the time this book was written.

Read Ephesians 6:10-19 (see sidebar).

1. As you read through the list of armor, you will notice no mention of armor for your backside. Why do you think that is?

    ☐ We don't run; we stand firm.
    ☐ We have someone guarding our back.
    ☐ Other: _____

2. Some of the armor Paul lists cannot be put on alone. Who do you think helps you put on the armor? What might this look like in our church communities?

---

1 CORINTHIANS 6:18-19

Flee from sexual immorality. All other sins a person commits are outside the body, but whoever sins sexually, sins against their own body. Do you not know that your bodies are temples of the Holy Spirit, who is in you, whom you have received from God? You are not your own.

1 PETER 2:4-9

As you come to him, the living Stone—rejected by humans but chosen by God and precious to him—you also, like living stones, are being built into a spiritual house to be a holy priesthood, offering spiritual sacrifices acceptable to God through Jesus Christ. For in Scripture it says: "See, I lay a stone in Zion, a chosen and precious cornerstone, and the one who trusts in him will never be put to shame." Now to you who believe, this stone is precious. But to those who do not believe, "The stone the builders rejected has become the cornerstone," and, "A stone that causes people to stumble and a rock that makes them fall."

They stumble because they disobey the message—which is also what they were destined for.

But you are a chosen people, a royal priesthood, a holy nation, God's special possession, that you may declare the praises of him who called you out of darkness into his wonderful light.

Read Hebrews 3:11-13 (see sidebar).

In these verses, we are told to be sure not to get an unbelieving heart that turns away from God. Encouragement and admonition from other believers help us make sure this doesn't happen.

3. Who in your life gets to see the real you and speak into what you are going through?

DAY TWO REVIEW

1. What stood out to you or convicted you from today?

2. Have you ever experienced a hard situation that felt like an attack you never saw coming? How could it have gone better if you had had someone fighting alongside you?

3. Consider the analogy of being brought together as living stones. Who in your life is that support and strength for you?

4. Who is someone you have been a support and strength for? Who might God be revealing as someone He might want you to come alongside and support in that way?

EPHESIANS 6:10-19

Finally, be strong in the Lord and in his mighty power. Put on the full armor of God, so that you can take your stand against the devil's schemes. For our struggle is not against flesh and blood, but against the rulers, against the authorities, against the powers of this dark world and against the spiritual forces of evil in the heavenly realms. Therefore put on the full armor of God, so that when the day of evil comes, you may be able to stand your ground, and after you have done everything, to stand. Stand firm then, with the belt of truth buckled around your waist, with the breastplate of righteousness in place, and with your feet fitted with the readiness that comes from the gospel of peace. In addition to all this, take up the shield of faith, with which you can extinguish all the flaming arrows of the evil one. Take the helmet of salvation and the sword of the Spirit, which is the word of God.

And pray in the Spirit on all occasions with all kinds of prayers and requests. With this in mind, be alert and always keep on praying for all the Lord's people. Pray also for me, that whenever I speak, words may be given me so that I will fearlessly make known the mystery of the gospel.

HEBREWS 3:11-13

"So I declared on oath in my anger,
   'They shall never enter my rest.'"

See to it, brothers and sisters, that none of you has a sinful, unbelieving heart that turns away from the living God. But encourage one another daily, as long as it is called "Today," so that none of you may be hardened by sin's deceitfulness.

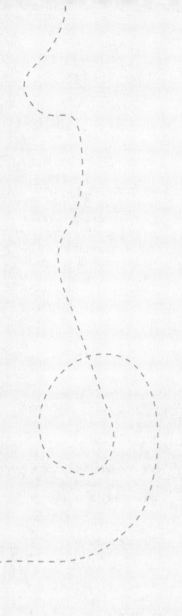

Day Three

THE DEVIL'S METHODS OF FIGHTING

GETTING STARTED

Yesterday we talked about the importance of abiding in Jesus and in His church. Being interconnected with the body of Christ helps empower us with the strength we need to fight the enemy, who works against us in many ways. Today we are looking at the weapons God has provided us to utilize in this spiritual battle we face.

> *Lord Jesus: Help me see what You want me to see today. Expose any lies I may believe and lead me to Your truth. Help me trust and obey You and walk out what I'm learning in every sphere of my life.*

So far this week, we've learned that the enemy consistently works in a few ways:

- He works in our minds directly either to discourage us (*I am unworthy to rely on the Lord*) or to puff us up with pride (*I can do it myself*). His goal is to get us to disconnect from God as our source of direction and supply of power.

- He works through sinful people to create a culture that entices us away from faith in God. The culture designed by humanity offers us earthly treasure, short-term relief, and escape. We all have our own internal sinful bent, and it can be tempting to allow it to control our actions. Like a carnival trying to lure you into various tents, the world is full of people who have been captured by the devil for his purposes and are attempting to lure us into one kind of sin booth or another.

- The enemy works through individual people to influence us away from faith in Christ.

As we look at Ephesians 6, we see that one of the pieces of armor we must put on is the helmet of salvation. In other words, we must constantly remember that we are saved—not by our good works or because we deserve it but because of what Jesus has done for us.

WHO YOU ARE

As believers, we must constantly remember who we are: children of God who are "in Christ." Our identity comes from that.

At Jesus' baptism God had just declared Jesus His Son and that He was proud of Him. But in the wilderness, when Jesus had been without food for forty days, the devil sought to make Jesus doubt who He was, saying, "If you are really the Son of God . . ." In a sense the devil was saying, "If you are really God's Son, then why did your Father leave you so hungry? You must have done something wrong. You must be failing Him as His Son." How did Jesus respond? Out of His identity.

We will make mistakes in this life, and the enemy will beat us down with guilt and shame, telling us we don't have the right to expect God to walk with us. But as believers, we must constantly remember who we are: children of God who are "in Christ." Our identity comes from that. Abiding means continually remembering and embracing this truth.

Paul tells us in Ephesians 6 that we are in a battle with a spiritual enemy. In Galatians, Paul explains further that though we are Christians, we are not free from this internal battle—we are called to fight it.

> I say, walk by the Spirit, and you will not gratify the desires of the flesh. For the flesh desires what is contrary to the Spirit, and the Spirit what is contrary to the flesh. They are in conflict with each other, so that you are not to do whatever you want. But if you are led by the Spirit, you are not under the law.
>
> The acts of the flesh are obvious: sexual immorality, impurity and debauchery; idolatry and witchcraft; hatred, discord, jealousy, fits of rage, selfish ambition, dissensions, factions and envy; drunkenness, orgies, and the like. I warn you, as I did before, that those who live like this will not inherit the kingdom of God.
>
> But the fruit of the Spirit is love, joy, peace, forbearance, kindness, goodness, faithfulness, gentleness and self-control. Against such things there is no law. Those who belong to Christ Jesus have crucified the flesh with its passions and desires. Since we live by the Spirit, let us keep in step with the Spirit.
>
> GALATIANS 5:16-25

As we enter the battle, we must be sure to know what is of the Lord and what is of the enemy. We have accepted Jesus as Lord and Savior and have been given the gift of the indwelling Holy Spirit to help us become mature and effective for the Lord (Acts 2:38; 1 Corinthians 6:19), but the old sinful nature still lurks within us. The devil will use that nature to bring confusion to our minds about which voice is speaking.

Because of our experiences and bents, we each have different sinful desires that cry out more loudly than others. The devil seeks to entice us—in a variety of ways—to remember and give in to those old desires, telling us that if we do, we will feel more alive and satisfied. But that is a lie. If we give in, these desires actually get stronger and we want more and more rather than being satisfied. Giving in leads to addiction (spiritual and physical slavery) and more severe consequences (James 1:13-15). As the old analogy says, the dog that barks loudest and is the most dangerous is the one who has been fed the most.

The two natures will battle, but we have the power to win against our sinful nature. How? The old sinful nature is present in us, but so is the Holy Spirit.

1. What does your sinful nature desire?

_____

_____

2. What have you done, or what are you willing to do, to kill the growing sin in your life?

_____

_____

ACTS 2:38

Peter replied, "Repent and be baptized, every one of you, in the name of Jesus Christ for the forgiveness of your sins. And you will receive the gift of the Holy Spirit."

1 CORINTHIANS 6:19

Do you not know that your bodies are temples of the Holy Spirit, who is in you, whom you have received from God? You are not your own.

JAMES 1:13-15

When tempted, no one should say, "God is tempting me." For God cannot be tempted by evil, nor does he tempt anyone; but each person is tempted when they are dragged away by their own evil desire and enticed. Then, after desire has conceived, it gives birth to sin; and sin, when it is full-grown, gives birth to death.

We don't have to rely on our own righteousness. We rely on what Jesus did for us—this is the gospel.

After the devil tempts you to sin, he loves to step in and say, "You are guilty of sin! You haven't changed—you have disappointed God too many times." Don't forget that the devil is a liar and the father of lies—he is the accuser of believers. Satan does this so we feel unworthy and will stop abiding in Christ. Scripture tells us we are unworthy in and of ourselves, so this shouldn't come as a surprise to us! But we don't have to rely on our own righteousness. We rely on what Jesus did for us—this is the gospel.

Paul's teaching on the fruit of the flesh and the fruit of the Spirit equips us to test our own actions and motives. The flesh is death and sin, but the fruit of the Spirit is life and peace. Because we know what to confess—what to fight—we can start to see growth and Christlikeness in ourselves and even in others as we grow in Christ.

In my own life, I often look back at who I used to be and am encouraged that God has indeed grown me. Whenever I begin to become prideful, I look to Jesus as I abide in Him (through Scripture, prayer, and fellowship with believers in worship). Who Jesus is reminds me that I have so far to go. Abiding humbles me.

Show me a disciple who is proud, and I will show you a believer who is not abiding with Jesus. When you do abide in Christ, you see what good really looks like and you know you are far from it.

A maturing disciple is on a journey. At the beginning of the journey, Jesus shared the gospel with us. We received it and got into the discipleship relational vehicle with Him. We started a journey together in connection with Him and others. We are learning to love and to work together. We are connecting to God's Word and growing in obedience.

As we walk with Jesus, we start to become ministers rather than consumers. We go from immaturity (ignorance and self-absorption) to maturity, to having a heart to serve. As we walk with Jesus, we become more intentional about how and when we serve our Lord on His mission to save the world and bring us all home.

DAY THREE REVIEW

1. What stood out to you or convicted you from today?

2. At the beginning of this section we talked about three ways the devil works in our lives. Which one of the three do you feel he uses most often in your life?

3. Share about a time when you felt unworthy or were made to doubt your relationship with God. Did you want to isolate yourself? How could someone have helped you during that time?

4. Is there someone you know who tends to isolate themselves? What could you do to help them connect with you? How could you remind them of who they are in Christ?

Day Four

DEALING WITH TEMPTATION

GETTING STARTED

Yesterday we talked about our battle with both the enemy and our old sinful nature. Today we will talk about how to deal with those temptations that appeal to our old nature that Satan likes to put before us. We will see that he did the same thing to Jesus, and we can learn much from Jesus' response to those temptations.

Lord Jesus: Help me see what You want me to see today. Expose any lies I may believe and lead me to Your truth. Help me trust and obey You and walk out what I'm learning in every sphere of my life.

Scripture tells us that we were saved from the empty way of life that our world offers us (1 Peter 1:18). In the beginning, the devil succeeded in tempting Adam and Eve to believe that there was something better than what God offered and that we humans could achieve it on our own. Satan continues to try to convince us today that we can be lord of our own life and that we will be the better for it. The truth is that when we allow the enemy to direct us, to lead us as we drive our spiritual cars on our own road trip, we end up in the wrong places—not only in this life but for eternity.

Let's look again at how the devil worked when he faced Jesus in the desert.

> The devil led him up to a high place and showed him in an instant all the kingdoms of the world. And he said to him, "I will give you all their authority and splendor; it has been given to me, and I can give it to anyone I want to. If you worship me, it will all be yours."
>
> Jesus answered, "It is written: 'Worship the Lord your God and serve him only.'"
>
> LUKE 4:5-8

The devil tells Jesus that if He will worship him, he will give Jesus the world.

1. Does the devil really own the world? Has it really been given to him, and can he give it to whomever he wants? Why or why not?

The truth was that Jesus was already going to get the world. The devil was offering Him an easier way than going to the cross—and at a much faster pace.

1 PETER 1:18

You know that it was not with perishable things such as silver or gold that you were redeemed from the empty way of life handed down to you from your ancestors.

EPHESIANS 6:18

Pray in the Spirit on all occasions with all kinds of prayers and requests. With this in mind, be alert and always keep on praying for all the Lord's people.

2. What does the devil's temptation here imply about those who are in positions of leadership and think they are successful in the world we live in?

    _____

    _____

3. Why did Jesus reject the devil's offer? What truth did He know and hold to as He responded?

    _____

    _____

We live in a world that offers half-truths and less-than-perfect perspectives on what is really going on. Agendas and impure motives rule the day. Jesus tells us the truth about how we are to live on planet Earth in relation to the world's culture and what it offers.

> [Jesus said,] "The eye is the lamp of the body. If your eyes are healthy, your whole body will be full of light. But if your eyes are unhealthy, your whole body will be full of darkness. If then the light within you is darkness, how great is that darkness!
>
> "No one can serve two masters. Either you will hate the one and love the other, or you will be devoted to the one and despise the other. You cannot serve both God and money.
>
> "Therefore I tell you, do not worry about your life, what you will eat or drink; or about your body, what you will wear. Is not life more than food, and the body more than clothes? Look at the birds of the air; they do not sow or reap or store away in barns, and yet your heavenly Father feeds them. Are you not much more valuable than they? Can any one of you by worrying add a single hour to your life?
>
> "And why do you worry about clothes? See how the flowers of the field grow. They do not labor or spin. Yet I tell you that not even Solomon in all his splendor was dressed like one of these. If that is how God clothes the grass of the field, which is here today and tomorrow is thrown into the fire, will he not much more clothe you—you of little faith? So do not worry, saying, 'What shall we eat?' or 'What shall we drink?' or 'What shall we wear?' For the pagans run after all these things, and your heavenly Father knows that you need them. But seek first his kingdom and his righteousness, and all these things will be given to you as well. Therefore do not worry about tomorrow, for tomorrow will worry about itself. Each day has enough trouble of its own."
>
> MATTHEW 6:22-34

> Do not love the world or anything in the world. If anyone loves the world, love for the Father is not in them. For everything in the world—the lust of the flesh, the lust of the eyes, and the pride of life—comes not from the Father but from the world. The world and its desires pass away, but whoever does the will of God lives forever.
>
> 1 JOHN 2:15-17

Our fallen culture is built to entice our sinful natures to act. There are temptations all around us, but what the enemy offers is temporary and ultimately unfulfilling. He wants to use those things to lead us away from what we need most: a relationship with God that will fill that hole in us that only God can fill.

Our sinful nature will kill our relationships with others. Scripture tells us clearly that we must be careful what we believe. We must not be gullible. We must take into consideration that we have an enemy working behind the scenes.

We are in a battle, and we cannot win spiritual battles with physical tools. In Ephesians 6:18 we are told to be alert and pray on all occasions. We pray alone as we abide, and we also pray with other believers. Prayer gives us God's perspective as we combine it with God's revealed Word.

Many people accept the fact that we are in a battle, but they fight against people and governments first and foremost. Paul tells us that we don't primarily wrestle or war against those things. In fact, unless we fight the enemy spiritually first, we will neither know how to fight nor have the tools to fight the physical issues we face.

DAY FOUR REVIEW

1. What stood out to you or convicted you from today?

2. Consider a time in your life when you were either tempted to or did take a shortcut to achieve something you were going after. What did you choose to do? What did you learn from that experience?

3. Whom in your life can you ask to pray for you? Whom do you trust to help you process your decisions and work your way through the devil's falsehoods? Name two or three people and which sphere of your life they come from.

4. What are some different ways you can see the Abiding Sphere and the Church Sphere working together to arm you for the battles in the Spiritual Sphere?

5. This week, ask God to show any areas in your life where you might be fighting against the people around you when the real battle is in the spiritual realm. What do you sense Him directing you toward?

Day Five

HOW DOES THE ENEMY WORK?

GETTING STARTED

So many times, temptations come up because we have neglected to place boundaries or protection around ourselves in the circumstances we find tempting. Keeping in step with the Spirit daily and having accountability with others are vital components of avoiding temptation and not allowing it to develop into sin.

> *Lord Jesus: Help me see what You want me to see today. Expose any lies I may believe and lead me to Your truth. Help me trust and obey You and walk out what I'm learning in every sphere of my life.*

The enemy works in our minds by enticing our sinful nature. He works in our culture to feed sinful natures and entice people to act out—and encourage those around them to do the same. Our most important defense is to receive Jesus as our Lord and Savior and then keep in step with the Holy Spirit daily (Galatians 5:25). As we do, the Holy Spirit directs our actions and Scripture becomes our guide for life.

Proverbs 7 contains a disturbing story of how the enemy works, as well as an admonishment to battle his schemes.

Read Proverbs 7.

1. According to Proverbs, what is the source of wisdom? (See also Psalm 119:9-16; 2 Timothy 3:16-17.)

———————————————————————

The writer of this proverb is telling his reader the story of a foolish young man. This message is rooted in a level of relationship: The writer acts as a father to the "son" to whom he is writing.

2. What makes the young man in this story foolish?

    ☐ He is not where he is supposed to be (within his own house, as the writer is in his own home).
    ☐ He is alone without accountability.
    ☐ He is near the adulterous woman's corner (rather than standing where it is safe, he is trying to get as close as he can to sin without crossing over the thin line).
    ☐ He is in the dark, acting in secret.
    ☐ All of the above.

GALATIANS 5:25

Since we live by the Spirit, let us keep in step with the Spirit.

PSALM 119:11, NLT

I have hidden your word in my heart, that I might not sin against you.

2 TIMOTHY 3:16-17, NLT

All Scripture is inspired by God and is useful to teach us what is true and to, make us realize what is wrong in our lives. It corrects us when we are wrong and teaches us to do what is right. God uses it to prepare and equip his people to do every good work.

3. Whom does the adulterous woman represent?

   ☐ The devil.
   ☐ A person who is unfaithful to the Lord.
   ☐ Both or either.
   ☐ Other: _____

4. Where can the adulterous woman in the story be found?

   _____

   _____

The adulterous woman is everywhere except where the storyteller is (safely in his house, looking out his window). We even read that she was in the temple—she made her religious vows and fulfilled them! This proverb is cautioning the reader that even if you walk near her corner but think you are safe because you didn't step over the line, the adulterous woman will cross over to you. Being near her corner is an invitation to the enemy.

5. The adulterous woman makes several promises. Fill out the chart below to compare what she wants the young man to believe versus what is actually true.

Promise	What she wants the young man to believe	What's actually true
"I was looking for you personally."[i]		
"This will be the most amazing experience you've ever had."[ii]		
"My husband is away and won't be back."[iii]		

6. Which of these false promises has the enemy used against you the most?

   _____

7. Consider a time when you believed the lie. What was the cost—to you and to those you care about—as a result?

   _____

   _____

As the woman uses persuasive words, the young man doesn't give in immediately. Instead, we see that falling into sin is a process.

- At first, the young man listened and did not act—but he didn't flee either.
- Then he takes time to contemplate the woman's words.
- He spends time alone without protection.
- Eventually his resolve lessens, and then he rushes in.
- Sin is always progressive—it leads to deeper and deeper issues.

JOHN 10:10

The thief comes only to steal and kill and destroy; I have come that they may have life, and have it to the full.

1 CORINTHIANS 6:18

Flee from sexual immorality. All other sins a person commits are outside the body, but whoever sins sexually, sins against their own body.

1 CORINTHIANS 10:14

Therefore, my dear friends, flee from idolatry.

1 TIMOTHY 6:11, NLT

You, Timothy, are a man of God; so run from all these evil things. Pursue righteousness and a godly life, along with faith, love, perseverance, and gentleness.

1 JOHN 1:9

If we confess our sins, he is faithful and just and will forgive us our sins and purify us from all unrighteousness.

Notes and Thoughts

- Like an archer's arrow that pierces the liver, sin leads to a slow, painful death.
- The devil's desire is to steal, kill, and destroy (John 10:10).

When we try to handle temptation by relying on our own wisdom and self-control, we will fail. The apostle Paul tells us how we should immediately respond to the devil's schemes: we should flee (1 Corinthians 6:18, 10:14; 1 Timothy 6:11).

8. Is there something in your life that you are playing with right now that you should be fleeing from? What is it?

_____

_____

Here is a truth we need to embrace: We will all fail as believers. And there may be earthly consequences to sin: Some people will not forgive us; sometimes we may face consequences in our jobs or even with the law. But Jesus always accepts us when we turn away from the devil and sin and return to Him.

The devil will tell us that because the world doesn't forgive us and let us get past sin, we can't come back to God. That is one of the devil's lies. God will forgive you (1 John 1:9) and even walk through those consequences with you.

As believers, we face a battle with an enemy who is crafty and a schemer. But God has provided us with the weapons that can give us victory. If you will allow mature believers within His church to disciple you, you will grow to become effective with all the weapons Jesus has given us.

DAY FIVE REVIEW

1. What stood out to you or convicted you from today?

_____

_____

2. Consider a time when you tried to see how close you could get to the line of right and wrong or when you thought you were safe on the right side of the line but found out you weren't. What happened? What did you learn?

_____

_____

3. Share about a situation where you have had to deal with the consequences of something you did, even though you knew you were forgiven.

_____

_____

4. Look at the close relationships in your life. How many people would you say tend to help you walk closer to God? Are there any that tend to lead you further away from God?

_____

_____

---

i. Answer: a. She wants him to believe he is special. The truth is she was looking for anyone on any corner.

ii. Answer: b. She overpromises how great sin will be. The truth is that sin will never satisfy.

iii. Answer: c. She convinces the young man that there will be no consequences—that he won't get caught. The truth is that sin always has consequences.How Does the Enemy Work?

BRINGING IT ALL TOGETHER

Day One

BALANCING THE FIVE SPHERES

You have made it to week 12! Congratulations on your persistence and hard work—you have come a long way on your journey! As you go through today's lesson, think back over the past few weeks. Have you noticed any shifts in your thinking about being and making disciples? Have you made any changes to any of your spheres of life?

Lord Jesus: Help me see what You want me to see today. Expose any lies I may believe and lead me to Your truth. Help me trust and obey You and walk out what I'm learning in every sphere of my life.

As we have gone on this journey together, we have referred many times to the analogy of a road trip. As disciples of Jesus, we are on a journey to make disciples of Jesus ourselves, moving together toward a destination of becoming mature in Christ in every sphere of our lives.

1. Read the verses about spiritual maturity, and fill in the blanks in the statements that follow:

   We have much to say about this, but it is hard to make it clear to you because you no longer try to understand. In fact, though by this time you ought to be teachers, you need someone to teach you the elementary truths of God's word all over again. You need milk, not solid food! Anyone who lives on milk, being still an infant, is not acquainted with the teaching about righteousness. But solid food is for the mature, who by constant use have trained themselves to distinguish good from evil.

   HEBREWS 5:11-14

   a. We are all to grow to become _____.

   Since we are surrounded by such a great cloud of witnesses, let us throw off everything that hinders and the sin that so easily entangles. And let us run with perseverance the race marked out for us, fixing our eyes on Jesus, the pioneer and perfecter of faith. For the joy set before him he endured the cross, scorning its shame,

Someday we will no longer have to deal with our sinful natures, a culture that entices us, or people who would lure us into sin.

Scan QR code to access video podcasts and other content that accompanies this week's session.

and sat down at the right hand of the throne of God. Consider him who endured such opposition from sinners, so that you will not grow weary and lose heart.

HEBREWS 12:1-3

b. We are on a _____ that has been marked out for us.

We are on a journey, and God sets the track, or the map, to the finish line.

DISCIPLINE AND DISCIPLESHIP

The root word of *discipleship* is *discipline*. We choose to reject certain roads and ways of living because we follow Jesus and know He is right about which way to go. We say no to many things the world suggests and commands. We allow the Lord Jesus to be our Architect for life. Someday we will no longer have to deal with our sinful natures, a culture that entices us, or people who would lure us into sin. But until we reach eternity with Jesus, we live within the Five Spheres for our protection and our good.

OUT OF BALANCE

The other day, a man asked me to meet with him for coffee. This man was a young, financially successful businessman who had recently become a believer. He had not grown up in a Christian family, and he didn't feel like he had the time to be in a life group. "I've started going to church, and I know God wants me to do something more," he told me, "but I don't know what that is."

The reason this man wanted to talk was because he needed help with some issues in his life. He and his wife had recently had their second child, and he was feeling tension between work and home. His wife was less than satisfied with their relationship, but at the same time his business mentoring group told him not to step back from taking ground in business. They told him he could have it all—no need to spend less time at work. All his wife probably needed was a couple of vacations a year.

As we sat there in the coffee shop, I took him through the Five Spheres.

Then I asked him to draw what he thought his current spheres looked like. It looked something like this:

2. Considering what you have learned in this workbook, what do you think the spiritual disadvantages of this man's current lifestyle are?

_____

_____

3. Abiding gives us God's architectural plans for life, His definition of words, and the strength to live all those things out. Without those things, what is the inevitable conclusion of this man's current trajectory?

_____

_____

Our abiding relationship with God works as the creator and regulator of the other spheres. It also works as the power source.

4. What would happen to your computer if it were not plugged in? What would happen if you didn't have the chip within your computer that told the rest of the parts how to work and what to do? What are the implications of this idea for our life?

_____

_____

Abiding keeps everything else in balance. When you do not abide, the other spheres get larger or smaller than they should be. A lack of abiding will reveal itself in how you spend your time, money, and energy.

The abiding relationship with God works as the creator and regulator of the other spheres.

5. What advice would you have given this young man?

Part of discipleship is realizing when we're looking through a distorted lens. When life feels out of balance, we should make sure we're not looking to the world for wisdom instead of Scripture. Let's be like this young man and listen to the Holy Spirit's promptings to seek spiritual guidance.

DAY ONE REVIEW

1. What stood out to you or convicted you from today?

2. One way you can tell what is important in someone's life is by looking at their calendar and their bank account. In the space below, draw an honest picture of what you think your own spheres of life look like.

3. If one of our spheres has enlarged to the point that it has diminished our abiding time with God, what serves as our power source for the other spheres instead? How can we change that dynamic?

BALANCING YOUR WORLD SPHERE

GETTING STARTED

In today's lesson we will talk about making sure your sphere is balanced. The pendulum can swing either way in this area—some want to take themselves completely out of the world, and others may be so entrenched in it they have no margin for the other areas of life. God calls us to be in the world, just not of it. He wants to lead us to live a balanced life in this sphere.

> *Lord Jesus: Help me see what You want me to see today. Expose any lies I may believe and lead me to Your truth. Help me trust and obey You and walk out what I'm learning in every sphere of my life.*

Yesterday we looked at the story of a young man who, through the guidance of the Holy Spirit as well as the teaching he was getting from church, was identifying some misalignment in his life. Once he saw that misalignment clearly, he asked me if I thought he should step back from his group of friends—because he respected these men in business, he was beginning to feel pulled toward their way of living life.

Here's the thing: Eliminating the World Sphere is both impractical and at odds with the calling of discipleship. We all must make a living and interact with people of differing views. Our role is to use the world as our mission field rather than just step out of it altogether.

So, to help this young man rightsize his World Sphere, I walked him through adding God's design for the church into his spheres. We talked about how making time for consistent investment with spiritually mature men who lived out God's design for the home could help him balance his spheres as God intended. I shared that building a godly Church Sphere would empower him to live out God's plans for his home, while also perhaps allowing him to reach coworkers with his strengthened view rather than being influenced by their view.

1. What would this man have to do to rightsize his World Sphere?

    ☐ Spend less time at work than the men from his business mentor group were spending.
    ☐ Make time for deeper relationships with godly men so that he could be honest about his questions with them and receive better wisdom.
    ☐ Nothing—just keep doing what he has been but be more aware of the situation.
    ☐ Go to the group, declare they are all wrong, and share the gospel with them.
    ☐ Begin pressing into abiding with Jesus and committing to becoming a more mature believer with men who invest in him.
    ☐ Listen to more Christian podcasts and attend church more regularly, as well as read Scripture more often, but don't cut back on business to spend more time at home.

I invited the young man into a men's group I had going on Wednesday mornings, and I asked him to start attending a life group with his wife, so they both would be able to observe more mature Christian couples living out the Five Spheres from Jesus' perspective. I also encouraged him to stay in his secular group and to ask different questions. These men were effective and could help in some ways, but he needed to learn to eat the chicken and spit out the bones—in other words, to test everything by God's Word and with godly, wise counsel. "As time goes on," I told him, "you will become a steady influence in the lives of these people as their advice gets lived out and the results become apparent to them. At some point they will reap what they sow, and then you can sow something different in them."

2. What would you have told the young man to do?

_____

_____

DAY TWO REVIEW

1. What stood out to you or convicted you from today?

_____

_____

2. Does this story reveal anything to you about your own life? Have you been tempted to pull yourself completely away from the people in your World Sphere to avoid being influenced by them?

_____

_____

3. Do you think you have enough wise counsel and fellowship with other believers in your life to balance out your World Sphere? Why or why not?

_____

_____

4. Do you need to share this story with someone in your life? If so, who and why? Commit to a time to talk with them about their World Sphere.

Day Three

BALANCING YOUR CHURCH SPHERE

GETTING STARTED

It might seem that filling your life with church at the expense of all other areas would be a worthy and noble way to live—but that is not what God has called us to do. Today we will talk about the importance of having balance in our Church Sphere and some of the dangers that can arise if we don't.

Lord Jesus: Help me see what You want me to see today. Expose any lies I may believe and lead me to Your truth. Help me trust and obey You and walk out what I'm learning in every sphere of my life.

Not long ago, I was talking with a man who was deeply involved in our church—he volunteered for almost everything. I knew he was married and had two teenage kids who did not come to church much, so I took the opportunity to ask him about his life.

When I am getting to know other believers, I ask questions with the Five Spheres in mind. A life not built on God's design will show itself in a variety of ways. As I asked this man about work, I could tell he worked hard but tried to maintain a work/life balance. His identity was not in his work for sure. But when I began to ask about his family, he shared his struggle in that area. He shared that he loved to serve the Lord and wanted to lead his family toward serving the Lord well, but they were not interested. Because he felt that they didn't have the same values he did he just did things without them and spent his time at church.

AN OFF-BALANCE CHURCH SPHERE

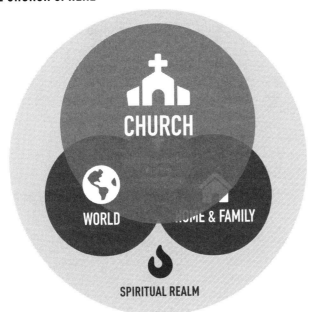

A life not built on God's design will show itself in a variety of ways.

Growing up with a pastor father, I got used to people calling or stopping by and interrupting us during family dinner. So often when I'd get time with my dad to play catch or a game, someone would stop by and need his help. I would just stand or sit and wait, watching him pray for them or take off to counsel them rather than prioritizing our time. I began to hate the church because it stole my father.

A situation like this happens when people are spending too much time working *for* God rather than spending time *with* God. If we are truly abiding, the Holy Spirit along with Scripture and God's people help us live out God's architectural plans for each sphere.

In my conversation with the man from our church, I shared that he might want to become curious and discover if his kids were angry with God—or just with the version of God he was showing them. My parents learned as they grew (while they were in ministry, they had never been discipled), and as they became more mature, I began to see the church and serving differently.

DAY THREE REVIEW

1. What stood out to you or convicted you from today?

2. What are the consequences of letting your Church Sphere get too small or too big?

3. After going through this workbook, do you believe your Church Sphere is too small, too big, or just right?

4. Do you know someone who is struggling in this area? How can you begin a conversation with them about the consequences of an out-of-balance Church Sphere?

Day Four

BALANCING YOUR HOME AND FAMILY SPHERE

GETTING STARTED

As you have figured out by now, we can become off-balance in any sphere, and the Home and Family Sphere is no exception. Today we will discuss two key areas that will help us assess our situation at home and lead us to God's wisdom for how to work through issues and bring balance in this sphere.

> *Lord Jesus: Help me see what You want me to see today. Expose any lies I may believe and lead me to Your truth. Help me trust and obey You and walk out what I'm learning in every sphere of my life.*

The Home and Family Sphere can be particularly difficult to balance because it is easily thrown off by the other spheres. The World Sphere can pull us away through work, comparison, or a lack of spiritual influences. An unbalanced Church Sphere can cause our family to either resent the church or feel that it's not important.

When we come to the Home and Family Sphere, we must intentionally focus on abiding in God to determine what needs to change. In partnership with the Holy Spirit, we must allow others in God's family to walk with us through a deliberate process of assessing different home and family situations, discerning what is going on, and listening to what God would have us do.

The process we're going to look at today involves two key steps:

- understand the situation; and
- affirm and examine (head, heart, hands, feet).

To learn this process, we're going to work through a hypothetical situation as a disciple-maker. While this example looks at how we do this with someone else, we should also pay attention to how it applies to our own lives and welcome this intentionality as we are discipled.

STEP 1: UNDERSTAND THE SITUATION

Imagine that the person you are discipling tells you they are having a problem in their Home and Family Sphere. Their oldest son is fifteen and wants to go to a party with his friends. The son discovers the party will have alcohol but does not mention this to his parents. His father finds out about the alcohol and knows that his son is holding the information back. Now his dad is wondering how you think he should respond to his son.

STEP 2: AFFIRM AND EXAMINE

First, tell the person how proud you are of him for being willing to seek counsel. We may be tempted to hide home struggles because they are particularly painful and can feel embarrassing, but that is the devil trying to lie to us with shame. Affirming a person's honesty and humility keeps the devil from getting a foothold and helps the person you are discipling be more confident to share struggles in the future.

Second, because this person is married, you can ask him what his wife thinks about it. This is important because he is a spiritual leader in his home, and God has given him a spiritual partner to work with.

Finally, you proceed with four kinds of questions that will guide him in discerning his response:

1. *Head*: What do Jesus (our head/authority) and His Word (the Bible is our inspired guide for life; 1 Timothy 3:16) say about this issue?
2. *Heart*: What is your motive or purpose in the issue?
3. *Hands*: What skills or understanding might you need to address the issue?
4. *Feet*: What should you do to apply head, heart, and hands to the issue?

Head Questions

Jesus is Lord, and Scripture contains His commands in every sphere of our lives. When someone is discerning how to respond in a home situation, we begin with asking them to look into God's Word on the subject we are dealing with.

Examples:

- "What does our head (Jesus) say in Scripture about being a husband and a father?"
- "How did our head (Jesus) model this kind of situation in Scripture (e.g., dealing with discipline of one of His disciples)?"

What verses would you point your friend to that would give him help? I often give people Scripture passages to read on their own so that they learn to read for themselves rather than just relying on me to provide the answers. I tell them that we will discuss what they learned after they do their own study.

As a disciplemaker, remind them that as we abide in Jesus, He not only gives us the directions but also the power for living out those directions. We don't want them to start with, *My friend Jim is so wise and I need his counsel.* We want them to learn to think, *I need to*

1 TIMOTHY 3:16, NLT
Without question, this is the great mystery of our faith: Christ was revealed in a human body and vindicated by the Spirit. He was seen by angels and announced to the nations. He was believed in throughout the world and taken to heaven in glory.

walk with God and seek His will through Scripture. The goal is for them to learn to seek God's Word first and then confirm and clarify what they've read with more mature believers.

Heart Questions

Next, we ask heart questions to help the person discern their motives and purposes.

Examples:

- *"What is your motive for following God's will?"* Understanding motive is important because sometimes we don't get what we want from doing what Jesus asks. If our heart is seeking God's will to "get," rather than because we love and are thankful for what God has already done for us, then our motives are off.

- *"How does Jesus see the people in this situation?"* As we discern motive, we must also help the person pay attention to their heart toward the other people involved. Sometimes when we deal with complex home dynamics, we will disagree with our spouse on how to handle it. Remembering that the other person is not our enemy but our partner who helps us get on a wise course—and fight against the enemy spiritually—is important.

- *"What is your reason for being angry or fearful?"* When the heart motive is self-centered, we react in ways that undermine the relationship. Does the person want change because the child is causing stress and ruining peace or because the person loves them? Is the person upset because they are being embarrassed in front of people? We must help the person understand if they are in the right place to address the issue or if they must address their own internal response first.

When someone looks at what is happening under the surface in their Home and Family Sphere, they may realize that they are upset at God or others because they don't see immediate change or agreement with their spiritual purposes. Each of us must choose to trust God ourselves when dealing with our children, remembering that they are also on a journey and that God isn't done with them yet. Our reactions often reveal what we ourselves believe, and although God wants to use us in the lives of our kids, He is also working on us at the same time.

Hands Questions

When we help a person with hands questions, we help them determine issues of skills. Sometimes those we are discipling don't know how to do something we assume they know how to do. For example, if I say, "Have you prayed with your wife about this?" I am assuming they know how to pray with their wife—but maybe they do not. They may have never seen it modeled in their family of origin.

Examples:

- *"Have you told your wife your real fear in this situation so she knows your heart?"* We are assuming that he has opened up and shared his heart with his wife before. We may need to model what that conversation would look like.

- *"Have you ever told your son why you are so concerned about early exposure to alcohol?"* Often parents have not told their kids their past because they think it permits their children's decisions. Our role is to tell them the appropriate amount of truth so that they learn from the pain our choices caused.

- *"Have you ever done a Bible-centered devotion with your family or with your son specifically?"* If he says no and you simply tell him to start doing this, you are assuming that he knows what a family devotional practice looks like.

- *"How do you think your wife will respond to this plan with your son?"* If the man indicates that he expects his wife to be resistant, he may not know how to understand and resolve underlying tension in his marriage. I may ask, "Why do you think she will respond this way? What is she afraid of? In your past have you disregarded her advice, or have you just let her take care of things but griped about how she handled them later?" You may assume the person knows how to care for his wife's heart and resolve conflict with her, but he may never have experienced that. Now that the Lord is changing him, you may need to equip him to ask for forgiveness and share his heart.

Hands questions address the practical actions people take as they grow in their understanding of their responsibility. Don't discourage people by assuming they know things they may not; instead, walk them through how to grow.

Feet Questions

Feet questions get us to the practical application of the head, heart, and hands insights. These questions deal with specific places and situations where we implement what we are learning. It can be easy to keep knowledge at a head level if we aren't making a specific plan for when and where we will put it into practice.

Examples:

- *"What do you think your next step is in this situation with your son?"*

- *"Do you need help planning a time when you and your wife can sit down with your son to talk about the situation?"*

- *"How will you handle the situation if your son goes to the party?"*

- *"How can you address the deeper issue of your son's secretiveness in the future?"* This question is meant to prompt self-awareness when it comes to his relationship with his son. Has he set time aside in his week where he can have conversations with his son to deepen their relationship? Has he made himself an approachable, safe place for his son to share things with him?

- *"Who does your son have in his life to talk with?"* We need to help him look at the people his son may be seeking wisdom from. Is the son involved in a youth group at church where he has other wise adults to talk with? Does the son spend more time with nonbelievers than with believers? How can the father begin to surround his son with more people who are abiding in Christ?

As you walk through situations like this with people, pray with them to ask God to help them do their part. Ask God to give the wisdom and prepare the way with the others involved. The situation may take time and continued support and debriefing, and they will come back to you for further prayer.

Over time, a person who goes through this process will begin to grow in the issues within all five spheres of life. As they do, they will start to see the pattern. At the head level, they realize that they can discover Jesus' plans in Scripture for themselves through abiding in Him. Through abiding, the Holy Spirit is changing them at the heart level—in their perspective and motives. As they walk through what they do in these situations, they begin to see growth and purpose in their skills (the hands level). Then, as they experience different situations with God's help, they learn that they can help others in the same way.

If you are the person dealing with a difficult home situation, the process will look very similar, except you must approach it with the humility to listen and learn:

- **Understand the Situation:** Ask your disciplemaker or a trusted friend to talk it through with you. Processing the dynamics of what is going on and how you feel about it will help your friend know what questions to ask and how to best come alongside you.

- **Affirm and Interrogate:** Be encouraged that you are seeking godly counsel. If your disciplemaker or trusted friend is unfamiliar with the process, share the four kinds of questions you want to explore.

    Head: Abide with Jesus through studying Scripture and prayer, and process with your disciplemaker what you are noticing regarding your situation.

    Heart: Consider what motives may be getting in the way of approaching the situation with God's perspective, and ask your disciplemaker to hold you accountable in how you respond.

    Hands: As you and your disciplemaker think through your response, be honest with yourself about areas where you may need to grow in your skills or understanding, and pursue growth in those things.

    Feet: Work with your disciplemaker to discern practical next steps to apply what you have observed about your situation.

In every sphere, we all need other people to hold us accountable to what we have already learned. If all we do is read Scripture or human-created materials in isolation—no matter how well intentioned and biblical they are—that is not discipleship. We cannot expect to merely check a box labeled "belief" and be changed forever. The Bible warns us about sliding away (Hebrews 2:1-4; 3:12-13), and on this journey of discipleship we need other believers as rails or rumble strips to keep us from going to sleep at the wheel or drifting over into a ditch. We never grow past our need for accountability, exhortation, or encouragement in our lives.

HEBREWS 2:1-4

We must pay the most careful attention, therefore, to what we have heard, so that we do not drift away. For since the message spoken through angels was binding, and every violation and disobedience received its just punishment, how shall we escape if we ignore so great a salvation? This salvation, which was first announced by the Lord, was confirmed to us by those who heard him. God also testified to it by signs, wonders and various miracles, and by gifts of the Holy Spirit distributed according to his will.

HEBREWS 3:12-13

See to it, brothers and sisters, that none of you has a sinful, unbelieving heart that turns away from the living God. But encourage one another daily, as long as it is called "Today," so that none of you may be hardened by sin's deceitfulness.

DAY FOUR REVIEW

1. What stood out to you or convicted you from today?

2. What is a situation in your Home and Family Sphere that would benefit from the process we walked through today?

3. Whom can you walk through this process with?

4. Who are the barriers, rails, or rumble strips in your life? If you don't have any people who help keep you accountable, will you commit to your group to seek someone out?

LET'S REVIEW

As we wrap up our time together, let's review some of the key points from this workbook. Each of these is a road marker on the journey of discipleship. Understanding the terrain will equip us not only to continue to grow toward maturity but also to pass along what we've learned and help others grow as well.

REVIEW SCMD

On your journey, Jesus has used a disciplemaker to invite you to go through the SCMD process toward spiritual maturity.

- *S* stands for _____. Someone shared the message of the gospel and you received it, believed it, and pledged your allegiance to Jesus as your King and Savior.

- *C* stands for _____. You are connected in a relational vehicle for the journey of discipleship and are learning to love God and others in authentic relationships. You are becoming known for your love.

- *M* stands for _____. You are becoming a humble servant/minister who knows you were given abilities and resources for a purpose: to serve. You are learning how to use those abilities and resources in every sphere of life.

- *D* stands for released to make _____. You understand the journey you are on and how to show others what the journey looks like.

REVIEW THE SPIRITUAL STAGES OF DEVELOPMENT

The spiritual stages of development help us know where we and others are on the journey of discipleship:

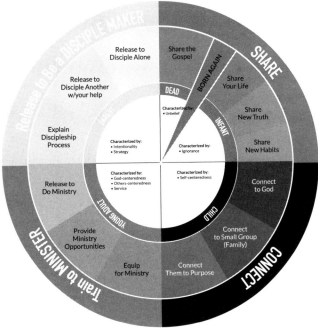

1. When a person is born again, they move from _____ to infants.[i]

2. Infants are characterized as _____ to the things of God, no matter how much they know about the world.[ii]

3. We move from the infant stage into the _____ stage. The characteristics of this stage are _____, and we will do what is right as long as _____.[iii]

4. As we move into the young _____ stage, we are learning to minister to others. We can be zealous and idealistic, and because of that we will struggle with discouragement and/or pride. We need someone to help us recognize our gifts and abilities and put us to work serving.[iv]

5. Finally, we become a spiritual _____. We are intentional and aware of our role as one who spiritually parents in the Five Spheres.[v]

6. We make _____, but we don't justify them. We abide in Christ and ask for forgiveness and move on.[vi]

7. We are learning to follow our Creator and Architect's plans for life in the Five Spheres as we come alongside others on this lifelong journey to maturity in Christ.

REVIEW THE FIVE SPHERES

1. Abiding in Jesus helps us remember who we are _____.

2. It allows us to spend time with God, who gives us His architectural _____ for each part of our lives as well as the _____ to build according to His plans.

Remember, we can be immature in one area and more mature in another, but we are never done growing as a believer.

FINAL THOUGHTS

As you have gone through this workbook, it is my prayer that you know not only how to live out the journey but also how to describe it and even help others live it out. I am praying that you have become more aware of the Lord's presence in your life and have developed real relationships you can experience in your Christian life.

Write out a game plan to grow and pray for God's help and the help of others as you continue on your journey, and share it with your group.

DAY FIVE REVIEW

1. Consider your drawing of your current spheres from day 1 of this week. What do you think the Lord is asking you to do in balancing the spheres? Share with your group.

2. As you are coming to the end of this study, what is something new you've learned?

3. What is something God has shown you about yourself?

4. What is something you either have changed or are changing in your life because of what you've learned?

5. Has the Lord brought someone to mind for you to courageously ask to join you in a group with this material? The key to learning is repetition. Studying something again drives the truth into us more deeply, and teaching those principles helps us learn in whole new ways. List the names of some people you sense the Lord may prompting you to invite.

---

i.   Answer: spiritually dead
ii. Answer: new (or ignorant)
iii. Answer: child; self-centered; it makes us happy (or we get what we want)
iv. Answer: adult
v.   Answer: parent
vi. Answer: mistakes

A NOTE FROM JIM

My prayer is that you have grown and will continue to grow as you move from infant, to child, to young adult, to spiritual parent of others—from sitting in the back seat or in the passenger seat to taking the role of driver (as Jesus drives through you), and finally into the ultimate role of a parent teaching someone else to drive. And remember: We never advance past the need for spiritual relationships. Jesus sent His trained disciples out by twos to start churches where people became God's family and together accomplished the mission.

God bless you!

Jim Putman

You can find more tools and podcasts to go along with this workbook at realliferesources.org/the-disciples-journey.

SHARING THE GOSPEL THROUGH THE FIVE SPHERES

To participate in God's mission, every disciple must understand the gospel story laid out in Scripture from beginning to end and learn how to explain it to those around them.

The book of Genesis reveals that God created a perfect world, an ideal place for us to live with Him forever. This relationship with Him would enable us to receive His directions for every part of life, as well as the strength provided to live out our designs. As we walk through the book of Genesis, we discover that God intended for us to have relationships with other humans as well. We also find that within that first human relationship came the ability to create a community of people. Not only are we supposed to have a relationship with God, a home life with family relationships, and a growing community, but we are also meant to work together with God and one another to cultivate and manage creation.

As the story goes along, we come to understand that God had a good way for us to live in every part of our lives. Eventually we are introduced to the fact that there is also a spiritual realm with spiritual beings, where things are happening that we can't see. We call these areas of our lives in God's creation the Five Spheres.

In the Bible, we also discover that God created us unique in all of creation. We were created like God (in His image), which means that though we have a beginning (unlike God, who has no beginning), we will live forever in a conscious state as a soul that has no end. We also find that we are like Him in that we are relational beings who can choose love . . . or not. We have a free will and can decide to listen to and obey God or rebel against Him and do things our own way. We are even told what would happen if we chose poorly: We would die. If we have read the story of God's interactions with His creation in the Scriptures, then we know how that freedom played out.

We discover that God's enemy, the devil (the serpent), tempted God's most precious possession to step out of His design and choose one of their own making. This all took place in the first chapters of God's Word, and everything that comes after explains God's historical attempts to pursue and lead us back into His good and right design for every part of our lives.

If we would have obeyed God in the beginning, our lives on planet Earth would have been much different. We would have each matured as a person, as couples, as people in community and as workers, and we would have understood and dealt rightly with the spiritual realm. This is the Five Spheres designed as God intended:

In the center of His creation was the Garden, and that is where humans were able to abide in a relationship with God, walking and talking with Him daily. That is represented by the sphere with a cross in the center of the graphic.

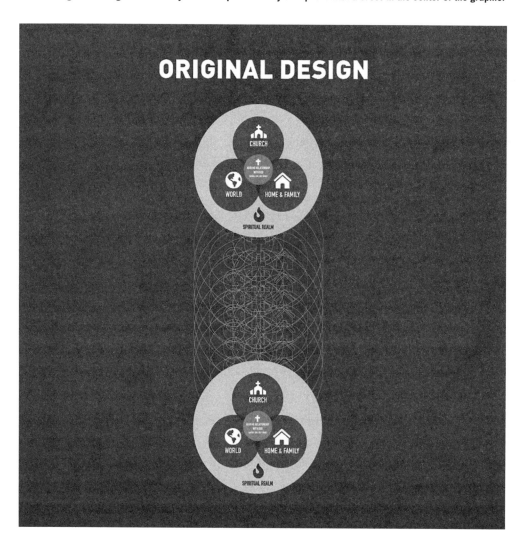

God also created the world we were to live in and filled it with plants and animals. In Genesis 1:28-29 and Genesis 2:15, God charges humans with the work of ruling over and caring for all the creatures on land and in sea and sky. He also gives humans the task of caring for the land and getting their food from it. Work was God's idea from the beginning! This area of our lives is represented by the World Sphere.

God then, in Genesis 2:18-25, created the Home and Family Sphere. He deemed that man and woman would be one flesh, and He commanded them to multiply.

The third sphere represents community. God's plan always included people in relationship together—a community supporting and caring for one another.

As we know from Genesis 3, humans did not choose to go with God's plan. Because of that choice, we started on a trajectory that was opposed to God's design for us (Romans 3:9-23).

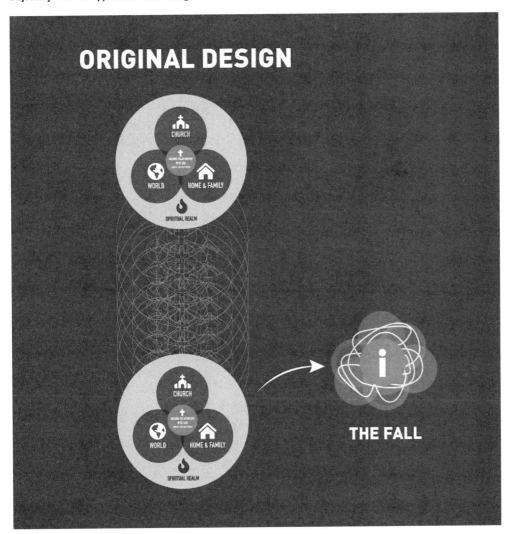

That is where Jesus stepped in to rescue us from darkness and bring us back into the light, using His model of discipleship to lead us back to God's original design for us (Isaiah 53; Romans 5:6-11). Our part in this is placing our trust in Jesus and accepting Him not only as our Savior but also as Lord of our lives (John 3:16).

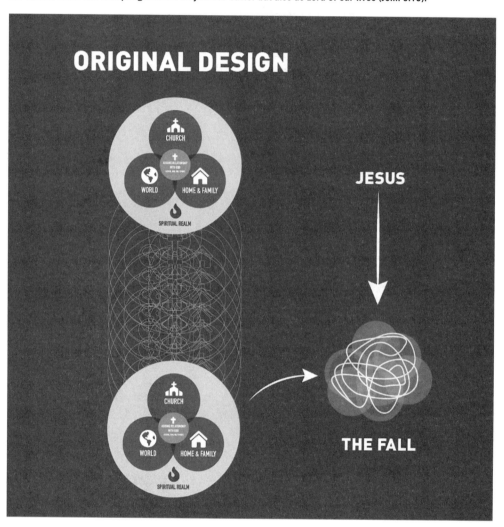

When we humble ourselves, submit to Jesus, and accept His invitation to become a disciple, He can begin the journey of bringing us back into alignment with God's original design for every sphere of our lives. Then we can be His ambassadors, helping reconcile all His creation back into relationship with Him and His design for their lives.

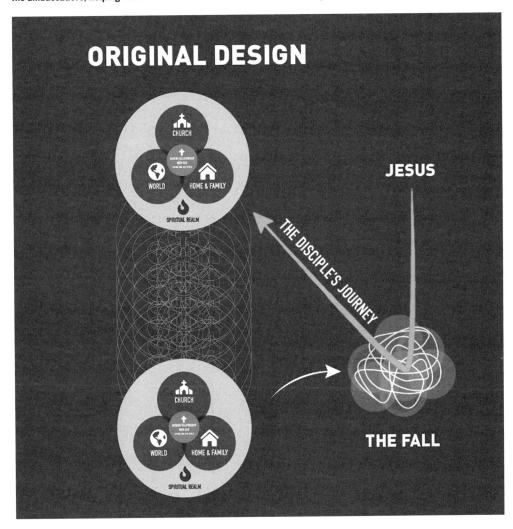

A FULL LINE OF
DISCIPLE-MAKING RESOURCES

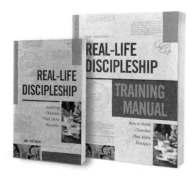

Real-Life Discipleship
Make disciple-making come alive in your church!

Real-Life Discipleship Training Manual
A practical, 14-week workbook for small-group leaders.

The Power of Together
Learn to live in authentic, relational communities— the kind that Jesus modeled.

The Power of Together Workbook
A 9-week workbook to practice authentic, relational discipleship.

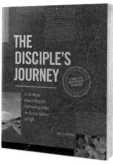

The Disciple's Journey
A transformative workbook for every member of your church.

NavPress

CP2016